SOCIETY FOR NEW TESTAMENT STUDIES
MONOGRAPH SERIES
General Editor: G. N. Stanton

63

EPHESIANS: POWER AND MAGIC

Ephesians: Power and Magic

The Concept of Power in Ephesians in Light of its Historical Setting

CLINTON E. ARNOLD

Assistant Professor of New Testament
Talbot School of Theology
Biola University

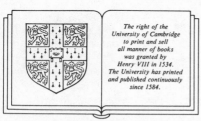

The right of the
University of Cambridge
to print and sell
all manner of books
was granted by
Henry VIII in 1534.
The University has printed
and published continuously
since 1584.

CAMBRIDGE UNIVERSITY PRESS

CAMBRIDGE
NEW YORK   NEW ROCHELLE
MELBOURNE   SYDNEY

21

Published by the Press Syndicate of the University of Cambridge
The Pitt Building, Trumpington Street, Cambridge CB2 1RP
32 East 57th Street, New York, NY 10022, USA
10 Stamford Road, Oakleigh, Melbourne 3166, Australia

First published 1989

Printed in Great Britain at
the University Press, Cambridge

British Library cataloguing in publication data

Arnold, Clinton E.
Ephesians.
1. Bible. N.T. Ephesians. Critical studies
I. Title   II. Series
227'.506

Library of Congress cataloguing in publication data

Arnold, Clinton E.
Ephesians, power and magic: the concept of power in Ephesians in
light of its historical setting / Clinton E. Arnold.
     p.   cm. − (Society for New Testament Studies monograph series
63)
Bibliography.
Includes index.
ISBN 0 521 36236 9
1. Bible. N.T. Ephesians − Criticism, interpretation, etc.
2. Magic − Biblical teaching. 3. Powers (Christian theology) −
Biblical teaching. 4. Power (Christian theology) − Biblical
teaching.   I. Title.   II. Series: Monograph series (Society for New
Testament Studies): 63.
BS2695.2.A76   1989
227'.506−dc19   88−15608

ISBN 0 521 36236 9

WS

To my dearest friend — my wife, Barbara

CONTENTS

PREFACE

This work represents the revision and abbreviation of a thesis presented to the Faculty of Divinity of the University of Aberdeen in June 1986. Consequently, I would like to acknowledge a number of people who gave valuable assistance throughout that period of research.

Above all, I express my deepest gratitude to my wife, Barbara. She supported this work from beginning to end by supporting me — with constant encouragement, by working for two years to help pay our expenses, by listening to virtually all my ideas, and by applying her own writing skills to several complete proofreadings which resulted in many stylistic improvements.

I also express my gratitude and appreciation to my supervisor, Professor Howard Marshall, for three years of wise guidance. Professor Marshall provided exceptionally insightful comments and suggestions at every stage of this project. In addition to some helpful advice at the outset of my research, I extend my thanks to Professor Ernest Best for providing many valuable suggestions for the revision of the thesis for publication. I am also indebted to Dr Ruth Edwards for her insight and expertise with material pertaining to the extra-biblical data and to the late Dr Colin Hemer for many engaging and profitable discussions on the social and religious milieu of Asia Minor in the Hellenistic era. Thanks are also due to Professor Graham Stanton for including this work in the Society for New Testament Studies Monograph Series.

Grants and contributions were provided by a number of groups and individuals in support of this research. The Committee of Vice-Chancellors and Principals of the Universities and Colleges in the United Kingdom provided an overseas research student grant. The Tyndale Fellowship for biblical and theological research not only provided a generous grant, but also paid my expenses for a number of trips to Cambridge to use the Tyndale House library and the

University Library of Cambridge. The Institute for Biblical and Archaeological Studies (Bakersfield, California), a non-profit foundation, supplied a research grant; more important was the encouragment given to me by its founder and my close friend, Stephen Reimer. Certainly not least is the abundant support received from our families, Mr and Mrs Wayne Arnold, Mr and Mrs George Erickson, and Mr Paul Erickson. Finally, the members of Deeside Christian Fellowship (Milltimber, Scotland) gave to us in countless ways through their love.

La Mirada, California   Clinton E. Arnold
Easter, 1988

ABBREVIATIONS

As listed in the *Journal of Biblical Literature* 95 (1976), 339–44, with the following additions:

AA	*Archäologischer Anzeiger*
ANRW	*Aufstieg und Niedergang der römischen Welt*
APF	*Archiv für Papyrusforschung und verwandte Gebiete*
CGTC	Cambridge Greek Testament Commentary
CIG	*Corpus inscriptionum graecarum*, ed. A. Boeckhius (Berlin, G. Reimer, 1843)
EPRO	Etudes préliminaires aux religions orientales dans l'Empire Romain
ERT	*Evangelical Review of Theology*
FiE	*Forschungen in Ephesos veröffentlicht vom Österreichischen Archäologischen Instituts* (Wien, Alfred Holder, 1906–)
FS.	Festschrift für
FTS	Frankfurter theologischen Studien
FzB	Forschung zur Bibel
HDB	*A Dictionary of the Bible*, ed. J. Hastings (Edinburgh, T. & T. Clark, 1906)
IGSK	Inschriften Griechischer Städte aus Kleinasien
Ist Mitt	Istanbuler Mitteilungen Deutsches Archäologischen Institut
IvE	*Die Inschriften von Ephesos*, ed. H. Engelmann, D. Knibbe, and R. Merkelbach, IGSK 13, parts 1–8 (Bonn, Rudolf Habelt, 1980–84)
IvS	*Die Inschriften von Smyrna*, ed. G. Petzl, IGSK 23 (Bonn, Rudolf Habelt, 1978)

JhhÖArchInst   *Jahreshefte des Österreichischen Archäologischen Instituts in Wien*

JSNT   *Journal for the Study of the New Testament*

JSNTSS   Journal for the Study of the New Testament Supplement Series

M–M   *The Vocabulary of the Greek Testament*, ed. J. H. Moulton and G. Milligan (London, Hodder and Stoughton, 1930)

NCB   New Century Bible

NTApoc   *New Testment Apocrypha*, 2 vols., ed. E. Hennecke and W. Schneemelcher

ÖTK   Ökumenischer Taschenbuch-Kommentar zum Neuen Testament

OTP   *The Old Testament Pseudepigrapha*, 2 vols., ed. J. H. Charlesworth (New York, Doubleday, 1983; 1985)

PGM   *Papyri graecae magicae. Die griechischen Zauberpapyri*, ed. Karl Preisendanz, 2nd revised edn by A. Heinrichs (Stuttgart, Teubner, 1973–4)

QD   Quaestiones disputatae

SUNT   Studien zur Umwelt des Neuen Testaments

TB   *Tyndale Bulletin*

TTS   Trierer Theologische Studien

Umwelt   *Umwelt des Urchristentums*, 3 vols., ed. J. Leipoldt and W. Grundmann (Berlin, Evangelische Verlagsanstalt, 1971)

WBC   Word Bible Commentary

ZBK   Zürcher Bibelkommentar

ZPE   *Zeitschrift für Papyrologie und Epigraphik*

After the first reference, commentaries on Ephesians will appear in the notes by the surname of the author only followed by the page number(s) being referred to. Subsequent references to all other works will include the author's surname, a shortened version of the title, and the appropriate page numbers. English translation of the Greek magical papyri is based on *The Greek Magical Papyri in Translation Including the Demotic Spells* (ed. H. D. Betz, vol. 1: Text, Chicago, 1986). Unless otherwise indicated all other English translations of other languages (including Greek, German, and French) are my own.

1

INTRODUCTION

There is a strong emphasis on the power of God and the "powers" of evil in Ephesians. This includes a lengthy section instructing believers about engaging in a "spiritual warfare" against these "powers."

This "power-motif" is first apparent in a significant concentration of power terminology. Words for power abound. The writer frequently speaks about δύναμις (5), ἐνέργεια (3), ἰσχύς (2), κράτος (2), and ἐξουσία (4). He also uses the verbs δύναμαι (5), ἐνδυναμόω (1), ἐνεργέω (4), κραταιόω (1), and ἐξισχύω (1).

This represents a substantially higher concentration of power terminology than in any other epistle attributed to Paul (the sole exception is 1 Corinthians – but it is nearly three times longer). When the occurrences of power terminology in a given book are considered in proportion to the size of that book, Ephesians is found to contain a greater percentage of power terminology than any other NT book. This percentage is not limited to one word group. Each word group denoting power in Ephesians contains a higher percentage of power terms than is contained in all other epistles attributed to Paul.

This high concentration of power terminology can partially be explained by the emphasis on the "powers" in Ephesians. These forces are emphasized in Ephesians far more than in any other NT epistle. The devil and various categories of "powers" are mentioned sixteen times in the epistle. The terms ἐξουσία and ἀρχή are both used three times in this sense in Ephesians. Four other power-denoting terms are also used in this way – δύναμις, κυριότης, ἄρχων, and κοσμοκράτωρ. This number would be increased substantially if we were to include the references to τὰ πάντα, τὰ ἐν τοῖς ἐπουρανίοις (τὰ ἐπὶ τοῖς οὐρανοῖς), and "every name that is named." Markus Barth rightly observes, "these powers are mentioned with disturbing frequency and given greater attention than they have received in earlier epistles."[1]

Ephesians is also loaded with many concepts and theological constructs conveying the notion of divine power. It is well known that Ephesians (and to a large degree Colossians) propound a "cosmic Christology" (denoting the power and authority of Christ) and a "realized eschatology" (denoting the believers' share in the power and authority of Christ). Ephesians also highlights the role of the Holy Spirit, who is frequently represented as the agent of divine power in Paul. Furthermore, the epistle also abounds with other concepts highlighting the presence of God's power. Specifically, the author of Ephesians employs terms which can be used with a "power slant" out of their possible range of meanings – πλήρωμα, glory, light, blessing, grace, the head – body imagery, mystery, the various pieces of the armor of God, et al.

These observations compel us to ask why the epistle appears to emphasize "power" to such a great extent – especially the power of God as juxtaposed with the "powers" of evil. The answer to this question could give us further insight into the background and purpose of the epistle.

Does this power-motif betray the influence of Gnosis on the author, or perhaps upon the readers, or both? Could the epistle have been written to a number of churches to provide a safeguard against the inroads of a heresy similar to that threatening the church at Colossae? Perhaps the author is addressing some kind of spiritual crisis in Asia Minor where he sees the readers in intense conflict with demonic agencies? Maybe there is no "situation" at all, but the power-motif reflects an integral and customary part of early Christian baptismal liturgy or catechetical training. We might also ask if this emphasis on the power of God and the "powers" of evil is consistent with a view which regards the epistle as a summary of the salient points of Pauline theology, either as an introduction to the Pauline corpus or as an authentic testament written during Paul's imprisonment. What about the style of the epistle? Could the apparent verbal emphasis on power in Ephesians be explained as a Semitic stylistic trait of stringing together synonyms and plerophoric expression?

The goal of this book is to acquire a more complete understanding of the nature of and motivation for the inclusion of the power-motif in the epistle by studying the author's development of the theme against the backdrop of the spiritual environment of western Asia Minor in the first century A.D. The results of this study may in turn give us an additional clue into the "life setting" of the epistle, and therefore also a better understanding of the message of the epistle in general. Most scholars would agree that the question of why the epistle was written is at the root of the continuing problem of how to understand the message of Ephesians.[2]

Our method of research will be historical, exegetical, and theological. We will begin with a detailed historical study of the religious milieu of the readers, highlighting those aspects particularly germane to an understanding of the first-century A.D. Jewish and Hellenistic notions of divine power and spirit "powers." Additional historical research will be carried out at various other points to determine possible sources for certain terms or concepts. Particular attention will be given to developing a more accurate picture of the mind-set, fears, and religious understanding of the readers. A variety of sources will be employed which may provide insight into the religious climate of the time the epistle was written.

In particular, I will explore the relevance of the Hellenistic magical tradition to understanding the spiritual setting. Our primary source for this is the collection of papyri published by Karl Preisendanz in the two-volume set, *Papyri graecae magicae: Die griechischen Zauberpapyri* (*PGM*), which is contained in a second revised edition by A. Heinrichs. An English translation of these papyri, plus many discovered since Preisendanz's edition, has been published in a volume edited by Hans Dieter Betz entitled, *The Greek Magical Papyri in Translation Including the Demotic Spells* (Chicago, 1986). In addition to this, we will make use of some of the valuable studies conducted and published under the auspices of the Austrian Archaeological Institute in Vienna, namely the older multi-volume work *Forschungen in Ephesos* (*FiE*), the journal *Jahreshefte des Österreichischen Archäologischen Instituts in Wien* (*JhhÖArchInst*), and the inscriptional material gathered in the multi-volume *Inschriften von Ephesos* (*IvE*), a part of a larger series known as Inschriften Griechischer Städte aus Kleinasien (IGSK).

These sources will be employed together with the relevant OT and Jewish material to discern the background to the variety of terms for the principalities, powers, and authorities in Ephesians. We will also conduct a careful analysis of the passages which refer to these "powers" in order more accurately to discern the essence of the author's message to the readers about these "powers."

Three passages where the language of power is particularly prominent will be discussed exegetically. Stress will be placed on providing a precise analysis of these passages, determining the function of the power-motif in these respective contexts, and finally explaining how a given passage relates to the rest of the epistle. A special exegetical analysis of the section on "spiritual warfare" will be undertaken for the potential light it can throw on understanding the power-motif and the overall message of the epistle.

We will not presuppose Pauline authorship of Ephesians as a basis for the study. Neither will this study presuppose any particular theory of the relationship of Colossians to Ephesians. Ephesians will be examined in its own right with the terminology and concepts frequently compared to those in Paul. A conclusion will be drawn at the end of the work stating whether or not we have found a line of continuity between Paul and Ephesians with regard to this power-motif.

Finally, a synthesis of the results of the historical and exegetical investigation into the power-motif of Ephesians will be taken into account in a final chapter. Here we will seek to explain some of the theological peculiarities of Ephesians in light of the results of the research in the preceding chapters regarding the power-motif.

2

THE RELIGIOUS CLIMATE OF WESTERN ASIA MINOR IN THE FIRST CENTURY A.D.

A profound interest in supernatural power and the demonic realm gripped the inhabitants of the Hellenistic world in the first century A.D. This can be seen in a number of traditions, but especially in the magical beliefs and practices of the time. Western Asia Minor was not exempt from these influences; on the contrary, the area was renowned for its flourishing magical activity which involved the spiritual "powers." The purpose of this chapter is not only to substantiate and illustrate these assertions, but also to show how this milieu is relevant to a better understanding of the Christian communities to which the Epistle to the Ephesians was addressed. We will seek to bring out the local flavor of the epistle, which seems sometimes to be lost when the homogeneity of the first-century Hellenistic world is overemphasized. Specifically, we will focus our attention on the concepts of divine power and supernatural "powers" within the context of religious belief in first-century Asia Minor with the hope that this might give us some insight into the themes of the power of God, the "powers" of evil, and "spiritual warfare" in Ephesians.

1. The destination of the epistle: western Asia Minor

There is unanimous agreement among interpreters that the Epistle to the Ephesians was written to western Asia Minor (as opposed to Palestine, Macedonia, Syria, etc.). There is also a strong likelihood of an Ephesian readership, whether the epistle was composed at Ephesus by Paul[1] or by one from his circle,[2] or whether it was written by Paul from Rome (or Caesarea?) as a circular letter to be distributed from Ephesus.[3]

Although it is sometimes argued that the epistle was intended specifically for Ephesus,[4] the internal evidence of the epistle[5] and the divided witnesses over the text-critical problem of 1:1 make it unlikely

5

that the believers of Ephesus were intended as the sole recipients of the letter.[6]

The most plausible conjecture for the destination of the epistle is that it was intended by the author as an encyclical, with copies (or perhaps, the original) being sent to various churches. If the epistle was intended as a circular to the Roman province of Asia it may very well have been sent first to Ephesus – the hub for communication throughout the province (see below, section 3). This probability is heightened by the fact that according to Luke (Acts 19:10) Ephesus had also been the center for Paul's evangelistic work for two and a half years from which "all who lived in Asia heard the word of the Lord."

One needs to be cautious not to assume that there was only one local congregation in Ephesus. By the time Ephesians was written there may have been a network of new churches established within the city. This consideration is made all the more plausible by recognizing that the lower estimates for the population of Ephesus in the first century begin at a quarter of a million.[7] It is also possible that churches existed in villages in the immediate vicinity of Ephesus, e.g. throughout the Cayster valley (viz. Metropolis, Hypaipa, Diashieron, Neikaia, Koloe, and Palaiapolis). These considerations greatly expand the potential "Ephesian" readership.[8] There has been a stronger consensus, however, that Ephesians circulated to a number of the western Asia Minor cities where churches were known to exist (e.g. in addition to Ephesus: Laodicea, Pergamum, and Sardis).

Of more significance for our purpose is the importance of discerning whether the churches of western Asia Minor faced a common spiritual problem or crisis. Some interpreters have answered this query in the affirmative. On the basis of internal evidence, Schnackenburg, for example, reached the conclusion that the epistle, having the character of a "catholic epistle" written by an unknown author, was obviously (*offensichtlich*) written to Christians in a specific spiritual situation. Schnackenburg thinks that it could hardly have been intended by the author as a general manifesto for all Christianity.[9] The churches he sees facing this common spiritual crisis are in the Lycus valley (Colossae, Laodicea, and Hierapolis) *and* in the general region of Ephesus. There does appear to be some evidence, both internal and external, pointing to a set of homogeneous problems facing the churches of western Asia Minor. Further study would then be warranted in seeking to determine whether the emphasis on divine power/spiritual warfare in Ephesians may have been prompted by a situation common to the churches of western Asia Minor.

2. Gnosticism in first-century Asia Minor?

Since F. C. Baur promulgated the view that the epistle to the Ephesians belonged to the latter half of the second century A.D. because of its dependence on Gnostic thought, the question of Gnostic influence upon Ephesians has occupied the forefront of the literature dealing with the epistle. Scholars such as R. Bultmann, P. Pokorný, H. Schlier, E. Käsemann, W. Schmithals, E. Norden, and a host of others are well known for their handling of this question with regard to Ephesians. Such terminology and concepts in the epistle as the head–body imagery, mystery, fullness, αἰών, ἄρχων, the once–now schema, and the so-called spatial eschatology are the main candidates for a Gnostic interpretation. Our purpose here is to take into account in a general way the course of recent scholarship on the hotly disputed question of whether some beginning form of Gnosticism actually existed in the first century A.D., and consequently, whether it could have been an influential factor on the author of Ephesians or on the communities to which the epistle was addressed. There is more thorough discussion of the Gnostic concept of the cosmic "powers" in chapter 3. The question of Gnostic influence on other specific terms and concepts will be discussed under the relevant exegetical sections.

Definitions

Any concise discussion of Gnosticism is difficult since scholars have still not reached a consensus on a definition of "Gnosticism." The Messina conference in 1966 urged a distinction between "proto-Gnosticism" and "Gnosticism."[10] R. McL. Wilson would like to gain greater precision by using the term "Gnosis" for the inchoate phenomena in the first century and reserve "Gnosticism" for the fully articulated systems in the second century.[11] Still others would like a much broader definition of Gnosticism which emphasizes its continuity over stages of development. Rudolph in particular adopts what he sees as a common practice in Germany of understanding "Gnosis" and "Gnosticism" as the same thing, while still using "the first as the self-designation of a religion of redemption in late antiquity, [and] the latter as a newer form of it."[12] To avoid confusion I will follow Rudolph's distinctions in the ensuing discussion of Gnosis.

Even since the publication of the Nag Hammadi documents and the continuing discussion about Gnosis, there is still widespread debate on what particular elements combine to comprise the Gnostic system. The diversity within Gnosis itself makes it rather difficult to give a coherent picture. Hans-Martin Schenke has distilled what he considers to be the main elements of the Gnostic system:[13] (1) the unknown God; (2) Sophia as world creator; (3) the seven planet-rulers; (4) the descent and raising again of the soul; (5) dualism of light/darkness; (6) dualism of soul/body and spirit/matter; (7) the teaching of the God *"Mensch"* (= the creation of the first man); (8) the redeemer concept (Schenke finds the concept of a "redeemed redeemer" unsuitable, however); (9) hypostasis teaching or emanation concept. This delineation is a helpful summary as a reference point for understanding Gnosis for our discussion.

Apart from what can questionably be interpreted as Gnosis in the biblical text, there is no extant evidence of Gnosis as having existed in Asia Minor in the first century. Even more problematic is the fact that no pre-Christian Gnostic texts have been found in any locale.[14] This evidence does not necessarily imply that the beginnings of Gnosis did not yet exist, but it should caution us against *assuming* that it did exist and then interpreting Ephesians in light of the second- and third-century systems. Certainly some elements of Gnosis must have been in vogue in the first century; it would have been impossible for it to develop so rapidly in the second century without some foundation. It is precisely this question of what served as the foundation and what motivated its development that is difficult to answer, chiefly because we lack any conclusive evidence.

Dualism in Gnosis

Some recent research on one of the cornerstones of Gnosis − anticosmic dualism − casts doubt on the pre-Christian origin of Gnosis as even a loosely coherent system. C. Colpe and H.-M. Schenke were the first to shake Bousset and Reitzenstein's assumption of *one* Iranian mystery of redemption.[15] They pointed the way toward extreme and decadent Jewish notions as a partial explanation of Gnosis.[16] I. Culianu has taken this lead in searching for a motivation for the type of dualism evident in Gnosis. His research led him to suggest that the background of the Demiurge in Gnosis is Jewish and that the catalyst for the development of the thoroughgoing dualism is the disillusionment after the Jewish Wars. He explains:[17]

> After the events of [A.D.] 70 and 135, even the most conservative Jewish circles, when confronted with the problem of

theodicy, may have rejected a God who failed, if only in order to preserve the idea of transcendence itself. Because the Jewish God had a strong national character, he was the heavenly guardian of Israel, in opposition with the mere angels, who were the guardians of the other nations. A defeated god is no almighty god. That is why such a god might have been sacrificed in order to save the idea of divinity.

He gathers adequate support to demonstrate the existence of a pre-Christian Jewish binitarianism – with God's lieutenant gaining increasing prominence. He sets forth further evidence to show that in the *apocalyptic* legends, God's lieutenant came mistakenly to be exchanged for God himself, and in the *cosmogonical* legends, God's lieutenant is assigned the creation of the world.

This overall approach to finding the source of Gnostic dualism seems to be moving in a plausible direction after the waning of the *religionsgeschichtliche* school's postulation of an Iranian (Zoroastrian) provenance. This is essentially also the approach of A.F. Segal, who sees the radical dualism as having its roots in degenerate Judaism. Segal's thesis is that, "The radicalization of gnosticism was a product of the battle between the rabbis, the Christians and various other 'two powers' sectarians who inhabited the outskirts of Judaism."[18] Yamauchi has endorsed this approach, but he would specifically emphasize the disappointed messianism after the Bar Kochba Revolt (A.D. 135), because of evidence of continuing apocalyptic hopes after A.D. 70.[19] He points to the dualistic sentiments associated with the apostate rabbi, Elisha ben Abuyah, and suggests that there were probably other unnamed rabbis who went even further in the direction of dualism than Elisha.[20]

If such an interpretation of the origin of Gnostic dualism could be firmly established, the view that Ephesians reflects Gnosis would need to be drastically reworked. Additional doubt on the previous Gnostic interpretations of Ephesians is cast by two considerations: (1) the syncretistic character of Gnosis makes it more likely that it drew on Ephesians rather than the reverse, and (2) many of the "distinctively Gnostic" terms in Ephesians can be shown to have a different provenance.

Gnostic use of Christian material

I have emphasized the alleged Jewish roots of Gnosis in the preceding discussion. This must be balanced by the fact that in a number of ways the entire Near East served as an ancestor to Gnosticism.[21] Not least of all, Christianity provided significant input to Gnosis.[22] M. Krause seeks to establish some objective criteria for the discernment of the Christianizing of Gnostic texts. The results of his analysis of the Nag Hammadi Library leave him with five Gnostic works reflecting Christianization.[23]

One important example of the Gnostic use of Ephesians is the frequent citation and allusion to Eph 6:12.[24] It is quoted in *Hypostasis of the Archons* 86:20−25 as a thematic introduction. It is also cited in *Exegesis on the Soul* 130:35−131:13 and in *Testim. Truth* 32:22−33:4. The Valentinian use of the verse is also demonstrated by its appearance in *Exc. Theo.* 48:2 and in Irenaeus, *Adv. Haer.* 1.5.4. A Manichean use is also probable.[25] The attribution of this text to "the great apostle" by the writer of the *Hypostasis of the Archons* makes it unlikely that Eph 6:12 was originally a Gnostic text. Rather, the writer of the *Hypostasis* seems to be appealing to the authority of the apostle. If he can effectively line up the apostle Paul with his exposition on the Gnostic archons, he can gain a Christian hearing and greater credibility (or, perhaps he naively believes that the apostle taught such a system). The upshot of this evidence would seem to suggest that there would be a temptation and a resultant tendency for Gnostics, and especially Christian Gnostics, to take "Paul's" teaching on spiritual "powers" (e.g. Eph 6:10) and use it for their own purpose in promoting a Gnostic view of the "powers," or archons.

The few occurrences (1:17; 3:19; 4:13) of the terms for knowledge in Ephesians, thought to reflect "Gnosis," are in no way a definitive proof that Ephesians reflects Gnostic thought. R. McL. Wilson warns, "All religions profess in some sense to convey a knowledge of God, hence a *gnosis*; but it is precisely the nature, content and significance of this *gnosis* that is in question."[26] For those who had heavily imbibed magical beliefs, "Gnosis" is not a knowledge of the divine kernel present within them, but "Gnosis" is above all the recognition of names as the most significant aspect of magical knowledge."[27]

While Gnosis drew on Christianity and Judaism, it also took terms and concepts from magic and the mysteries.[28] The converse of this statement is not necessarily true, however, i.e. that magic and the mysteries borrowed from Gnosis. The magical tradition itself can be sharply distinguished from Gnosis. The magic writings possess an essentially different tone. A. D. Nock quips that while the Gnostics were passionately eager to know how wheels went round, the authors and readers of the magical papyri desired simply to be able to make them turn.[29] The magical papyri were unconcerned about systematizing and making sense of the supernatural realm and the heavens; their chief concern was utilitarian — manipulating the "powers" for individual interest. This is especially conspicuous in the tendency of the magical papyri to give long strings of "magical" names which seem to have no coherent connection other than the fact that they are believed to be laiden with power.[30] Nock also points out that whereas the Gnostics were concerned about ultimate salvation, the magical practitioners were more concerned about the here and now and safety from the threatening supernatural "powers."[31] C. Colpe has therefore warned against the inadmissible broadening of our understanding of Gnosis by comparing a magical papyrus with a Gnostic text.[32] The magical papyri are original documents and primary sources enhancing our understanding of magical beliefs and practices in the Greco-Roman world. While the Gnostic and Hermetic groups used magical books, "most of their material vanished and what we have left are their quotations."[33]

Jewish Gnosis?

Various strands of Judaism are thought to be reflected in the so-called Colossian heresy. Most notably, some interpreters see a "gnosticized" Judaism behind the heresy.[34] F. F. Bruce has gone even further by attempting an identification of this apparent gnosticized Judaism with "Merkabah Mysticism"[35] — a Jewish development on the theme of heavenly visions patterned after the vision granted to Ezekiel (Ezek 1:15–26). G. Scholem, who has written the major work on Merkabah Mysticism, describes it as having been thoroughly influenced by Gnostic speculation concerning the ascent of the soul through the spheres of the hostile planet-angels and rulers of the cosmos.[36]

There are two serious difficulties in seeing a Gnosis-infected Judaism in the first century — the problem of dating and also the problem of whether the allegedly "Gnostic" Judaism truly was Gnostic. We have already seen that the existence of a first-century Gnostic dualism is shrouded in uncertainty. Thus, the question of any kind of Gnostic influence on Judaism at this time is still an open question. A major objection has been leveled against reading Merkabah Mysticism back into the first century by I. Gruenwald. He contends that some of the remains of Merkabah Mysticism may well go back to the second century A.D., but not to the first century. He also objects that "The material as it lies before us today reveals clear traces of the work of later editors, who not only added new material to the old but also interfered with the old texts before them."[37]

Gruenwald has also challenged the assumption that Merkabah Mysticism even in its developed form was Gnostic. He points to what he considers as a total absence of anti-cosmic tones in the Hekhalot literature, thus an absence of the dualism so characteristic of Gnostic texts.[38] He notices that while Gnosis essentially longed for a final escape from the bonds of the material, evil world, the mysticism of Merkabah presupposes that the mystic always returns from his celestial adventures to his body on earth.[39] Furthermore, the Hekhalot writings are basically mystical writings with no immediate redemptive claims; therefore, "they are to be strictly distinguished from the gnostic concepts and writings which have an emphatic redemptive quality."[40] Here again, one needs to exercise caution in assuming the existence of a first-century Gnosis.

Summary and conclusions

(1) In spite of the fact that a great number of interpreters see Gnosis reflected in Ephesians, the existence of any relatively coherent Gnostic system which would have been capable of influencing either the author of Ephesians or the communities to which the epistle was addressed rests on a very weak foundation.

(2) A total dismissal of all Gnostic interpretations of Ephesians would not be the proper conclusion to draw, however. Even if the thoroughgoing dualism characteristic of fully developed Gnosis cannot be demonstrated as existing before A.D. 135 or even A.D. 70, other streams of religious influence (with permutations already in process) may have existed which had a profound impact on developing Gnosis. These streams may have been converging in the first century, forming the beginnings of Gnosis. One or a number of these merging streams may have influenced the content of Ephesians, perhaps in a way that would make certain aspects indistinguishable from Gnosis.

(3) A serious caution then needs to be exercised in the treatment of Ephesians – a caution which certainly does not *assume* a

flourishing Gnosis and perhaps gives the benefit of the doubt in an interpretational dispute to the line of evidence which does not depend on third- and fourth-century Gnostic texts of fully developed Gnosis for an explanation.

(4) It is highly questionable whether a gnosticized Judaism existed in the first century or indeed ever did exist. It is also dubious that Merkabah Mysticism existed in the first century. Undoubtedly, some forms of Jewish mysticism certainly did exist, but they need to be carefully distinguished from Gnosis.

(5) Therefore, in seeking to understand better the attitude of the people in western Asia Minor to supernatural power, we will explore the possible influence of other traditions. In particular, we will examine the role of magic and the mysteries in western Asia Minor.

3. Ephesus as the leading city of Asia Minor

The notion of Ephesus as the "chief" city of Asia Minor in the first century A.D. receives widespread support.[41] Evidence suggests that Ephesus had become the titular capital of Asia after Attalus III bequeathed the Pergamene kingdom to Rome in 133 B.C.[42]

Because of its active port on the mouth of the Cayster river and also owing to its strategic geographical position, Ephesus served the Roman senatorial province of Asia as the center for commerce[43] and communication.[44] Not only was Ephesus readily accessible from the Aegean, it was situated at the junction of two major highways leading to the interior – the Royal Road, which led across Mt. Tmolus from Sardis, and a second route with an easy pass leading through the Maeander valley and to the Southern Highway.[45] Even the Phrygian cities of Colossae, Laodicea, and Hierapolis were bound to this Aegean port for communication and commerce.[46] Almost a century ago Sir William Ramsay suggested that Ephesus was the communication and transportation hub of Asia Minor in the Imperial period – all roads led from Ephesus.[47] This conclusion has recently been upheld by D. H. French in his study of the Roman road-system of Asia Minor.[48] French concludes,[49]

> The first stage of development is represented by the roads built by the Romans within their newly acquired province of Asia. The evidence of this statement comes from milestones of M' Aquilius (129–126 B.C.). The administrative centre of the province was Ephesus. That the paved roads started at Ephesus and radiated outwards is demonstrated by the

high numbers on the milestones (CCXXIII at Yarash near Burder and CXXXI at Bergama). Mileages were measured from the *caput viae*, Ephesus.

Ramsay gathered geographical and literary evidence to support his contention that this natural communication route followed the order in which the seven churches appear in Revelation 2–3.[50] This conjecture could potentially give us insight into the readership of Ephesians.

J. Lähnemann summarizes well the importance of Ephesus in the first century:[51]

> Within "Asia," which in many respects was the most important province of the Roman Empire, Ephesus was the outstanding metropolis: it was not only the largest city (with a population of well over a quarter million), but it was also politically, culturally, and economically the leader – as the most important intersection between East and West. It was here the Roman proconsul had his official residence.

Thus, the influence of Ephesus on the rest of Asia Minor should not be underestimated. Of much more consequence for our study, however, is the significance of Ephesus as a religious center in the first century. The prominence of Ephesus was heightened by the city serving as the home for the "leading divinity" of Asia Minor – Artemis of Ephesus. No less important was the function of Ephesus as the leading magical center for Asia Minor. These two aspects of the religious life of the city will receive much more detailed treatment below.

4. Ephesus as a center for magical practices

Magical practices were prevalent throughout the entire Hellenistic world in the first century A.D. The city of Ephesus, however, bore the reputation for being something of a center for magical practices. B. M. Metzger states, "Of all ancient Graeco-Roman cities, Ephesus, the third largest city in the Empire, was by far the most hospitable to magicians, sorcerers, and charlatans of all sorts."[52] O. Meinardus concurs: "Perhaps even more than Pisidian Antioch, Corinth, and Antioch-on-the-Orontes, this city of traders and sailors, of courtesans and rakes, swarmed with soothsayers and purveyors of charms."[53]

In his account of Paul's two- to three year ministry at Ephesus (Acts 19), Luke implies that there were a substantial number who practiced magic at Ephesus. Quite a number of these magicians were converted and as an expression of their new allegiance to the Lord Jesus, gathered all of their magical books together and burned them. Luke places an incredibly high monetary value on the burned books (Haenchen: 50,000 days' wages) which may indicate the vast number of books burned and/or that the books were extremely valuable, reflecting a high demand for them.[54] The magical practices at Ephesus continued well into the Christian era since it was the subject of Christian prophecy (Clem. of Alex., *Exhort.* 2.19): "Against whom does Heracleitus of Ephesus utter this prophecy? Against 'night-roamers, magicians (μάγοι), Bacchants, Lenaean revellers and devotees of the mysteries.' "

The Ephesia Grammata

The reputation of Ephesus as a magical center may partly be derived from the fame of the proverbial "Ephesian Letters" ('Εφέσια γράμματα).[55] These "letters" constituted written magical spells and are well attested in the literature.[56] The genuine Ephesia Grammata amounted to six magical terms specifically named as ἄσκιον, κατάσκιον, λίξ, τετράξ, δαμναμενεύς, and αἴσια by Clement of Alexandria and Hesychius. The first mention of these Ephesian Letters occurs as early as the fourth century B.C. in a Cretan tablet.[57]

The letters (or names) seem to be laden with apotropaic power, that is, in the warding off of evil demons.[58] They could be used either as written amulets or spoken charms. Anaxilas makes reference to those "wearing fine Ephesian charms in little sewed bags."[59] Plutarch relates that the "magi" instructed those possessed to repeat to themselves the magic words in order to drive the demons out (Plut., *Quaest. conv.* 7.5).

The words were also used in superstitious ways to provide help on special occasions. For example, the Suda and Eustathius give an account of an Ephesian wrestler who competed in Olympia wearing the Ephesia Grammata on his ankles. He repeatedly defeated his Milesian opponent until the "letters" were discovered and removed. The Milesian then easily won three successive victories.[60] The same sources also report that the Lydian king Croesus is said to have saved himself from the funeral pyre by using the Ephesia Grammata. Menander records an instance of the Ephesia Grammata being used as "evil-averting spells" for the benefit of those who were getting married. On this occasion someone would walk around and around the couple repeating the magical names.[61]

The bearer or speaker of these words was clearly believed to have personal access to supernatural powers. McCown notes that for their literary tradition, the Ephesia Grammata are words of power and there is no evidence for their hypostatization. In popular usage, however, he finds them transformed from a mere magical formula into active and powerful beings whose characters and performances are known.[62] This interpretation is further justified by two of the Ephesian letters − "Lix Tetrax" − appearing in the *Testament of Solomon* (7:5). Here they are taken as one name (as in the Cretan tablet) and are placed in the category of the demonic.

It is difficult to determine how the Ephesia Grammata came to be affiliated with Ephesus. The most likely suggestion is that the six words were closely connected with the Ephesian Artemis (see below, section 5).

The Ephesian Letters are not the only evidence of magical practice in Ephesus and western Asia Minor.[63] A whole magical apparatus has been discovered at Pergamum consisting of a triangular bronze magical table, a bronze magical dish, a bronze spike, two bronze magical rings, two bronze magical plates, and three magical amulets. Each of the pieces is inscribed with magical names and figures.[64] A magical amulet with Jewish characteristics was found in the area around Ephesus.[65]

Additional amulets were reportedly discovered between Smyrna and Ephesus, also bearing Jewish characteristics.[66] It is also interesting to note that Ignatius' only use of the word μαγεία occurs in his letter to the Ephesian congregation (Ign., *Eph.* 19:3): with the coming of Christ "all magic was dissolved." If the climatic conditions were more conducive to the preservation of papyri, we could doubtless have numerous documents of magic from the Asian capital.[67] Consequently we are forced to rely on the Egyptian papyri, which were probably quite similar to those used in Ephesus, to broaden our understanding of the nature and purpose of magic.

Sources

The primary source for our knowledge of how magic was practiced during the Hellenistic era is derived from a collection of papyri discovered in the last two centuries, mainly in Egypt. Those discovered up to 1940 have been collected and edited by K. Preisendanz in a two-volume work entitled, *Papyri graecae magicae: Die griechischen Zauberpapyri.*[68] An English translation of the magical papyri has recently been completed under the direction of Hans Dieter Betz. The new work, entitled *The Greek Magical Papyri in Translation Including the Demotic Spells*, includes an English translation of all of the papyri in Preisendanz's collection, the Demotic (Egyptian) spells, and a translation of forty more recently discovered Greek magical papyri.

Other sources for an understanding of Hellenistic magic can be found in the *tabellae defixionum* (i.e. cursing tablets), amulets, ostraca, and various extant magical apparatuses.[69] The Testament of Solomon is also a very important source, although it contains a number of Christian elements (see below, section 7).

There is no doubt that magical practices were flourishing in the first century A.D.[70] Suetonius records that Augustus ordered 2,000 magical scrolls to be burned in the year 13 B.C.[71] The personalities of the Olympian gods had begun to wane as early as the fourth century B.C. and were soon replaced in popularity by magic and the mystery cults.[72] This time also marked a rapid increase in astrological beliefs. The syncretism and strong belief in the influence of supernatural forces common to these three related traditions are reflected in the numerous Greek magical papyri extant today.

Most of these papyri date to the third and fourth centuries A.D., but there are a few which have been dated to the first[73] and second centuries A.D.[74] The third- and fourth-century date of many of these papyri is not a great problem for using them in the quest to discern the nature of magic practiced in the first century. There is little doubt that these more recent papyri actually contain formulas dating much earlier. The purported value of the magical papyri was their claim to possess ancient, reliable, and venerable formulas and recipes.[75]

The Egyptian provenance of most of the magical papyri in Preisendanz's collection does not imply that it would be essentially different in nature and content than the magic practiced at Ephesus. With Ephesus as the chief port city of Asia Minor there was frequent commercial contact between Ephesus and Alexandria. This had resulted in the dissemination of significant Egyptian religious influence in Ephesus which undoubtedly included the sharing of effective magical charms and recipes.[76]

Magic and the spirit world

The overriding characteristic of the practice of magic throughout the Hellenistic world was the cognizance of a spirit world exercising influence over virtually every aspect of life. The goal of the magician was to discern the helpful spirits from the harmful ones and learn the distinct operations and the relative strengths and authority of the spirits. Through this knowledge, means could be constructed (with spoken or written formulas, amulets, etc.) for the manipulation of the spirits in the interest of the individual person. With the proper formula, a spirit-induced sickness could be cured, a chariot race could be won, sexual passions could be enhanced, etc. Conversely, great harm could be brought to another person through the utterance of a curse.

Fear of the demonic realm was a very important factor in the use of magic. Howard Kee rightly draws attention to the recurrent use of the word φυλάσσω in the papyri and concludes that the aim of the formulas is largely apotropaic, i.e. to protect from demons.[77]

There can be no question that spirit beings were perceived as the functionaries behind the magic.[78] For example, notice the attempt to enlist the assistance of the spirits by a competitor in a chariot race:[79]

> I conjure you up, holy beings and holy names; join in aiding this spell, and bind, enchant, thwart, strike, overturn, conspire against, destroy, kill, break Eucherius the charioteer, and all his horses tomorrow in the circus at Rome. May he not leave the barriers well; may he not be quick in the contest; may he not outstrip anyone; may he not make the turns well; may he not win any prizes ... may he be broken; may he be dragged along by your power, in the morning and afternoon races. Now! Now! Quickly! Quickly!

Many times in the various formulas, specific names of spirits/divinities are called upon to carry out the request. The syncretistic character of the Egyptian papyri is evident through the variety of names called upon – those from Jewish influence (Iao, Sabaoth, Adonai), Egyptian (Osiris, Isis, Serapis), and Greek (Kronos, Zeus, Aphrodite), to give just a few examples.

Magical practices crossed all boundaries. "Magical" beliefs and practices can be found in the mystery cults and even in Judaism and Christianity. At this point it is essential to ask how one can differentiate between "religion" and "magic." The magical practitioner as well as the devotee of a given religion believed in the supernatural, exercised faith, and even prayed. On the surface the main difference appears to be that one is viewed as sanctioned, legal, and acceptable and the other is not. David Aune has recently sought to provide a more precise definition of "magic" in order to compare it to the dominant religion. He contends that magic has historically played a role as an integral substructure of the dominant religious institutions. He has formulated two criteria for deciding what is distinctively "magical." First, he defines magical practice as a deviation from the sanctioned religious practice. Secondly, and more germane to our study, is this contention:[80] "Goals sought within the context of religious deviance are magical when attained through the management of supernatural powers in such a way that results are virtually guaranteed." We find this definition generally acceptable and particularly appropriate in putting the stress on "the management of supernatural powers."[81] For monotheists, both Jews and Christians, reliance on the aid of "powers" betrays a lack of confidence in the one God. The one God ("Iao," "Sabaoth," or "Adonai") is given a place equal to strings of other divinities in the magical formulas and recipes. The definition is accurate not only in stressing "powers," but also by highlighting "management." In religion one prays and requests from the gods; in magic one commands the gods and therefore expects guaranteed results.[82]

It is also highly significant for our purposes to note that magic appears to have been far more popular among the lower classes in the Greco-Roman world than among the upper classes.[83] It was therefore not reserved for the philosophers and the educated, but was widely diffused and practiced among the common people of the cities, villages, and countryside. Aune remarks,[84]

> Those who were educated and affluent associated magical practices with the uneducated and poor in the lower strata of society (Origen contra Celsum 6.41; 7.4; Philostratus vit. sophist. 523, 590). Certainly the Greek of the magical papyri is the unpretentious common language of the people, not the cultivated, literary and atticistic language of the educated. Since the Graeco-Roman literature which is extant was produced and transmitted by the educated, rarely are the views of the common people adequately represented.

The magical papyri are therefore extremely valuable in reflecting the language and beliefs of a great number of the common people in the

Hellenistic world. Betz is therefore correct when he comments, "Magical beliefs and practices can hardly be overestimated in their importance for the daily life of the people."[85]

Summary

(1) Ephesus had a reputation for a prolificity of magical practices. Since Ephesus was the leading city of Asia Minor, its influence in the sphere of magic very likely extended throughout the province.

(2) Magic was primarily concerned with the acquisition of supernatural powers and the manipulation of the spirit world in the interest of the magician. The magical papyri give us a rare insight into the beliefs and fears of the common people in the Hellenistic world.

(3) Hellenistic magic is therefore quite relevant to our study in Ephesians. It was widely practiced in the area to which the epistle was written and it was chiefly concerned with "power" and supernatural "powers."

5. The cult of the Ephesian Artemis

Her significance

Antipatros lauded the temple of Artemis at Ephesus as one of the seven wonders of the world (Antipater of Sidon, *Anth. Pal.* 9.58). The grandeur and fame of the temple was only exceeded by the influence of the cult itself, not only in Ephesus, but throughout all of Asia.[86] The Ephesian Artemis, or Diana (her Roman name), was worshiped more widely by individuals than any deity known to Pausanias.[87] The spread of the cult throughout Asia was assisted by the annual Artemisia — a monthly festival held in the month of Artemision in honor of Artemis.[88] Adherents gathered from all over for festive celebration and worship of their goddess. The dissemination of the cult was also aided by a strong missionary outlook by its devotees. Scores of missionary sites were established throughout the world where worshipers patterned their local Artemis cult on the model of the Ephesian cult.[89] She was even worshiped in the Lycus valley in the cities of Colossae, Laodicea, and Hierapolis.

The influence of the Ephesian Artemis extended beyond the religious sphere into a domination of Asian life and culture. The temple wielded tremendous power through its function as a banking and financial center. Large amounts of money were deposited and borrowed from the Artemision. The cult also obtained a sizeable income from the large amount of property owned in the environs of Ephesus. After citing much inscriptional data in this regard, Oster concludes, "So through economic means the religion of Artemis became an indispensable pillar in the cultural structures and life of Asia, and was therefore a crucial factor in the lives of all individuals whom Christianity hoped to convert."[90]

Her power

One undisputed characteristic of the Ephesian Artemis is the unsurpassed cosmic power attributed to her. She was worshiped at Ephesus as πρωτοθρονία, supreme in divine power and place.[91] Oster has summarized well the inscriptional evidence extolling her transcendent power:[92]

> The veneration of the Ephesian goddess did not come solely from her ability to be sympathetic and involved in the human problems and predicaments of her worshippers. This aspect of her character was equally matched in the eyes of her suppliants by her transcendent power ... her ability to help her worshippers stemmed, in fact, from her awesome power. It was because of her supra-natural powers that she could intercede between her followers and the cruel fate which plagued them. To those who called upon Artemis she was Savior (Σώτειρα), Lord (Κυρία), and Queen of the Cosmos (Βασιληΐς κόσμου). She was a heavenly goddess (οὐράνιος θεὸς Ἄρτεμις Ἐφεσία), whose being and character could only be described in superlatives: μεγίστη, ἁγιωτάτη, and ἐπιφανεστάτη.

Her power was symbolically represented to her worshipers by certain ornamentation on her dress and by her necklaces. The rows of lions, steers, and other animals depicted by relief on her skirt demonstrate the compelling authority she was believed to have possessed over all powers since mythical antiquity. Likewise, the fact that the signs of the zodiac were so prominently displayed around her neck would assure the devotee that Artemis possessed an authority and power superior to that of astrological fate.[93] This promise of power over fate was extended by many of the mystery religions, but the Ephesian Artemis is the only divinity to depict visually her divine superiority with the signs of the zodiac.[94]

A prayer to the Ephesian Artemis recorded in the Acts of John by Pseudo-Prochorus may preserve something of the mind-set of the worshipers of Artemis with regard to her power:[95]

> O Great Artemis of the Ephesians, help! Display your power (δύναμιν) upon this young man who has died. For all the Ephesians know, both men and women, that all things (τὰ πάντα) are governed by you, and that great powers (δυνάμεις μεγάλαι) come to us through you. Give now to your servant what you are able to do in this regard. Raise up your servant Domnos.

Although the date of this work is well into the Christian era, the attribution of resurrection power to the Ephesian Artemis may very well reflect the beliefs of the Artemis devotees in the first century.

One of the reasons for the belief in the transcendent and superior power of the Ephesian Artemis may stem from the legend that she came directly from heaven – Διοπετής (Acts 19:35). The Suda describes her place of origin as ἐξ οὐρανοῦ.[96]

Artemis and magic

We have thus far characterized Ephesus both as a center for magical practices and as a center for the cult of Artemis for Asia Minor. One may wonder if there was any connection between the two, and if so, what type of relationship the Artemis cult had with the practice of magic.

Although it has been claimed that the Ephesian Artemis was not by nature a goddess of magic,[97] she does seem to have had a direct link with the magical practices of the time. She was considered a supremely powerful deity and could therefore exercise her power for the benefit of the devotee in the face of other opposing "powers" and spirits. Her power in this respect is well illustrated in a papyrus containing a magical formula apparently for the purpose of compelling the passion of a woman toward a man. Directly under the text is a crude drawing of the Ephesian Artemis, indicating that she is the power called upon to fulfill the wish (line 4: "take a leaf of lead and with a nail write the figure ...").[98]

Artemis plays an important role in Greco-Roman times as a goddess of the underworld. This role is particularly evident in the magical papyri. She possesses authority and control over the multiplicity of demons of the dead and also the demons of nature. She is virtually identified with Hekate, Selene, and the Babylonian goddess Ereschigal, who are even more widely renowned as goddesses of the underworld.[99] Pliny informs us that an image of Hekate was even present in the precinct of the temple of Artemis at Ephesus (Pliny, *Nat. hist.* 36.4.32). It is also significant that the magical apparatus found at Pergamum, while containing images of the goddess Hekate on the three corners of the bronze table, also contains an epithet peculiar to Artemis under one of these images.[100] C. Bonner also gives examples of magical amulets bearing the images of the Ephesian Artemis and Hekate.[101]

There is some evidence which points to a direct connection between the Ephesian Artemis and the Ephesia Grammata. Pausanias, the Atticist lexicographer, records that the "letters" "seem to have been written indistinctly and obscurely on the feet, girdle, and crown of Artemis."[102] Doubt has been cast on the accuracy of Pausanias' statement since the Ephesia Grammata have not been found inscribed on any of the extant images of Artemis.[103] The magical papyri provide confirmation to the statement, however. The great Paris magical papyrus mentions certain permutations of the Ephesia Grammata Δαμναμενεύς that were inscribed on the scepter of Artemis-Selene.[104] It is certainly possible that magicians and silversmiths did engrave the letters on various parts of the many images of the Ephesian Artemis, in spite of the fact that none has survived to this day. Unfortunately, the great image in the Artemision has also long since been destroyed. McCown does find the evidence sufficiently compelling to conclude that an Anatolian provenience should be assumed for the words which were at some point taken over by the worship that developed around Artemis of Ephesus. He remarks, "for the Hellenistic age, certainly, the might of Ephesian Artemis lay behind the ancient formula, but, more than that, the power also of primitive magic and religion."[105]

The close relationship of the Ephesia Grammata to Artemis-Hekate is strongly supported by the magical papyri. The names ἀσκει κατασκι occur in a magical charm of Hekate Ereschigal.[106] The word Δαμναμενεύς is twice used as a magical name in a hymn to Hekate-Artemis (*PGM* IV.2709-84; see also lines 2773, 2779). It is also used in a spell in *PGM* III.434−35 instructing the practitioner, "on the 13th, say the 13th name Ἄρτεμι Δαμνο Δαμνο Λύκαινα [= "she-wolf," and epithet of Artemis]."

The best illustration of the close connection of Artemis to the Ephesia Grammata occurs in a more recently discovered magical text published by Dierk Wortmann.[107] The text also serves to illustrate and substantiate the nature of Artemis as an underworld goddess and her connection with Hekate and Ereschigal. The text invokes the aid of the goddesses of the underworld which it specifically names as Artemis, Hekate, Persephone, and Ereschigal to provide their help and power in securing the love of an unwilling maiden for an impassioned lover. Three of the Ephesia Grammata are given as the magical names to be uttered. The combination ἀσκι κατασκι at line 64 and Δαμνομενια with eight other variations of the word appear at lines 40−44 after the phrase: "because I conjure you by the κυρίας, according to Artemis."[108] These goddesses are attributed with possessing the keys to the fort of Hades (lines 11ff.) and therefore authority over the underworld gods and demons.

Some of these Ephesia Grammata may have originally been connected with Cybele, the "Great Mother" of Phrygia, who we know exerted a significant influence on the development of the Ephesian Artemis. Clement of Alexandria attributes them to the wizards of Cybele and Rhea, known as the Idaean Dactyls.[109] Wünsch thinks that the figures engraved on the two bronze plates which are part of the Pergamum magical apparatus are the Idaean Dactyls.[110] The plates were probably used as apotropaic amulets functioning in much the same way as amulets bearing the names of the Ephesia Grammata.

As we can see from the preceding, there is a very close correspondence between the cult of the Ephesian Artemis and what we call "Hellenistic magic." In many instances there seems to be little or no difference between calling upon Artemis to accomplish a certain task and utilizing a "magical" formula. Magic appears to be less a substructure of the cult of Artemis than it is an integral aspect of her "religion." The "magical" aspects of her cult which I have highlighted would certainly not be viewed as unsanctioned or "illegal" as a part of the belief structure affiliated with her worship.

Although the "religion" of Artemis has many elements corresponding to what we know as "Hellenistic magic," it would be erroneous to think that the magic practiced in Ephesus and throughout western Asia Minor was linked solely to the cult of Artemis. The images of the many gods and goddesses found in the Prytaneion at Ephesus demonstrate the syncretistic milieu of even the home city of Artemis.[111] All known divinities are named in the magical papyri − any name which was thought to have power.[112] I have surveyed a number of sources, however, establishing an explicit link between Artemis and magic.

The cultic image of the Ephesian Artemis

A more precise explication of the nature of the Ephesian Artemis is intertwined with the disputed interpretations of the adornment on her extant images.[113] Numerous interpretations (sometimes quite imaginative) of the bulbous objects on her chest have been postulated. Among the various views are: breasts, bee eggs, ostrich eggs, steer testicles, grapes, nuts, acorns, et al.[114] Most scholars agree that this ornamentation in some way illustrates her well-attested role as goddess of fertility.

E. Lichtenecker offers a plausible explanation of the significance of the "breasts" which is consistent with the Ephesian Artemis' connection with magic. She observes that in the fertility cults of Asia Minor, the sexual organs seemed to acquire magical significance. She therefore concludes with regard to the Ephesian Artemis, "Just as the amputated genitals were used in the fertility cults, it is also certain that the false breasts of the Ephesian goddess and the related cultic images bore a *magical character*" (italics in original).[115] As such, Lichtenecker thinks the "breasts" would have apotropaic significance as well as signifying the impartation of magical, nourishing power to the suppliants of Artemis.[116] This view is partially confirmed by later Christian interpretation, viz. Hieronymus, who explained that the "breasts" symbolized nourishing power.[117]

The "breasts" undoubtedly had varying significance in different epochs. Originally they may have served strictly as a symbol of fertility and fruitfulness. During the Hellenistic age, however, the adherents to the cult may have ascribed more of a magical significance to this prominent ornamentation.

The next most striking part of the decoration on the cultic image of the Ephesian Artemis is the rows of animals sculpted on her skirt. The frightful-looking creatures should probably be understood as representations of the harmful spirits of nature over which Artemis wields authority.[118] In *PGM* IV.2288, Artemis-Hekate bears the title, "Deliverer from fear," which Hopfner explains thus: "As the most powerful ghost-goddess, she can naturally deliver people from any peril involving spirits."[119] Hopfner continues by explaining how the names of various animals (dog, wolf, horse, bull, lion, etc.) occur throughout the spells to demonstrate that Artemis-Hekate is on the one hand herself a ghost-goddess (*Gespenstergöttin*), but on the other she is also the most powerful of these dangerous spirits.[120] In attempting to find some line of distinction between Artemis, Hekate, and

Selene in the magical papyri, Hopfner sees them as possessing three contiguous kingdoms with Hekate ruling under the earth, Artemis on the earth and Selene over the earth.[121] It must be remembered that this is a very thin line of distinction, but it does substantiate the background of Artemis as a goddess over the spirits of nature.

Artemis and the mystery religions

It is important to point out that an equation cannot be made between the Ephesian Artemis and the Artemis known to Greek mythology. The Ephesian divinity appears to be a hybrid of Asian influences — perhaps chiefly from "the Great Mother" (Cybele, Meter, Ma) of Phrygia and Lydia.[122] In fact, as a result of his excavation of the Artemis sanctuary in Ephesus, Anton Bammer has found some evidence pointing to the fact that the Artemision was originally dedicated to Cybele and Demeter sometime before the fifth century B.C.[123] Oster supposes that when the Greeks came to the Ionian coast they imposed the name of the Homeric Artemis upon the indigenous Mother Goddess whom they found there, and thereby gave birth to the Ephesian Artemis.[124]

The Ephesian Artemis has, however, retained some of the characteristics of the Greek huntress-goddess.[125] This is brought out especially in the animal motifs on her image demonstrating her power over the wildlife, which we have already briefly noted. It is therefore difficult to discern whether she had been ascribed a primary function among the three roles variously attributed to her — mother goddess, fertility goddess, and nature goddess.

There is a substantial amount of inscriptional evidence indicating the performance of certain mysteries in the cult of Artemis, e.g. ἐκτελέσαν τὰ μυστήρια.[126] On the basis of evidence from Strabo (14.1.20), Oster concludes that one of the occasions for the performance of the μυστήρια was at the annual festival celebrating the birth of Artemis.[127] Apart from this, there is virtually no other source giving us an insight into the nature of her mysteries. It could be assumed that her mysteries followed the general pattern of mystery rites, best known from their performance at Eleusis. This might partially be supported by Artemis' occasional identification with Persephone in the magical papyri.[128] Further understanding of her mysteries might also be attained by observing what took place in the mysteries of Cybele, especially the Taurobolium. In this rite, the blood of a slaughtered bull was drained through the lattices of the altar onto the neophyte below, where the strength of the beast was allegedly transferred into the limbs of the devotee.[129] The worship of Artemis is also thought to have been orgiastic in nature, with sacred prostitution as part of the ceremony.[130]

Artemis and Christianity

Later Christian writers certainly had no problem in linking Artemis with the evil demonic realm. The *Acts of Andrew* speaks of a large crowd of demons which lived on a rock next to an image of Artemis and made the nearby road impassable.[131] A Christian inscription specifically refers to Artemis as a "demon" and records the valiant action of a certain Demeas, who tore down the image of the Ephesian Artemis.[132] The Christian interpretation of Artemis as a demon as well as her connection with magic and sorcery is further attested by the apocryphal *Acts of John*:[133]

> Where is the power of the demon [Artemis of Ephesus]? Where are her sacrifices? Where are her dedication-festivals? — her feasts? — her garlands? Where is all that sorcery and poisoner's art that is sister to it?

Few NT scholars have referred to the Artemis cult as relevant to the background to Ephesians, much less as relevant to the teaching on the hostile "powers."[134] Most scholars quickly dismiss seeing any reference to the Artemis cult in Ephesians since neither the name "Artemis" nor specific and unique details of the cult are mentioned.[135] This may prove to have been an erroneous assumption. I would tentatively suggest that an understanding of the cult may also give some insight into why the author emphasized the "powers" in Ephesians. It may also be helpful in understanding one of the terms for the hostile "powers."[136]

Summary

(1) The prominent and widespread cult of the Ephesian Artemis was closely linked with magical practices and beliefs. The devotees of Artemis feared the demonic realm, or the spirits of nature, and considered their goddess more powerful than these forces and thereby called upon her as their protector and deliverer.

(2) Adherents to the cult of Artemis also practiced mysteries perhaps similar to those performed in conjunction with Cybele.

Artemis was also thought to have power superior to the astral powers who were believed to control the fate of people. Thus, magic, mysteries, and astrological beliefs overlap and work in confluence in this cult.

(3) The influx and expansion of Christianity eventually wrought the demise of the cult of the Ephesian Artemis. The Christians regarded the goddess herself as a "demon."

(4) Because of her strong links with the "demonic" realm we would suggest that it is not an impossibility that the writer of Ephesians could have had the cult in mind when he referred to the hostile "powers." This idea will therefore warrant further examination.

6. Astrology

There can be no doubt about the existence of astrological beliefs in the first century.[137] As with magic, astrology became an increasingly dominant spiritual force after the collapse of classical Greek religion in the fifth and fourth centuries B.C. An awareness of the movements of the stars was believed to give one the key to unlocking the mysterious outworking of fate. In popular belief, the stars and planets were thought to bear a close association with angelic intermediaries. This opened up the possibility of altering one's fate through manipulating the astral "powers." In this respect, astrology is closely connected with magic which sought to harness and utilize the power of these so-called deities.[138] Helios (sun) and Selene (moon), the planets, and the twelve animal-type images in the heavens (the zodiac) were regarded as most powerful. The rays of the sun and moon were also thought of as spirits, demons, or angels.[139] Even exorcism was in some cases linked to the planets (*PGM* IV.2490).[140]

A distinctive feature of the cult of the Ephesian Artemis was its close association with the astrological beliefs of the time. Our knowledge of this aspect of the Artemis worship is not mediated by literary sources, but rather through the extant images of the goddess. The signs of the zodiac were prominently displayed around the neck of the cultic image. This ornamentation was intended to signify that Artemis was lord of these cosmic "powers." The devotee of the Ephesian Artemis would find assurance in worshiping a goddess who was unaffected by the grip of astrological fate. This association with the zodiac indicates too that one could also seek oracular advice from her about one's future plans.[141] It is also possible that the numerous "breasts" on the image may be laden with astrological significance.[142]

It is not unusual to see astrology closely connected with an oriental religion. To a large degree the popular success of astrology was dependent on the mystery religions which lent it their support.[143] The "mysteries" offered a new way of propitiating the evil "powers" populating the heavens. Fate could now be conjured by powerful and mysterious processes. Magic developed alongside the "mysteries" as an additional and complementary means of manipulating the "powers."[144]

The astrological beliefs of western Asia Minor are illustrated by a planetary inscription (*CIG* 2895) found in the theater at Miletus, about 40 km south of Ephesus. The inscription is divided into six sectors which give the signs of planets. Each of the sectors contains the inscription, "Holy one, protect the city of the Milesians and all those inhabiting it." A further inscription stands below these six sectors which reads, "ἀρχάγγελοι, protect the city of the Milesians and all those inhabiting it."

There is strong evidence that Judaism was influenced by astrological beliefs, especially during the Babylonian exile.[145] The fact that first-century Judaism did contain astrological elements is well attested. Zodiacal signs have been discovered even among the symbols of first-century Palestinian Judaism.[146] A Hebrew horoscope was found among the scrolls at Qumran (4Q 186) which assumes that body and soul are influenced by the signs of the zodiac.[147] Astrological beliefs are given prominence in Jewish works such as *1 & 2 Enoch, Jubilees, Ascension of Isaiah*, and in the *Testament of Solomon*.[148]

7. Some aspects of Judaism in Asia Minor

In continuing our quest for a better understanding of the spiritual environment to which the Epistle to the Ephesians was addressed, it is necessary to consider the nature of Judaism in western Asia Minor.[149] Josephus puts the foundation of the Jewish community in Ephesus (the largest in the area) in the mid third century B.C. (Josephus, *Antiq.* 12.3.2).[150] Early Jewish presence in Ephesus has been confirmed by subsequent archaeological discoveries,[151] although a synagogue has not as yet been discovered.

Acts 19

With a high degree of relevance to our theme of power and spiritual "powers" is Luke's account of a striking incident regarding a number of Jewish exorcists during Paul's ministry at Ephesus (Acts 19: 11–20). Luke tells us that there were a number of Jews who went from place to place driving out evil spirits by the name of Jesus (19:13). He then illustrates this with a specific account of a certain Sceva, who with his seven sons also traveled about exorcising demons (19:14–16). They reportedly encountered extraordinary physical resistance by the evil spirits on one occasion which left them naked and bleeding. Luke asserts that the story became well known to the inhabitants of Ephesus.

It is very interesting that Luke associates such prolific demonic activity with Ephesus. He, in fact, has Paul conducting exorcisms (19:12), Jews wandering about casting out evil spirits (19:13), and finally Sceva and his sons having a dramatic encounter with evil spirits (19:14–16). The significance of this association is heightened by the fact that Luke does not describe any other location with so many accounts of the demonic in Acts. Apart from the exorcism at Philippi (Acts 16:16–18), there are no other accounts of exorcism or even references to "evil spirits" in Luke's account of Paul's missionary journeys (Acts 13–28). This evidence does not suggest that encounters with evil spirits and exorcisms were not known by Luke to have taken place elsewhere. The evidence does make us wonder why Luke would choose Ephesus to illustrate how the gospel of Jesus Christ has the power to overcome the demonic realm. If Ephesus and its environs were reputed as a center for "demonic" activity, Luke's purpose of demonstrating the superior power of the gospel would be well established by this account. This point would be valid even if one doubted the historical details of Luke's account,[152] i.e. if Luke fabricated the account to demonstrate the power and growth of the Christian message, he probably chose Ephesus to relate the power of the gospel over the "demonic" because of its reputation. The existence of such roaming Jewish exorcists is well attested, however.[153] Likewise, there is substantial evidence of Jews practicing magic during this period (see below).

It is noteworthy that in his volume on the life of Apollonius of Tyana, Philostratus (4.10) has an extraordinary account about demonic activity in Ephesus. A plague-demon who had been wreaking havoc on the city was discovered by Apollonius in the form of a blind beggar. Apollonius instructs the Ephesians to stone the blind beggar, whose appearance immediately changes into the form of a mad dog. The Ephesians later erect a statue of an averting god, Apotropaios, where the mad dog was. Such an account serves to confirm the reputation of Ephesus as a place with abundant demonic activity and simultaneously provides an explanation for the itinerant Jewish exorcists there.

Jewish magic

Numerous strands of evidence point to the fact that the Judaism of the Hellenistic period had been heavily permeated by contemporary magical beliefs. H. D. Betz finds such a great amount of evidence that he can assert, "Jewish magic was famous in antiquity."[154] It is often difficult to decide what is distinctively Jewish magic as opposed to syncretistic pagan magic which invokes Sabaoth or uses other Jewish motifs. Much of the recent research on magic has been able to differentiate some "Jewish" charms and amulets from the pagan counterparts. The chief criterion employed is to observe where the text is centered; for example, if Ptah and Thoth are added to a charm that is otherwise essentially Jewish, the provenance of the text can be said to be Jewish. A good example of this is the *Prayer of Jacob*. It has been mediated to us as a magical papyrus in Preisendanz's collection of texts (*PGM* XXIIb). It has recently been included in the second volume of *The Old Testament Pseudepigrapha* edited by J. H. Charlesworth[155] because of the prominence of Jewish ideas and terminology in the text. It is of significance that although the "Prayer" is extant only on a fourth-century papyrus, Charlesworth finds adequate reason to conjecture that the actual prayer could date as early as the first century A.D.[156]

M. Simon, followed by Goodenough and Charlesworth, saw three features which characterized Jewish magic: (1) a great respect for Hebrew phrases which seemed to some Jews to have magical power; (2) a sense of the efficacious power of the name; and (3) an overwhelming regard for angels and demons.[157] These aspects are present in the *Prayer of Jacob*, a number of other charms in Preisendanz's collection, and numerous magical amulets discovered throughout the Mediterranean world. A relatively recent discovery confirming the Jewish preoccupation with magic in antiquity is the *Sepher Ha-Razim*, or the "Book of Mysteries." While inspecting some Kabbalistic texts from the Genizah collection, Mordecai Margalioth discovered a number of magical fragments which he used to reconstruct a magical handbook from the early Talmudic period.[158] There is a conspicuously close similarity between the material preserved in the *Sepher Ha-Razim* and that of the *PGM*. Although the text has been dated to the late third or early fourth century A.D., it is widely recognized to contain a much earlier folk tradition.[159] Gruenwald considers the *Sepher Ha-Razim* and similar books more reliable than the rabbinic writings for transmitting to us the nature and scope of occult practices among the common people. He notes, "We may well assume that the common people were less conscientious in restricting their use of magic."[160] While the rabbis were more bound to maintaining certain standards of doctrinal integrity, the typical Jew was probably more susceptible to conforming to some of the habits and beliefs of pagan neighbors.

In his discussion of Judaism at Ephesus, Kraabel's treatment is taken up almost entirely with the question of Jewish involvement in the prevalent magical practices of the area.[161] Indeed, there is a substantial amount of evidence pointing to Jewish involvement in magic in this locale. In many of the amulets found in the region of Ephesus there are distinct Jewish elements. In the amulet published by J. Keil which is dated to the imperial period, one side contains an invocation in Greek to the "ever-living 'Αδωναῖε." The reverse side contains eleven letters in a Hebrew cryptographic scheme known as At-Basch.[162] E. R. Goodenough gives credence to the detailed report of a missionary published in 1870 who claims to have seen many signet stones all coming from the region between Smyrna and Ephesus and all bearing the same inscriptions. Each bore a fine representation of the menorah along with a number of magical names which included a crude transliteration of "Yahweh."[163] It is also significant in this connection to note that the name of Solomon appears on the magical apparatus found at Pergamum.[164]

Testament of Solomon

One further source which may provide some evidence about Judaism in Asia Minor relevant to our theme is the *Testament of Solomon*.[165] It is one of the sources most frequently referred to as reflecting the kind of Jewish angelology by which Paul or the Jews in the Hellenistic world may have been influenced.

Some scholars postulate an Asia Minor (perhaps Ephesian) provenance for the Testament, most notably C. C. McCown and M. R.

James.[166] The Testament does contain a number of elements linking it to Ephesus, and also elements quite similar to the Epistle to the Ephesians. In 7:1−8 the Ephesia Grammata "Lix Tetrax" appears as a demon of the wind and is interrogated by Solomon. The demon is subsequently thwarted by the angel Azael. Artemis is referred to in 8:11, where Solomon is threatened by a spirit with being bound by the bonds of Artemis. Clearly, either the author of the Testament was aware of the magical/demonic tradition at Ephesus which his readers could accept or he himself wrote from that milieu.

It is true that there appeared to be an ancient widespread tradition linking Solomon with magic and the manipulation of demons.[167] This tradition was deeply imbedded in western Asia Minor. We have already observed that the name of Solomon appears on the magical apparatus found at Pergamum. It is also significant to note that an amulet has been discovered which depicts the underworld goddess of Asia Minor, Hekate, on one side while showing Solomon practicing hydromancy on the other.[168] In three of the four occurrences of the name "Salaman" in Preisendanz's collection of magical texts, the name is used in conjunction with other magical names for the binding of "the scorpion Artemis."[169] This evidence serves to increase the plausibility of the western Asia Minor provenance for the Testament of Solomon, but it can certainly not confirm it.

The Testament uses much of the power language of Ephesians. It contains one of the earliest references to κοσμοκράτορες (18:2). It also makes reference to "the ruler of the spirits of the air" (16:3; 18:3; 22:1) and principalities, powers, and authorities in heaven (20:15). It bears similarity to many other aspects of the language of Ephesians. There is difficulty in attempting to decide whether the Testament used Ephesians or a similar Christian tradition. This question is quite complex and has occasioned substantially differing opinions. Most do acknowledge the presence of Christian additions and perhaps complete recensions (McCown), thus rendering it very problematic if not impossible to be sure what reflects first-century pre-Christian Judaism. Many do, however, see the Testament as displaying first-century Jewish demonology. McCown, for example, views it as a Christian combination of Jewish and heathen demonology.[170]

The Testament is therefore important for our study because it serves as an indirect witness to the demonic/magical tradition of western Asia Minor and because it reflects a first-century Jewish demonology. Unfortunately, past attempts at unraveling the Jewish elements from Christian developments have not occasioned much mutual agreement among interpreters.

Qumran and Asia Minor

A number of scholars have undertaken a comparison of Ephesians with the Qumran scrolls and have discovered many similarities.[171] The possibility of Qumran influence is certainly not impossible and needs to be considered as a lively option.[172] Benoit, for example, has postulated that Asia Minor, and especially the region of Ephesus, was a locale which would have been likely to come into contact with the documents. The difficulty with this view is that there is no external literary evidence for it. His reasons are based on internal evidence, that is, he sees Ephesians, Colossians, John, and 1 John as heavily influenced by the Qumran literature. He conjectures that the Alexandrian Apollo and/or the disciples of John at Ephesus (Acts 18:24–25; 19:2–3) may have introduced the documents to the region.[173] We will examine the various postulated points of contact between Ephesians and Qumran in the relevant exegetical sections.

Summary

One aspect of Asia Minor Judaism that stands out in the first century is a lively demonology. It appears that these Jews of the diaspora utilized a number of magical practices, including a Solomonic magical tradition, to cope with the "powers" in their daily existence.

8. The first-century interest in divine power

A keen interest in supernatural power was especially characteristic of the adherents of Artemis and those who practiced magic in the Hellenistic era. We would be overstating our case, however, to limit the interest in divine power to these two groups – this emphasis was typical of the entire Hellenistic world. The term δύναμις has accurately been described as one of the most common and characteristic terms in the language of pagan devotion.[174] A. D. Nock has demonstrated how an interest in divine power came to supersede even an interest in the divine personalities in the evolution of the Roman Empire.[175] The people of the era did not have a passive attitude toward divine power, they desired to be strengthened by receiving it.[176] They desired access to supernatural power that would protect them from their opponents and from evil "powers" that could harm them or bring sickness to them. This emphasis eventually gave way to a lessening of exclusiveness in Imperial paganism for the beginnings of the tendency to invest one deity with the attributes of others.[177] Nock even finds this predominant interest in power displayed in the common attitude toward the triumph of Christianity:[178]

> The popular hagiographical stories of the conflict are couched in terms of the victory of a superior δύναμις. There can, moreover, be no doubt that the demonstration by cures, exorcisms, and the like of the superior nature of this power was a most effective cause of conversions. The common people could argue that since Christ showed himself stronger than Artemis, Christ and not Artemis (since Christ would not be *primus inter pares*) must be worshipped, and readily learned to believe that those they had worshipped were δαιμόνια and inferior.

We certainly see this emphasis on divine power in first-century Asia Minor along with the tendency toward the generalization of the deities. The magical papyri clearly demonstrate no real preference for particular deities − the importance comes in addressing the names of all relevant deities which would be able to assist the magician with certain requests. The Ephesian Artemis does seem to possess an aura of primacy for her suppliants in western Asia Minor, however, as evidenced by the many ascriptions to her of superior power. This could have been on the wane prior to the introduction of Christianity into Asia Minor, however, and her reputation as a supreme deity certainly did falter after her encounter with Christianity. The presence of so many other worshiped deities at Ephesus in the first century also calls into question the assumption that she was considered as supreme by all (or the majority) of the inhabitants of Ephesus. Inscriptions and terra-cotta statues have revealed a substantial number of other gods and goddesses associated with Ephesus, e.g. Meter Oreia, Zeus, Athena, Aphrodite, Asklepios, Apollo, Hephaistos, Dionysos, Demeter, Hestia, Leto, Nemesis, Serapis and Isis, Tyche, and Poseidon.[179] Artemis may or may not have been worshiped as the leading deity of Asia Minor and as the deity possessing supreme power, although it seems likely for the time of Paul on the basis of Luke's account of Paul's encounter with the Artemis devotees (Acts 19:27). The most salient point for our study is that she was, in fact, worshiped as a deity possessing cosmic power who was willing to dispense it to her worshipers. Ramsay published an inscription of Artemis-Leto found at Dionysopolis extolling the strengthening power of the goddess: "Γνείος Ἀφιὰς Θεοδότου δυνατῇ θεῷ εὐχαριστῶ Λητῷ, ὅτι ἐξ ἀδυνάτων δυνατὰ ποιεῖ."[180]

This is well illustrated by an early account of the saving power of the Ephesian Artemis, who rescued the city of Ephesus from the seige of the Lydian king, Croesus. In reponse to the threatening situation, Pindaros of Ephesus took a rope and bound the gates and walls of the city to the columns of the temple of Artemis for protection from the ensuing attack (Herodot. *History* 1.26; Polyan. *Strateg.* 6.50). The city survived. Nilsson cites this as an example of the "substance" notion of power common in the Greek-speaking world.[181] Nilsson explains that Pindaros would have assumed that the power of the goddess would flow through the rope and protect all that was encompassed by it.

A "substance" concept of power prevailed throughout the Hellenistic world of the first century. This concept has been summarized well in a *religionsgeschichtliche* study of the meaning of δύναμις by O. Schmitz.[182] Schmitz classifies the concept of δύναμις into two basic streams of thought: (1) a magical-mystical line representing Hellenistic thought (and having influenced Diaspora Judaism to a large degree) which had a "substance" notion of δύναμις, viewing it as a power-fluid, or as electricity, and (2) the prophetic-salvation-historical line of the OT (as was operative in early Judaism), in which instance the locus of power was in the personal God who used his power to accomplish his own will and mediated his power to those who exercised faith.[183] Schmitz coined two terms to describe these variant concepts, *gegenständlich* ("objective") and *nightgegenständlich* ("non-objective"). One may further describe the contrast in terms of impersonal versus personal power. For Schmitz, the OT text portrays a unique concept of power quite distinct from that in the Hellenistic world. He finds Paul not at all influenced by the "substance" (*gegenständlich* or "objective") view of power found in the magical tradition. Schmitz roots Paul deeply into the OT concept of power, but with one decisive "objectivizing" difference — the coming and indwelling of the Holy Spirit in believers. He then describes Paul's view of power in terms of a *pneumatische Gegenständlich* ("Spirit-objectivity") concept.[184]

No one has attempted to build a case to the contrary of the position of Schmitz (and Grundmann et al.) by suggesting that Paul was influenced by and reflects a *Hellenistic* "substance" view of power.

Is Ephesians in this mainstream of Pauline tradition in its numerous references to "power"? At the outset, this does appear to be the case, but this hunch needs to be tested by a thorough analysis of the "power" references. If Ephesians was written to a milieu which held to an "objective" or "substance" view of power, could it be that the author of Ephesians was consciously seeking to correct in a subtle and careful manner those in the community holding to a Hellenistic notion of power?

9. The ruler cult in Asia Minor

Smyrna boasted of having the first temple dedicated to Roma as early as 195 B.C. (Tacitus, *Annals* 4.56). Augustus permitted Pergamum to erect a temple to Roma and to him for the use of the Roman citizens in the province in 29 B.C. (Dio Cassius 51.20.6). This marked the first time that a Caesar was deified and linked with the goddess Roma, the deification of the Roman people.[185] The Greek population of Ephesus wanted a temple of their own. A temple of Roma and Augustus was later constructed in, or adjoining, the Artemision by 6 B.C.[186] However, Ephesus could not have had its provincial temple (νεωκόρος) by A.D. 26 since it was vying in Rome then for the temple of Tiberius (Tacitus, *Annals* 4.56).[187] Tacitus records an interesting reason why Ephesus was refused permission for a temple: the senate adjudged the city as fully occupied with the cult of Diana (Artemis of Ephesus). Pergamum stood as the center for the Imperial cult in the province of Asia.

It is important to realize that the cult of Roma or the ruler cult did not bear the same religious significance as the cult of Artemis or the cult of Apollo or any of the other traditional religions of pagan antiquity. There are no *ex voto* proofs of fulfilled prayer involving any emperors on their own, alive or dead.[188] The establishment of the Imperial cult was essentially political. It enhanced the status of the city and usually its more influential citizens.[189] Mellor writes:[190]

> For the Greeks such cults were political and diplomatic acts, sometimes sincere, sometimes not, as is the custom in politics and diplomacy ... the cult of Roma covered the entire range of political emotion: enthusiastic affection, servile flattery, gratitude, suspicion, naked fear. It was a cult based on political, rather than religious, experience.

The ruler cult offered no protection or safeguard to its adherents from the threatening evil "powers." Those seeking salvation, healing, oracular advice, or genuine religious experience would turn elsewhere.

10. The influence of the religious climate on Christianity

Apart from some of the NT documents, we have very little evidence for discerning the early influence of the pagan religions and belief on the fledgling Christian communities. We do know, however, that there was a tendency for some Christians either to retain or take up magical beliefs and practices. This was true of Christians throughout the Hellenistic world and was probably true of the Christians of Asia Minor in spite of Luke's account of a large number of Christians burning their magical papyri in Ephesus.

F.W. Norris thinks that Acts 19:19 may indicate that some Christians within the Pauline congregations had been secretly practicing magical arts not merely prior to their time as Christians, but during their membership in that group.[191] Whether or not this is true, a substantial number of Christianized magical papyri have been discovered. Preisendanz published twenty-four of these papyri in his collection.[192] Interestingly, two of these depict Artemis as an intruding demon (*PGM* P2, P3). In *PGM* P3, the text begins with an adjuration that the "scorpion Artemis" would be bound. It continues with the aim that the household be protected from all evil and from the "aerial spirits." The text invokes the aid of "Mary (who gave birth to Christ)" together with Sabaoth, Solomon, and a number of other magical names. Most of these papyri give recipes for constructing amulets to protect the wearer from evil spirits.

Many of the church fathers give evidence of Christians becoming involved in magical practices. Origen records Celsus' accusation that Christians practiced magic:[193] "He says that 'he has seen in the hands of certain presbyters belonging to our faith barbarous books, containing the names and marvelous doings of demons.'"

11. Conclusions

(1) The Epistle to the Ephesians was written to western Asia Minor with the likelihood of Ephesus as one, or perhaps the first destination point. Ephesus functioned as a strategic center for Asia Minor — commercially, economically, in communications, and not least of all, in terms of its religious influence. In this respect, Ephesus served as

the center for the worship of Artemis and the widespread practice of magic. An understanding of the worship and cult of Artemis and the practice of Hellenistic magic may therefore be quite important to an understanding of the background of the converts to whom Ephesians was written.

(2) The worshipers of Artemis extolled their goddess as supreme in power, a "cosmic" power that was believed to be superior to that of any other deity, astrological fate, and evil spirits. Artemis was closely linked with Hekate as a goddess of the underworld. For this reason, she could be called upon for protection from pernicious "powers." She could also be invoked to raise the dead, heal the sick, and protect the city. In many respects, the descriptions of the nature of her power are quite similar to the concept of power in Hellenistic magic. In fact, much evidence closely links Artemis with the practice of magic. The proverbial Ephesia Grammata were inscribed on her image and she was closely affiliated with the Idaean Dactyls. We can infer that a discussion of magic in Asia Minor necessarily encompasses a discussion of some aspects of the cult of Artemis.

(3) A knowledge of Hellenistic magic may very well be the most important background for understanding why the author highlights the power of God and the "powers" of evil in Ephesians. This background may also help to explain the motivation for the lengthy admonition to prepare for engaging in "spiritual warfare" and the particular emphases in the way the teaching on power is expressed in the epistle. The reason this background is of paramóunt importance is threefold: (a) The epistle was written to an area famed as the *center* for magical practices in western Asia Minor; presumably (and according to Luke), many converts came into the church forsaking a background of magical practices. It is then certainly conceivable that the epistle could be concerned with addressing issues arising in the community related to the former (or, perhaps continuing) practice of magic on the part of some of the converts. (b) The subjects of "God's power" and "evil powers" were probably chief among these concerns. Ephesians strongly emphasizes the theme of power; the whole concern of Hellenistic magic was how to obtain access to and use supernatural power, a power gained by manipulating the spirit world. Ephesians, more than any other epistle in the NT, addressed the Christian response to the spirit world and provides teaching on the power of God. (c) With the widespread and popular cult of the Ephesian Artemis so closely linked to magical practices and beliefs, it is all the more likely that the first Christian congregations were composed

primarily of people coming from a similar background, a background having a "substance" concept of power and a lively interaction with the perceived spiritual world.

(4) The very existence of pre-Christian Gnosis is shrouded in uncertainty. It is well known, however, that Gnosis was eclectic and borrowed from many traditions. It may prove more worth while for us, in concentrating on the theme of "power," to stay with factors that were *known* to exist than to press for comparisons with the developed Gnosis of the second century. I do not deny the possibility of the existence and influence of elements of Gnosis in the first half of the first century. Neither do I deny the possibility of the influence of some beginning form of Gnosis on Ephesians. I have preferred, however, to explore the relevance of two traditions – Hellenistic magic and the cult of the Ephesian Artemis – consistently overlooked yet seemingly very significant for understanding the reason behind the emphasis on power and the nuances of the teaching on power/ "powers"/spiritual warfare in Ephesians.

(5) I am not suggesting that practices and beliefs were present at Ephesus that did not exist elsewhere in the Hellenistic world. A belief in the harmful influence of the "powers" is attested throughout the Mediterranean world of the Greco-Roman period. There is a particularly strong testimony, however, to the vibrancy of these beliefs in Egypt and western Asia Minor, particularly Ephesus. Unfortunately, neither Paul nor his fellow-workers wrote an epistle to Alexandria, Heliopolis, or Memphis for us to compare the emphasis given to a treatment of the "powers." We do have an epistle written to the churches of western Asia Minor, however, and in this instance the "powers" are given a prominent place.

3

THE REPRESENTATION OF THE "POWERS" IN EPHESIANS

As we have seen, virulent spiritual forces were perceived by the first-century inhabitants of western Asia Minor as troubling their daily existence. Artemis, amulets, charms, and various other forms of apotropaic magic were appealed to and utilized for relief from diabolical tyranny. Given such a climate, it will be instructive for us to discern how the author of Ephesians responds to Christian churches existing in this milieu, churches undoubtedly filled with converts having questions and continuing fears about these malignant forces.

There is no doubt that the author of Ephesians has a substantial amount to say about a category of beings I have referred to as the "powers." This is evidenced in the amount and variety of his references to them. Some reference is made to the "powers" in 1:10, 21; 2:2; 3:10, 15; 4:8, 27; 6:11, 12, and 16 by a diverse collection of terms: δύναμις, ἀρχή (three times), ἐξουσία (three times), κυριότης, πᾶς ὄνομα ὀνομαζάμενος, πνεῦμα, ἄρχων, πατριὰ ἐν οὐρανοῖς, τὰ πάντα, διάβολος (twice), κοσμοκράτορες, πνευματικά, and ὁ πονηρός. Ephesians has much more to say about the "powers" than any other NT epistle. As will soon become apparent, few interpreters have sought to discover *why* there is such prominence given to a discussion of the "powers" in Ephesians. The significance of an answer to this question remains to be tapped for its likely contribution to interpreting the "powers" and ultimately for a better understanding of the argument of the Epistle to the Ephesians.

In the following pages I will make an attempt to uncover the author's teaching on the "powers." I will also seek to detect the author's intention in providing the particular kind of instruction given in this epistle. The question of the source of some of the terms and the basis of the author's thinking on the "powers" will be important to consider for the evidence it can provide in answering our primary question, i.e. Why are they stressed in Ephesians? It will also be important to discern how the author himself viewed the "powers" –

did he perceive them as mythological abstractions or as actual beings, either spiritual or human? Was it clear to the readers that the author referred to good or evil "powers" in the various pericopae, or would they have sensed some ambiguity in his means of expression?

I will begin by reviewing a select portion of the contributions made to the understanding of the "powers" in Ephesians in the past century.[1]

1. Previous interpretations of the "powers"

The foundational works of Everling, Dibelius, and Grundmann

Any discussion of the "powers" would be incomplete without reference to the foundational work of Otto Everling published in 1888 entitled, *Die paulinische Angelologie und Dämonologie*.[2] Everling sees the "powers" terminology and thought in Ephesians rooted in "an unmistakable connection to pre-Christian Jewish and heathen religious designations and cultic activity" (p. 119). In his treatment of the specific passages, however, he argues forcefully against Gnostic influence on the author and sees the author taking over the kind of Jewish demonology found in such pseudepigrapha as *1 Enoch* and *Jubilees*. Everling devotes twelve pages of his monograph to a treatment of the passages in Ephesians (although neglecting 4:8), expending most of his effort on a discussion of 2:2. He concludes that Ephesians teaches, "the existence of a multitude of devilish beings which live in the air under the supreme command of Satan" (p. 109). What for Everling was implicit in the *Hauptbriefe* is made more explicit by the author of Ephesians. It is unfortunate that he does not follow up this observation by seeking to discern the *reason* for this heightened emphasis.

In a much larger monograph Martin Dibelius builds upon the work of Everling, to which he acknowledges a great indebtedness.[3] The title, *Die Geisterwelt im Glauben des Paulus*, indicates one of the ways he expands on what he considers to be a deficiency in Everling's study, that is, relating the significance of Paul's view of the spirit world to his religious and theological thought. Dibelius clearly states the specific significance of this in a warning (p. 5):

> The place of the belief in the spirit realm (*Geisterglaubens*) in the religion of Paul is of special significance for eschatology

and Christology. One may not push it aside as peripheral, for every single concept reaches into the center of his piety: one loses a portion of the Pauline faith when one rejects it.

Dibelius also seeks to supplement the study of his predecessor by giving a greater weight to the rabbinic literature and by accomplishing a more painstaking sifting of the religions-historical sources. He endeavors to determine whether there is "an analogy or a genealogy" to the possible source of each term for the "powers," viz. whether it comes from the OT, late Judaism, or Hellenism.[4]

In his fifty-page treatment of Ephesians (and Colossians), Dibelius concludes that in comparing the spirit-world teaching in Ephesians to that in the *Hauptbriefe* there is no compelling ground for denying the Pauline authorship of Ephesians.[5] With Everling, Dibelius concludes that the source for Paul's thinking with regard to the spirit world has a multiplicity of roots but can primarily be traced to Jewish apocalyptic (p. 182). Dibelius is careful, however, to draw a firm distinction between the view of Paul and that of Judaism. Jewish apocalyptic was tantalized by speculation about heavenly details and differences between the classes of angels. Quite to the contrary, Paul laid great emphasis on what to him was the most important question, "Where does Christ stand in relation to the spirit world?" (p. 182).

Dibelius affirms that all the references to the spirit world in Paul have a very important connection to the life and faith of the Christian community. He finds this practical emphasis carried out by Paul in Colossians and even uses it to defend the authenticity of the epistle (p. 170). Dibelius accuses those who deny the authenticity of Colossians of overlooking the fact that the peculiar statements of Colossians (regarding the spirit world) have their purpose in the aim of the epistle, which takes the form of a struggle against false teaching. Dibelius then finds insurmountable problems with Ephesians since the peculiar statements regarding the spirit world in Ephesians cannot be explained by a situation in his view. For Dibelius, Ephesians has the shape of a positive teaching on the unity of the church and lacks specific warnings.

Perhaps Dibelius is looking for the wrong kind of "situation" in Ephesians and narrows the field of possibilities too much in his analysis. It is highly instructive, however, to note that in Dibelius' opinion a given situation may be sufficient to explain unique twists in a language and thought in an epistle attributed to Paul.

A frequently overlooked work, but one having a great deal of importance for interpreting the "powers" in Pauline thought, is the monograph written by Walter Grundmann, *Der Begriff der Kraft in der Neutestamentlichen Gedankenwelt*.[6] Grundmann agrees with Everling and Dibelius on most points of consequence and tends to supplement their evidence, thereby confirming their conclusions. One significant way he supplements their work is by highlighting and incorporating the Greek magical papyri as evidence for the common beliefs about the "powers" in the first century A.D. He correctly observes, "The whole magical conception is indeed based directly on the notion of demonic principalities and powers which one seeks to make serviceable ... the magical papyri give us an insight into the conceptions of the common people (*Volksvorstellungen*)" (p. 43).

Interpreting the "powers"

The majority of works since Dibelius and Everling treating the "powers" in Pauline thought have sought to interpret the meaning and significance of the "powers" in terms of contemporary life.[7] One of the first examples of this type of study is a monograph by Heinrich Schlier, *Principalities and Powers in the New Testament*.[8] Schlier endeavors to discover "which phenomena are meant by these 'powers' and which meaning or reality corresponds to the terms 'principalities and powers' " (p. 9). By his interpretation of "air" in Ephesians 2:2 as a kind of spiritual "atmosphere," Schlier concludes that Paul regards this medium as *the chief means* (my italics) by which the "powers" exercise their domination. He can then view this domination by the "powers" as a general spirit or attitude in a nation or locality which is passed to the institutions and is then propagated by the institutions.[9]

Schlier considers the morality of the "powers" in their every occurrence in the Pauline epistles as wicked and hostile to God (pp. 14–15). Ephesians holds substantial significance for the work of Schlier. This is seen in the pivotal importance he ascribes to 2:2 for his interpretation and it is also seen in a concluding chapter on the Christian response to the "powers" (pp. 53–68). This chapter is built largely on the basis of the Epistle to the Ephesians, which may reveal something of the tenor and significance of Ephesians with regard to the "powers."

Oscar Cullmann brought new light to the interpretation of the "powers" by suggesting that ἐξουσίαι refers *both* to human authorities and angelic "powers."[10] His hypothesis was developed as a way to explain Rom 13:1–7, but the implications of it are clear for the other references to ἐξουσίαι in the Pauline corpus. His pupil, Clinton Morrison, has attempted to provide the historical substantiation to such an hypothesis in a monograph which also furnishes a history of the interpretation of Rom 13:1–7.[11] Emphasizing an "angels of the nations" view in Jewish apocalyptic, Morrison goes far beyond this evidence by postulating that a similar view was commonly accepted in Greco-Roman thought. Thus, in his opinion, "a strong and significant relationship between civil rulers and spiritual "powers" was the popular view of the first century.[12] The dual-reference view, although accepted by many, has not gone without criticism.[13] Both Morrison and Cullmann have neglected to draw the implications of their view to the four passages referring to ἐξουσίαι in Ephesians, especially the apparent contradiction between subjecting oneself (ὑποτάσσομαι: Rom 13:1) to the "powers" and resisting (ἀνθίστημι: Eph 6:13) the "powers," which would arise in applying their view to Ephesians. Furthermore, this view ignores the fact that the meaning of the ruler cult to the common people was essentially political and not religious (see chapter 2, section 9).

An approach to the interpretation of the "powers" somewhat similar to the view of Heinrich Schlier was advanced by Hendrik Berkhof.[14] He proceeds one step further toward demythologizing the "powers" when he says, "One can even doubt whether *Paul* [my italics] conceived of the powers as personal beings. In any case this aspect is so secondary that it makes little difference whether he did or not" (p. 24). According to Berkhof, the "powers" are understood by Paul as "structures of earthly existence" (p. 23). A strong basis for Christian social action is then seen to be provided by the Epistle to the Ephesians.[15]

In his treatment of the "powers" in Pauline theology, G. B. Caird also emphasized a "structural" interpretation of the "powers."[16] O'Brien correctly observes, however, that Caird changed his position twenty years later in his commentary on Ephesians.[17] Caird later maintained that Paul was referring to *spiritual beings* which operated in and through the structures.[18]

A notable exception to the tendency to demythologize the "powers" is Peter O'Brien in his recent article, "Principalities and Powers: Opponents of the Church." His interpretation of Paul is quite similar to the view of Everling, i.e. Paul uses language and concepts similar to Jewish apocalyptic, which "describes supernatural cosmic forces, a vast hierarchy of angelic and demonic beings" (pp. 135–6). O'Brien does not see Paul as having begun to demythologize the "powers" and does not see the need for the modern interpreter to demythologize the language (given his own belief in the reality of this spiritual realm).[19]

Works treating the source of the "powers" thought

In his article, "Principalities and Powers: The Cosmic Background of Paul's Thought," G. H. C. MacGregor contends that astrological beliefs are the most important stream in Paul's thought concerning the "powers."[20] MacGregor roots Paul's use of στοιχεῖα τοῦ κόσμου, κοσμοκράτορες, the dimensional terminology of Rom 8:38–39, and other terms for "powers" in what he regards as the widespread first-century belief in astral spirits. He does not opt for one specific religious source for the concepts and terms; astral beliefs were prominent in all first-century traditions, even Judaism, which he finds confirmed by the close connection of *1 Enoch* and Poseidonius (p. 20). For MacGregor, Paul clearly admits the existence of these astral "powers," but denies their divinity (p. 22). MacGregor would therefore deny that Paul has demythologized the "powers" – this is the question facing the NT interpreter who seeks to give the instruction contemporary relevance.

MacGregor appears to be correct in drawing attention to the existence of astrological beliefs in the first century (see chapter 2, section 6). He may also be commended for rightly highlighting the importance and influence of the magical papyri in the first century and their connection with astrology (p. 21). One may wonder if his view is rather narrow by speaking *solely* of astral "powers" as a background to the Pauline concept, however. He also, as do many other interpreters, recognizes the prominence of teaching about the "powers" in Ephesians, but never seeks to discover why there is such an emphasis in this epistle.

J. Y. Lee sees a harmonious confluence of what he describes as Jewish apocalyptic (fallen angels behind the state) and the Gnostic astrological point of view (astral spirits).[21] He may have been more accurate to speak of "proto-Gnostic" or astral spirits since he does not refer to the developed Gnostic beliefs, but rather to the Babylonian and Persian influence on Judaism. He seeks to find middle ground between Cullmann and MacGregor/Knox.

In his endeavor to discern the sources for Paul's "powers"

terminology, Pierre Benoit has taken a rather skeptical stance.[22] After briefly examining the texts from the Pseudepigrapha and Qumran which are frequently cited as being possible sources for Paul's "powers" terminology, Benoit dismisses the majority of the Pseudepigraphal references as "too late" or as possible interpolations, and the Qumran references to the heavenly "powers" and angels he finds insufficient for explaining the particular Pauline terminology. He concludes with an agnostic position: "One must confess that the precise origin of the Pauline designations of the heavenly Powers is not yet entirely clarified."[23] Benoit may be faulted for not mentioning the astrological (Lee/MacGregor) and magical (Grundmann and see below) evidence which serves to corroborate the Jewish Pseudepigraphal evidence. Furthermore, he has too quickly dismissed much of the Pseudepigraphal evidence (e.g. *1 Enoch* 61:10; *2 Enoch* 20:1; *Test. Levi* 3:8 et al.) as dependent on Paul and anachronistic without sufficient proof. A number of the works he cites are well attested as predating Paul.[24]

Modern Pseudepigrapha research tends to confirm the value placed on the Pseudepigrapha by Everling, Dibelius, and others for gaining some insight into the Pauline demonology.[25] One of the distinctive traits of the early Jewish *Zeitgeist* is the fear of demons. Charlesworth comments on the demonology of the Pseudepigrapha,[26]

> The earth is full of demons. Humanity is plagued by them. Almost all misfortunes are because of the demons: sickness, drought, death, and especially humanity's weaknesses about remaining faithful to the covenant. The region between heaven and earth seems to be almost cluttered by demons and angels; humanity is often seen as a pawn, helpless in the face of such cosmic forces ...

The Pseudepigrapha thus accurately represent the *Zeitgeist* of Paul's time and also for the time of the composition of Ephesians. Specific care needs to be taken, however, in postulating a particular reference as a source for Pauline terminology.

The recent works of W. Carr and W. Wink

In a monograph specifically dealing with Paul's understanding of the "principalities and powers," Wesley Carr has taken a substantially different approach than any of his predecessors.[27] Carr argues that all of the Pauline references to the "powers" should be understood not as applying to evil, demonic "powers," but as references to the pure angelic host surrounding the throne of God. In fact, he contends that there was no concept of evil demonic "powers" in the thought world of the first century A.D. and before. Evil was personified only in the single figure of Satan; the idea of a multitude of demonic "powers" developed in the second century. With respect to Ephesians, which he regards as Pauline, Carr interprets the references to the "powers" in 1:21 and 3:10 as to good angels. The admonition to resist the "powers" in 6:12 is treated as a second-century interpolation. I have argued in a separate publication for the integrity of Eph 6:12 and seek to reveal that Carr's novel thesis rests on a very weak basis and should therefore be rejected. I attempt to demonstrate that belief in the demonic realm is substantially verifiable for the first century A.D. and that Carr's handling of the Pauline texts leaves much to be desired.[28]

At the time of this writing, Walter Wink has published the first two volumes of a three-volume work treating the "powers."[29] The first volume, *Naming the Powers*, provides ninety-seven pages of exegetical material supplemented by four detailed appendices which form the foundation for his interpretation of the "powers" given in the last section of the book. Wink does not present us with yet another novel view of the "powers." He endeavors to construct a more sure exegetical and historical footing to the demythologizing view of the "powers" first presented by Schlier and Berkhof. He states his thesis clearly at the outset of his handling of the NT evidence: "*Unless the context further specifies* (and some do), *we are to take the terms for power in their most comprehensive sense*, understanding them to mean both heavenly *and* earthly, divine *and* human, good *and* evil powers [italics in original]" (p. 39).

This interpretative key is derived from a brief analysis of the use of power terminology during the NT era (pp. 13–35). He finds the language for power imprecise and interchangeable and, because of this, one term (or a pair or a series) can be made to represent them all (pp. 10–11). In demonstrating the interchangeability of the language, for example, he draws attention to how John can use the term ἄρχων to designate Satan (John 12:31) and just a few verses later have it refer to Jewish "authorities" (John 12:42) (p. 9). For Wink, this example clearly demonstrates that ἄρχων can be applied to two different classes of beings in John's mind. But if we are faithfully to apply Wink's interpretive key, how can we be certain that we are not too quickly narrowing the scope of reference? Why is John not also making reference to the institutionalization of religious power in Judaism in 12:42 *and* 12:31 by his use of the term ἄρχων? Wink does not say.

It is at this point that the logic of his "comprehensive" understanding of power terminology is open to criticism. He does not provide any compelling examples of one term used in this comprehensive sense. The examples he does cite (Rom 8:39–39; 1 Cor 15:24; Col 2:10, 2:20) are all disputed in their own right. Further, because one term may have five different applications does not mean that all five applications may be used simultaneously. For example, the term ἄγγελος may refer to a human "messenger" as Luke used it for the disciples of John the Baptist (Luke 7:24), or it may refer to the supernatural attendants around the throne of God (e.g. Luke 12:9). It does not refer to both categories simultaneously in spite of the fact that in different contexts the term can be used in two different ways. The term ἄγγελος cannot bear a comprehensive sense in one context since man and the heavenly attendants do not share the same essence. The significance of this illustration is heightened when it is realized that Paul parallels ἄγγελοι and ἀρχαί in Rom 8:38. I would therefore infer that just as ἄγγελοι cannot refer at the same time to both humans and angels, neither can ἀρχαί.

I certainly do not deny that terms such as ἄρχων and ἀρχαί were used for human rulers. In fact, I could even add to the instances cited in Wink on the basis of their local use in Asia Minor.[30] I would maintain, however, that the magical practitioner would have something completely different in mind when he would call on the ἀρχαί than the citizen would have when he would speak of his state magistrate. The root difference is a difference in essence − a spirit being as opposed to a human being. Granted that both the spirit being and the human magistrate have in common a sphere of power, but the spheres represent two distinct dimensions.

The results of such a view of the "powers" terminology can be seen most clearly in Col 1:16. Wink describes Paul as having demythologized the language of power to such a degree that spiritual essences are no longer in Paul's mind. He sees θρόνοι as referring to the institutionalization of power; κυριότητες as spheres of influence; ἀρχαί as a non-personal symbol of an agent in office; and ἐξουσίαι as legitimations by which authority is maintained (e.g. rules, codes, constitutions).[31] Wink interprets Eph 1:20ff. in a similar way, where he sees the author (in the same vein as Paul) demythologizing the "powers," i.e. withdrawing "the mythic projection of the real determinants of human existence out onto the cosmos and their identifications as actual physical, psychic, and social forces at work in us, in society, and in the universe" (p. 62).

In seeking to navigate this middle course between the reductionist view of the liberation theologians (human structures and institutions) and traditional theology (spiritual beings) (p. 15), Wink not only seems to be imposing a post-Enlightenment mind-set on the first-century writers, but he winds up with a rather confusing view of the first century. He is willing to recognize that the ancients did actually believe in a real Satan, evil angels, and demons, yet he also wants to see Paul and his contemporaries as aware of the myth about the "powers." Wink is certainly not clear in explaining to what extent the "powers" were regarded as mythical in the first century. Were there just a few who were enlightened (as Paul appeared to be sometimes), or were all inhabitants of the Hellenistic world aware of the mythical nature of the "powers?" Further, is it not contradictory to see Paul emphasizing the mythical aspect in one passage and in another passage seem to be affirming the reality of personal beings? This question of Paul's view of the "cosmic powers" is taken up and treated in much greater detail in chapter 6.

Wink's monograph is seriously flawed by never taking into account the relevance of the magical tradition for a more accurate understanding of the first-century view of "powers." He refers to the magical papyri once in a footnote only to dismiss this evidence as too late.[32] Wink also neglects treating the evidence compiled by MacGregor and Lee affirming a widespread belief in astral spirits. The presence of magic in the Hellenistic world blatantly contradicts the demythologizing trend that Wink sees in the first century. The practice of magic implies a vibrant and flourishing belief in evil spiritual forces — forces that magicians in no way identified with humans or institutions. The magician believed in personal spirits that bore names. The spirits could be called upon to appear or to perform certain tasks. The spirits were greatly feared by the common people of the Hellenistic world in the first century A.D.

If Paul wished to make himself understood to his readers (even if he was somehow enlightened about the myth of the "powers"), he would certainly not speak of the "powers" as social structures when his readers would think of evil spiritual beings. He would leave his readers confused and bewildered. The vast majority of the readers of Ephesians were common people, not philosophers or the educated elite. Furthermore, I have demonstrated that the readers were immersed in a milieu where magical beliefs flourished. On this basis, we have every reason to suppose that when the author of Ephesians spoke of "principalities, powers, authorities," his readers would naturally think of the demonic "powers" they feared. The question of demythologizing the "powers" needs to be left to the modern interpreter who seeks to make the epistles relevant in terms of today.

Summary

(1) Of the many monographs and articles written about the "powers," most recognize and highlight the emphasis on the "powers" in Ephesians. None, however, seeks to find the reason they are referred to so much more frequently in Ephesians than in other epistles. The source-critical, religions-historical, and interpretational questions have compelled the bulk of attention in the past.

(2) There does seem to be some consensus that Paul reflects a Jewish view of the spirit world. This does not mean that first-century Judaism maintained a unique view of the spiritual forces in comparison to the pagan world. On the contrary, Judaism appeared to share the beliefs of the Hellenistic world about the "powers" in many respects. Judaism and the pagan world also shared a common reservoir of terminology to refer to the "powers."

(3) There has been no general agreement concerning how Paul himself understands the "powers." The references have been taken as all evil, all good, or a combination of the two depending on the context. Some see in Paul a tendency toward demythologizing the "powers." Although I do not find these arguments compelling, there has been no consensus in this respect.

2. The supremacy of Christ over the "powers"

In the remainder of the chapter, stress will be placed on determining the precise information communicated to the readers about the "powers." Why does the author mention them? What does he have to say about them? Equal stress will also be placed on discerning the possible sources for the "powers" terminology. Because of their pivotal importance for understanding the author's message regarding the power of God and the "powers" of evil, two passages treated below will be developed in much greater detail in chapters 4 and 5, viz. Eph 1:15−23 and 6:10−20.

Ephesians 1:15–23

In the prayer in Eph 1:15–23, the writer wants to impress indelibly upon his readers that no conceivable being can even come close to matching Christ in power or authority. Upon raising Christ from the dead, almighty God exalted him to a position of unrivaled authority from where he exercises his lordship. The significant Christological statements in the prayer are made by the author for their direct ecclesiological relevance – the church now shares in this resurrection power. The goal of the prayer is that the readers will be made aware of and appropriate this unsurpassed power which is available to them.

In formulating his prayer extolling the superiority of Christ over his enemies, the author quite fittingly alludes to Ps 110:1, the OT passage most frequently cited by early Christian writers. This Psalm was used to support God's vindication of the crucified and resurrected Christ through the exaltation to the right hand of God, where Jesus is in a continuing session with God. It was also used by the early Christians, who identified the "enemies" of the Psalm with the invisible "powers," to assert the subjugation of the "powers" to Christ.[33] The subjection of the "powers" was a typical aspect of the early Christian hymns and integral to the meaning of the Christological title "Lord." In his interpretation of the Psalm, the writer of Ephesians gives a substantial list of the "enemies" subjected to Christ.

He first characterizes them as ἀρχή and ἐξουσία, using the singular with πᾶς to denote the entire group. The author is fond of this pair of terms to describe the spiritual forces, employing it also in 3:10 and 6:12, but so also is the author of Colossians (see 1:16; 2:10, 15). The terms are familiar to Paul, who includes ἐξουσία in his list (1 Cor 15:24). 'Αρχαί occurs independently from ἐξουσίαι to denote "powers" in Rom 8:38. In 1 Pet 3:22, ἐξουσίαι is paralleled with ἄγγελοι and δυνάμεις in the list of subjected powers, a passage which is thought to be hymnic.

Our survey of the literature showed that there is some consensus that Ephesians, in line with Paul, reflects a Jewish view of the spirit world. This "Jewish" view, however, overlaps significantly with the Hellenistic world and in many ways is indistinguishable. There may be a connection between the use of ἐξουσίαι in Dan 7:27 (ἀρχαί in Theod.) and its use in Paul, especially if the term is synonymous with ἄρχοντες, which is used to describe the angelic "princes" against which Michael fights.[34] Such a connection is known to Paul in Rom 8:38, where he coordinates ἄγγελοι with ἀρχαί.

Early Christians could also have picked up this terminology for the "powers" from extra-canonical Judaism. The first-century *Slavonic Apocalypse of Enoch*, for example, has an enumeration of heavenly "powers" in 20:1: "And I saw ... the incorporeal forces (δυνάμεις) and the dominions (κυριότητες) and the origins (ἀρχαί) and the authorities (ἐξουσίαι), the cherubim, the seraphim, and the many-eyed thrones (θρόνοι)."[35] So also does *1 Enoch* 61:10: "And he will summon all the forces (δυνάμεις) of the heavens, and all the holy ones above, and the forces (δυνάμεις) of the Lord – the cherubim, seraphim, ophanim, all the angels of governance."[36] The *Test. Levi* 3:8 also has a relevant listing of angelic "powers": "there with him [the Lord] are thrones (θρόνοι) and authorities (ἐξουσίαι); there praises to God are offered eternally." We cannot state categorically that each of these Pseudepigraphical texts was immune from Christian influence, but it is indeed more probable that the Christian terminology for the "powers" reflects Jewish influence than vice versa. We have already documented Judaism's intense interest in the spirit realm around the time of the first century, which resulted in the development of elaborate demonologies with long lists of angelic names and categories. The early Christians probably drew from this reservoir of terminology. Thus, these texts may account for the source of the author's use of ἀρχαί and ἐξουσίαι and so also for δυνάμεις.

The term ἀρχή does not occur in the magical papyri in the plural and the singular does not appear to be used as a circumlocution for the "powers." Neither is the plural of ἐξουσία used in the magical papyri, but there are two occasions where the singular is hypostatized and made evil (*PGM* I.215; IV.1193). The latter passage is a prayer to Helios to protect the suppliant from every prominent ἐξουσία and from all harm.

The third expression for the "powers" in Eph 1:21 is δύναμις. This is the only such use of the term in Ephesians (and Colossians) for an angelic power (but see also 1 Cor 15:24, Rom 8:38, and 1 Pet 3:22). This particular use undoubtedly has its roots in OT thought as an expression for angels. The LXX often translates *yhwh tsebha'oth* with κύριος τῶν δυνάμεων. Yahweh is thus represented as king and lord surrounded by angelic armies. The LXX also uses δυνάμεις to refer to "the hosts of heaven" (2 Kings 17:16; 21:3, 5; 23:4f.), which Israel is prohibited from worshiping (Deut 4:19). The personalized significance of this term was then taken up by Judaism (*1 Enoch* 41:9; 61:1, 10; 82:8; *4 Ezra* 6:6; Philo, *Spec. leg.* 2.45, and *Plant.* 14, et pl.).[37]

The syncretistic magical papyri here seem to draw on Jewish material for the personalized sense of δυνάμεις as seen in the *Prayer of Jacob* (*PGM* XXIIb): "(1) A Prayer of Jacob. Father of the Patriarchs, Father of all things, Father of the δυνάμεων τοῦ κόσμου, creator of all, creator of the angels and archangels ... (8) Hear me, You the God of the δυνάμεων, God of angels and archangels." A similar use can be seen in an inscription found in Asia Minor: "There is one god in the heavens, great Men the Heavenly, μεγάλη δύναμις of the ever-living God."[38] The personalized sense of δύναμις was thus widely known.

The final term used in the list of subjugated "enemies" is κυριότης. It should be understood in coordination with the previous terms as "a special class of angelic powers."[39] Precedent for this use can be seen in *1 Enoch* 61:10 and *Slav. Enoch* 20:1. The term only occurs once in Preisendanz's collection of papyri, where it is found in a Christian text showing clear dependence on Eph 1:21 (*PGM* P21.3ff.).

All four of these terms show signs of OT and Jewish provenance which exercised a degree of influence on Hellenistic texts. This is not to say that a similar belief in angelic "powers" was not held in the surrounding pagan world. The evidence seems to suggest that Judaism furnished new labels for the perceived forces.

The author provides still another expression to emphasize the comprehensive scope of Christ's supremacy. "Every name that is named" (πᾶς ὄνομα ὀνομαζόμενος) is encompassed in the mighty reign of the Lord Jesus Christ — no conceivable power is outside of the dominion of Christ. This particular phrase is loaded with significance for exorcism and magical incantation both in Judaism and the pagan world. The use of this phrase also reaffirms the traditional understanding of the four previous terms as spiritual forces.[40]

The calling of the names of supernatural "powers" was fundamental to the practice of magic.[41] A knowledge of the six names of the Ephesia Grammata and then the employment of those names either by verbal repetition or by carrying them on inscribed amulets, charms, or gems was essential for enlisting the help of the "demons" they signified. This was the essence of magic. Supernatural "powers" were called upon by name through these means by one who desired access to their power and assistance. Every conceivable name of both known and unknown deities and supernatural "powers" is called upon in at least one of the magical papyri.[42] In fact, the very term ὄνομα is so important in the magical papyri that in the index to his collection, Preisendanz lists close to 400 occurrences of it.[43]

A parallel construction to Eph 1:21 using both the noun and the verb (ὀνομάζω ὄνομα) occurs in *PGM* LXI.2. Sometimes no specific names occur when the exorcist wants to be comprehensive in scope. For instance, "I conjure you by the 'great names' (ὀναμάτων μεγάλων) ..." (*PGM* CI.52, Wortmann, "Texte," 90) coordinates "names" with "powers": "You, these holy names (ὀνόματα) and these powers (δυνάμεις), confirm and carry out this perfect enchantment; immediately, immediately; quickly, quickly!" A typical example of the naming of names can be found in the instructions for the creation of an amulet to ward off demons and sickness (*PGM* VII. 580–90):

> A phylactery, a bodyguard against demons, against phantasms, against every sickness and suffering, to be written on a leaf of gold or silver or tin or on hieratic papyrus. When worn it works mightily, for it is the name (ὄνομα) of power (δύναμις) of the great god and his seal, and it is as follows: ... (fourteen magical names) ... These are the names (ὀνόματα).

F. C. Conybeare long ago suggested that the expression, "every name that is named" in Eph 1:21 comes from a milieu where it implied exorcism with the names of angels and patriarchs.[44] The evidence from the magical papyri published since Conybeare wrote would serve to underline his conclusion.

It is quite interesting to note that in the thirteen epistles attributed to Paul, the verb ὀνομάζω occurs six times, with *three* of these occurrences in Ephesians (1:21; 3:15; 5:3). It is of further significance to observe that the verb occurs only once in Acts, and, very interestingly, in Acts 19:13 – in the account of the roaming Jewish exorcists at Ephesus! In fact, the verb is here linked with the noun ὄνομα, just as it is in Eph 1:21.

Continuing his theme of Christ's supremacy over his enemies, the author cites Ps 8:6 (= 8:7 LXX), "And he put all things (πάντα) in subjection under his feet." The objects of the subjection include the material world in Ps 8:7ff. with the sheep, oxen, birds, and fish. Here, however, the "powers" serve as the interpretation of "all things." This interpretation is similar to that of Paul in 1 Cor 15:25–28 who refers to a list of "powers" and then also includes "death" (see also Eph 1:10; Col 1:16–17; 1 Cor 8:6). This understanding of τὰ πάντα would have been intelligible to a non-Jewish readership. In the first-century section of *PGM* XII, the expression is used in a recipe for an amulet (lines 302ff.): "I call upon you, great god, and through you τὰ πάντα, that you would give divine and mighty power to this carved stone.''

We may conclude about this list of "powers" that they are to be understood as evil and angelic in character. They cannot be interpreted as good or as both good and evil since the author makes them enemies of Christ through his allusion to Ps 110:1. This is also consistent with the other references to the "powers" in the letter, where they can only be understood as evil (6:11, 12, 16; 2:2; 4:8, 27). The emphasis on Christ's victory over the "powers" is affirmed here in order to substantiate the author's claim that there is a surpassingly great power effective in believers. The content of this prayer anticipates and is motivated by the admonition to engage in spiritual warfare (6:10–20).

For the person who has been converted out of a background of magical practices, Eph 1:21 would convey a powerful message. Christ's power and authority is cosmic in scope. His name *alone*, and not his name in addition to others, is sufficient for a successful confrontation with the "powers" of evil. The convert would no longer need to live with the fear that perhaps one or a number of supernatural "powers" could be equal to or superior to Christ – Christ's power and authority is exceedingly superior to all categories of "powers," indeed, "every name that is named"!

Ephesians 4:8–10

Christ's victory over his enemies is alluded to again by the author in Eph 4:8, "when he [Christ] ascended on high 'he captured a catch of prisoners.'" This is actually a citation of Ps 68:18, which the author uses to show that the exalted Christ is the source of spiritual gifts. Our concern is to determine whether he had the "powers" in mind when he spoke of "captives" (αἰχμαλωσία). The discussion generated by Eph 4:8–10 in recent literature has been concerned primarily with understanding (1) the change of terminology from the LXX, which reads, "you received," to the Ephesian reading, "he gave," and (2) the meaning of the midrash (vv. 9–10), esp. the descent to the lower parts of the earth: does it refer to the incarnation, the coming of the Spirit, or a *descensus ad infernum*?[45] Virtually no attention has been given to identifying the captives or understanding the relevance of the first part of the Psalm citation.

In light of the reference to Christ subjugating the "powers," his enemies, in 1:20ff., it would be natural to assume that these are the captives the author has in mind when he cites Eph 4:8. This is the conclusion reached by Dibelius, who refers to this as "the well-known triumph of Christ over the angel-powers in his exaltation."[46] Likewise, Mußner remarks, "The descent—ascent concept in Ephesians serves the kerygma of the lordship of Christ over the cosmic powers."[47] In the Psalm itself, God is depicted as leading a band of prisoners up to his holy mountain as a sign of his triumph. In Ephesians, the Psalm is given a Christological interpretation with Christ understood as the triumphant one and having ascended "above all the heavens." He has successfully triumphed over the demonic forces and they are his prisoners.

There has been a tendency among recent interpreters to understand the κατώτερα τῆς γῆς where Christ descended as the earth itself (4:9). In this view, the genitive τῆς γῆς is taken as epexegetical and the reference is understood as the incarnation of Christ or the descent of the Holy Spirit at Pentecost.[48] If this is the case, why did the author choose to use the comparative κατώτερα to modify "earth"? Would the point not have been made less ambiguously by merely referring to the earth alone? The failure to answer these questions is the chief difficulty of this particular view.

The phrase κατώτερα τῆς γῆς makes most sense in its first-century Hellenistic and religious context if it is understood as an expression for the underworld or Hades. Although the comparative κατώτερα does not occur in Preisendanz's collection of magical texts, the adverb κάτω is used in reference to the underworld. *PGM* LXX illustrates this use well while simultaneously using the adverb in conjunction with καταβαίνω to speak of a descent to the underworld:

> I have been initiated,
> and I descended (κατέβην) into the (underground)
>   chamber of the Dactyls,
> and I saw the other things down below (κάτω) ...

Hans Dieter Betz supposes that this papyrus preserves a record of the ritual connected with the mysteries of the Idaean Dactyls.[49] He suggests that the statement εἰς μέγαρον κατέβην assumes that the initiation took place by way of a descent into an underground crypt. This crypt apparently served as the entrance to the underworld comparable to the Ploutonion in Eleusis and the cave of Trophonius in Lebadeia.[50]

This text is particularly relevant to us for its implicit connection with Asia Minor. It is prefaced with the heading "Charm of Hekate Ereschigal" (line 5), the Ephesia Grammata ἄσκει κατάσκει are among the magical names invoked (line 13), and, as I have already mentioned, the text refers to a descent to the chamber of the Idaean Dactyls.[51]

Hekate, revered as goddess of the underworld, was considered to have the authority over "the keys of Hades."[52] G. Horsley thinks this phraseology finds a striking parallel with Rev 1:18, where Christ is said to have the keys of death and of Hades, an example of the figurative use of κλείς for which Moulton and Milligan could find no parallel outside the NT.[53] "Hades" was a place greatly feared by the people of Asia Minor, as evidenced in the references in the inscriptions on numerous gravestones found throughout the region.[54] Popular belief found the goddesses Artemis, Hekate, Selene, and Ereschigal the only sources to rely on to have their fears of Hades and the underworld partially alleviated. The morality of these goddesses, however, was not beyond reproach; they had to be carefully managed with the appropriate charms and incantations.

Eph 4:8−10 should therefore be seen as providing supplementary evidence to Eph 1:19ff. to establish Christ's supremacy over all the "powers" of evil in addition to its function of introducing Christ's gifts to the church. When this is viewed from the perspective of the first-century milieu and the fear of the underworld deities, one can gain a greater appreciation for the comfort the passage would bring to the readers. It underlines the cosmic supremacy of Christ in a fresh way. Christ is not only superior to the aerial spirits and the forces populating the heavens, but he is also superior to the so-called underworld deities. Christ alone holds "the keys of Hades," as another Christian writer wrote to believers in Asia Minor.

Ephesians 3:14

There is one additional passage which highlights the supremacy of God himself over the "powers." The author addresses his prayer in 3:14ff. to the Father from whom every πατριά[55] in heaven and upon the earth derives its name (ὀνομάζεται). The phrase is no doubt used in its most expansive sense, i.e. *every* living being finds the source of its life in God the "Father." The inclusion of ἐν οὐρανοῖς points unmistakably to the angelic realm, both good and evil. I have demonstrated above how the "naming" of names was important in magical practices. This passage affirms that every name, without exception, is derived from God. He is creator. There may even be a tinge of irony in the phrase, i.e. "It may be true that the so-called divinities have a name with power, but it is the Lord God, the Father of all, who gave them their name." Therefore, no conceivable "power" is outside of the parameters of his sovereignty. The people of God can approach him in full confidence when they pray knowing that no hostile force can prevent him from hearing their requests.

3. The realm of the devil (Eph 2:2)

The "powers" hold a very significant role in Eph 2:1ff., where the author provides his readers with an interpretation of life in relation to the "powers." He seeks to demonstrate to his readers that there are two possible realms in which people exist. One is the realm of death, which is controlled by an evil angelic prince, and the other is the realm of life, entered by faith in Christ Jesus. The author explains that the believer has experienced a transfer from one realm to the other, which he describes by a "once–now" (ποτέ–νῦν) schema (see chapter 6).

He vividly depicts the nature of the former realm in vv. 1–3. The compelling inspiration for this past way of life is described by two coordinated clauses in v. 2 (κατά ... κατά). In the first clause the author reveals that believers once conducted their lives according to the αἰών of this world. "Aion" is well known in Hellenism as a personal deity. The expression occurs numerous times in the magical papyri bearing this sense. It later came to be a very popular term for personal "powers" in the Nag Hammadi texts and other Gnostic documents. Certainly such an interpretation of the term would have been readily intelligible to Gentile readers.[56]

In spite of the appeal of this interpretation, it appears more accurate to view αἰών in the Jewish sense of a period of time as coupled with κόσμος, signifying the world existing in that particular span of time. The context mandates such an interpretation. In 1:21 the author uses αἰών when referring to the typical Jewish two-age schema. Likewise, he uses αἰών in a temporal sense in 2:6. It would be odd and confusing to the readers for the author to switch to a personalized sense just a few lines later and before a temporal usage. This would then also constitute the only clear use of αἰών in a personalized sense in all the epistles attributed to Paul. A Gentile reader who had been immersed in magical practices and was familiar with the name of the god Aion would still understand the author's use of αἰών in 2:2 after noticing that the author uses the term in a temporal sense in 1:21.[57] The author is thereby developing a contrast between the characteristics of the old age and the new age which is dawning in Christ Jesus.

Not only are non-believers pulled in to following all of the corrupt traits of this present age, but they are described as actually inspired and energized by personal evil forces. These forces are directed by τὸν ἄρχοντα τῆς ἐξουσίας τοῦ ἀέρος. The term ἄρχων is yet another expression for a personalized evil force. Here its etymological sense of "primary" or "prominent" should be taken into account. The term is used for the national, local, or tribal leader in the LXX from Genesis to 2 Chronicles. In the Theodotion text of Dan 10:13, 20f., and 12:1, the term denotes heavenly "powers" which represent earthly nations.[58] The author is here, therefore, referring to a chief or leader among the angelic powers. It may be a reference to the devil himself (cf. 4:27; 6:11) since the term is in the singular and because of the prominence ascribed to this being. The Synoptics describe the devil as the ἄρχων τῶν δαιμονίων (Matt. 9:34; 12:24; Mark 3:22; Luke 11:15). John refers to the devil as the ἄρχων τοῦ κόσμου τούτου (John 12:31; 14:30; 16:11).

This evil angelic prince is in control of the domain (ἐξουσία) of the air. In this instance, ἐξουσία is not used in a personal sense, but rather refers to the "realm" or "sphere" of the ruler's influence which is further defined as "air."[59] Some interpreters have understood ἐξουσία as a collective here denoting all the spirits of the air.[60] This idea is certainly not absent from the context — it is one of the chief characteristics of the devil's realm — but it is not the way ἐξουσία is used in 2:2.

The air was regarded as the dwelling place of evil spirits in antiquity. This is well attested in the magical papyri. *PGM* I.97–194 refers a number of times to demons or spirits in the air. Lines 179ff. say, "For no aerial spirit (πνεῦμα ἀέριον) which is joined with a mighty assistant (κραταιῷ) will go into Hades, for to him all things are subject."[61] Another magical text petitions for help from aerial "powers": "Protect me from every demon in the air ..." (*PGM* IV.2699).[62] *PGM* CI.39 (= Wortmann, "Texte," 100) may provide the closest parallel to Eph 2:2: "And again I conjure you by the one who is in charge of the air (κατὰ τοῦ ἔχοντος τὸν ἀέρα)." The air as the abode of demons is also well known to Judaism. This is seen clearly in the *Test. Benj.* 3:4: "For the person who fears God and loves his neighbor cannot be plagued by the ἀερίου πνεύματος of Beliar since he is sheltered by the fear of God."[63] There is no reason to see the author taking a step toward demythologization in this passage, as does Wink.[64] The religions-historical parallels would support the conception of actual evil beings populating the air as opposed to viewing the air as an evil atmosphere consisting of abstract ideas such as attitudes, peer pressure, licence, etc. Such a view appears to be more of a Western imposition onto the text.

The nature of this diabolical prince is further clarified by the author in the next phrase when he describes the ἄρχων as a spirit (πνεῦμα).[65] The manner of the operation of this evil spirit is described with a dynamic power term (ἐνεργέω). The devil is thus seen to exercise effective and compelling power in his work of inspiring disobedience among humanity. We cannot seek too much precision in how we translate the preposition ἐν. The gospels attest to a belief in the actual indwelling of evil spirits, on the analogy of someone dwelling in a house. The thought here is probably more expansive than the indwelling of an evil spirit and may be better translated "among." The emphasis of the author, however, is upon the *direct* mighty work of the "powers" on humanity. This diabolical force is so entirely effective in retaining its subjects that the author can describe these victims as "sons" of disobedience. The first-century A.D. section of the *Ascension of Isaiah* (2:2–4) may provide an illustration of what the author may mean regarding the nature of the control:

> And Manasseh ceased from serving the God of his father and served Satan and his angels and powers ... for the *prince* of unrighteousness who rules this world is Beliar, whose name is Matanbukus. Now this Beliar rejoiced in Jerusalem over Manasseh and *strengthened* him in his leading to apostasy and in the lawlessness which was spread abroad in Jerusalem (my italics).

This text demonstrates that it is not necessary to demythologize the belief in angelic powers in order to see institutions as "diabolic." Here the political foundation of Israel is seen as corrupt because of the direct influence of a hostile angel on the human political leader.[66]

The author describes the nature of the pre-Christian life from another perspective as well. In v. 3 he speaks of the role of the "flesh." This is balanced with v. 2 by the repetition of κατά. The writer now includes himself with the readers and remarks that they all once conducted themselves "in the lusts of our flesh" and accomplished "the desires of our flesh and of our minds." This description of the former life stands in strong connection with the *Hauptbriefe*, whereas the description of the past life in v. 2 as held in thrall by the devil and his "powers" is not as prominent in the accepted epistles of Paul.[67] Gal 5:16, 24 speak of the "lusts of the flesh" which are opposed to the desires of the Spirit. The "flesh," of course, holds a significant place in the Pauline anthropology to describe the power which leads man away from God. Here in Eph 2:2, 3, however, the influence of the flesh is coordinated with the influence of the evil "powers." The Pauline concept of flesh is thus not replaced in our epistle by another explanation for sin. On the contrary, our author sees the two influences as *complementary*. They both work together to lead individuals into sin, transgression, and disobedience (see chapter 6).

The motivation for this dual emphasis can be explained by the overall emphasis on the spirit "powers" in the epistle. If the author is indeed addressing a group of readers who are keenly aware of demonic "powers" at work and who are also in need of instruction about the place of these "powers" with regard to Christ and the believer, a satisfactory occasion can thus be envisioned for the nuances of this description of the former life.

This passage thus provides a significant insight into the author's conception of the spirit world. It may be helpful to summarize my interpretation of the passage by a paraphrase of 2:2: "You once conducted your lives according to the manner of this world-age and according to the prince of the kingdom of the air, the prince who is actually a spirit wielding effective and compelling power to lead humanity into disobedience from God." The devil is thus depicted as the "arch-power" among a host of "powers" sufficiently equipped to lead and keep individuals in a life of disobedience.

4. The existence of the church reveals God's wisdom to the "powers" (Eph 3:10)

After explaining his apostolic commission to proclaim the gospel to the Gentiles, "Paul" also comments that he is responsible for making known "the economy of the mystery" (ἡ οἰκονομία τοῦ μυστηρίου). The content of this mystery is that Jews and Gentiles have been united into one body in Christ Jesus (3:6).[68] He continues by affirming that the "powers" are also the recipients of enlightenment. They are now to be made aware of the manifold wisdom of God through the church. This passage raises two important questions, especially since there is no other similar statement given in the NT: (1) How does the church make God's wisdom known to the "powers"? and (2) Why is there an emphasis on "making known" his wisdom to the "powers"?

The church must hold either an active or a passive role with regard to making known God's wisdom to the "powers." The passive role better explains the meaning of this passage. The church is not passive in the sense of failing to resist the influence of the "powers," but in the sense that it does not act as a dispatched agent to proclaim the message of God's dominion to the "powers." The church visibly testifies to God's wisdom *by its very existence.*[69] This interpretation avoids the difficulty encountered by Wink, who finds the church's task articulated in this passage as "preaching to the Powers."[70] He finds this supposed duty of the church "puzzling," an "apparent non sequitur," and ultimately concedes that it cannot be explained: "Try as we may to place ourselves within the thought-world of the first century, the idea of the church preaching to heavenly powers is simply not intelligible."[71]

The author never states that the church is given the task of "preaching" to the "powers." He merely remarks that the wisdom of God will be made known (passive voice) through the church. Wink is correct in asserting that there is scanty evidence in the early Christian literature about the church teaching angels.[72] That is not what is communicated by this passage.

There is evidence that the angels are intimately concerned with and aware of the affairs of humanity. Paul claims that he and the other apostles were a spectacle to angels (1 Cor 4:9). The first epistle of Peter (1:12) speaks of angels longing to look into the matters regarding the gospel and salvation. The very term "watchers" used in much of the apocryphal and Pseudepigraphal literature to describe the angels who fell gives supporting evidence of this.[73] The church is therefore not instructed to make a conscious effort to preach to the "powers." The readers are here informed that their existence as a church provides a testimony to the "powers."

What kind of a testimony is given to the "powers," and why is this important? The writer does not make the answer to this question explicit, so we can only make a logical inference. A reading of 1 Cor 2:6–8, which bears a strong similarity to our passage, may help provide the answer.[74] Scott has provided an illuminating explanation of the relationship between the two contexts:[75]

> The hostile powers had sought to frustrate the work of God, and believed they had succeeded when they conspired against Christ and brought about his Crucifixion. But unwittingly they had been mere instruments in God's hands. The death

of Christ had been the very means He had devised for the accomplishment of His plan. So it is here declared that the hostile powers, after their brief apparent triumph, had now become aware of a divine wisdom they had never dreamed of. They saw the Church arising as the result of Christ's death, and giving effect to what they could now perceive to have been the hidden purpose of God.

The existence of the church thereby demonstrates to the "powers" that they are in fact powerless to impede the progress of the gospel to the Gentiles and consequently destroy the church, the body of Christ, which they thought they had already once destroyed on the cross.

The purpose of 3:10 in the context of the entire epistle is primarily for the comfort of the readers. Plagued by a fear of the "powers," the readers would find great encouragement in knowing that the "powers" can see that they have been devastatingly foiled by the emergence of the body of Christ, the church. This would also give the readers added assurance of victory over the "powers" as they engage in spiritual warfare and await the consummation of the age to come.

5. The church engages in warfare with the "powers" (Eph 6:10–20)

The concept of a spiritual warfare which envisions the church battling against the forces of evil is one of the distinctive contributions of the epistle. I will discuss the nature of this warfare as the author presents it in chapter 5, but here I will treat the nuances of the terms the author uses in describing the "powers."

The author refers first to the "devil" (διάβολος) by instructing his readers to resist the devil's schemes by putting on the armor of God (6:11). The occurrence of this particular term here has been used as a reason for objecting to the authenticity of this epistle, since it does not occur in the accepted epistles of Paul.[76] Van Roon has rightly pointed to the illegitimacy of such an objection since διάβολος and σατανᾶς are used indiscriminately and also since the word σατανᾶς occurs too few times (eight) in the *Hauptbriefe* for such a judgment to be made.[77] In addition, Paul does use other terms to make reference to "Satan," viz. βελίαρ in 2 Cor 6:15 and ὁ πειράζων in 1 Thess 3:5.

The source of this term is clearly rooted in the LXX, where it is employed as a translation of *hasatan* (see Job 2:1; Zech 3:1ff.; 1 Chron 21:1). It is used elsewhere in pre-Christian Jewish literature.[78] It is also found a number of times in the Synoptics, John, the Pastorals, Hebrews, James, 1 Peter, Jude, and Revelation. It was undoubtedly a well-known expression for the prince of evil in the first century A.D. The word should be understood as synonymous with ἄρχων in 2:2.[79]

The author of Ephesians uses διάβολος in 4:27, where he admonishes the readers not to give a place to the devil by lying, excessive wrath, or other sin. This concept of providing the devil with an opportunity was familiar to Judaism (see *Test. Reub.* 4:7; *Test. Sim.* 5:3). *Test. Dan* 4:7 specifically links it with anger and falsehood: "Anger and falsehood together are a double-edged evil, and work together to perturb the reason. And when the soul is continually perturbed, the Lord withdraws from it and Beliar rules it" (see also *Test. Dan* 2:4; 3:6; 4:5; 5:1; *Test. Gad* 4:7; CD 4:15).

In v. 12, the author further defines the nature of the spiritual (not blood and flesh) opposition with which believers will struggle. For the third time in this epistle he mentions the ἀρχαὶ καὶ ἐξουσίαι. He then adduces another group of "powers" which he has not spoken of before and which are referred to at no other place in all of the NT or LXX – οἱ κοσμοκράτορες τοῦ σκότους τούτου. The source of this term has baffled interpreters since it does not appear in Jewish writings until the Testament of Solomon[80] and since there is no use of the term in any extant pre-Christian literature or inscriptions. This leaves interpreters with two choices. Either (1) the author of Ephesians created the term himself on the analogy of παντοκράτωρ,[81] or (2) the use of κοσμοκράτωρ in some of the literature postdating the first century A.D. accurately reflects a usage of the term current in the first century A.D. and perhaps before. Both are viable options, but there may very well be sufficient evidence to opt for the latter. This evidence suggests that the term was current in both the magical tradition and astrology when the author wrote this epistle.

The term does occur a number of times in the magical papyri, with the earliest papyrus dating to the second century. I am convinced, however, that these occurrences reflect an earlier usage than the actual date of the papyri (see chapter 2). It is used as one of a number of descriptive titles for various gods/spirits called upon to aid the conjurer. In *PGM* IV.166, Nephotes writes a recipe to Psammetichos, king of Egypt, on how to conjure up a god – (κοσμοκράτωρ) –

to appear and answer any question. *PGM* III.35 uses it as one of the many titles of the deity Helios (see also *PGM* IV.1599 and 2198f., where it is used of Ra, and V.400, for Hermes). The term seems to be regarded as one of the names which could be "named" in conjuration. A good illustration of this can be found in *PGM* XIII.637ff.: "[Do this] for I am your slave and petitioner and have hymned your valid and holy names, lord, glorious one, κοσμοκράτωρ, of ten thousand names, greatest, nourisher, apportioner, Sarapis" (see also *PGM* XIII. 619). It is also significant that the title is found in passages in the *PGM* having astrological elements, as in the context of *PGM* XIII.619ff.:

> I call on you, lord, holy, my hymned, greatly honored, κοσμοκράτωρ, Sarapis; consider my birth and turn me not away, me, ... (magical words) ... who knows your true name and valid names ... (magical words) ... I hymn your holy power in a musical hymn ... (magical words) ... Protect me from all my own astrological destiny; destroy my foul fate; apportion good things for me in my horoscope; increase my life; and may I enjoy many good things, for I am your slave ... [cf. *PGM* XVII b.1ff., V.400f., for other uses with astrological associations].

F. Cumont and L. Canet have demonstrated that the term is deeply rooted in astrology.[82] Apart from its use in Ephesians, one of the earliest attested occurrences of κοσμοκράτωρ in extant literature is in the *Anthologies* of Vettius Valens (second century A.D.). This work, a compilation of more ancient texts, gives evidence of the use of the term by Pseudo-Petosiris in the second century B.C., who used it of the planets.[83] Cumont and Canet's primary concern in their article is to explicate the significance of an inscription found on the baths of Caracalla in Italy which reads: Εἷς Ζεὺς, Σάραπις, Ἥλιος, κοσμοκράτωρ, ἀνείκητος. The interesting aspect of this inscription is that the name "Mithras" has been engraved over the top of "Sarapis." Cumont and Canet conjecture that the change probably occurred after the death of Caracalla (217 A.D.), when the mysteries of Mithras became the most important.[84] The term bears a dual meaning for the deities to which it is applied. It denotes both omnipotence and universality. The κοσμοκράτωρ is both the master of the universe and the master of time.[85] The sun ("Helios") is therefore an appropriate image for the κοσμοκράτωρ, whether the title is applied to Sarapis, Mithras, or Artemis, since the sun is by far the brightest and most powerful luminary in the sky.

It is doubtful whether κοσμοκράτωρ was applied to the Roman emperors in the first century. The earliest evidence for this application is in an Egyptian inscription of A.D. 216 which calls Caracalla κοσμοκράτωρ.[86]

We have four remarks regarding the relevance of this material for an understanding of the use of the term in Eph 6:12. (1) The employment of κοσμοκράτωρ appears to be a clear example of the Ephesian author utilizing a term from the magical/astrological tradition. It is also a likely candidate for being one of "the names which are named" (1:21). (2) The author reinterprets the meaning of κοσμοκράτωρ for the Christian readers. There is not one κοσμοκράτωρ, but many (the term is plural). The κοσμοκράτωρ is not considered omnipotent, but is placed alongside the principalities and "powers" *under* the leadership of the devil! Far from being beneficial or helpful deities, the κοσμοκράτορες are regarded as evil spirits (πνευματικά) of "this darkness." (3) The way the term is used in this context may serve as the author's interpretation of the Ephesian Artemis.[87] It would certainly also seem to serve as the author's interpretation of Helios, Sarapis, or other deities claiming to possess cosmic power.[88] (4) Those who were once worshipers of Artemis (or other pagan deities) and/or those who formerly put their faith in magical practices and have since professed faith in Christ now have apostolic instruction about how they are to regard the deities or spirits in which they formerly trusted in light of their confession of Christ. The pagan deities are not imaginary or lifeless and therefore harmless, but neither are they omnipotent. They are powerful and evil emissaries of the devil himself who need to be resisted with the powerful armor of God.

It is important to note that the concept of evil "powers" behind the worship of pagan deities is present in Paul. He says to the Corinthians (1 Cor 10:20): "The things which the Gentiles sacrifice, they sacrifice to demons (δαιμόνια), and not to God; and I do not want you to become a sharer in demons." Paul believed that a Corinthian believer would actually be joined with demonic "powers" if he became involved in the table fellowship of pagan deities. Everling explains that for Paul, the heathen gods were nothing but chimeras, although an offering brought to them brought one under the influence of demonic "powers." This was because the heathen cults were the instruments of the kingdom of Satan.[89]

This close association of pagan gods with "demons" is also found in the LXX. Ps 95:5 reads: "For all the gods of the Gentiles are demons" (δαιμόνια; see also Deut 32:7; *Baraita* 4:7; *Jub.* 22:16–17).

The identification of the gods of the heathen with demons became even more explicit in later Judaism.⁹⁰

If the author of Ephesians had the worship of Artemis, Sarapis, Isis, or any other pagan deity in mind as he wrote κοσμοκράτορες, he accurately reflects the teaching of Paul in 1 Cor 10:20ff. – Artemis and the other so-called gods are animated by evil spiritual "powers."

The writer finishes this list of "powers" not with a new category, but with a comprehensive designation for all the classes of hostile spirits – τὰ πνευματικὰ τῆς πονηρίας. The term πνευματικά should probably be viewed as an alternate expression for πνεῦμα, not πνεύματα.⁹¹ Believers need to be prepared to engage all the forces of evil in battle.

Finally, the author uses yet another expression to denote a hostile force in 6:16. He uses a descriptive title for the devil, ὁ πονηρός, which is also known to Matthew (Matt 6:13; 13:19, 38), John (John 17:15; 1 John 2:13, 14; 3:12; 5:18, 19) and the writer of 2 Thessalonians (2 Thess 3:3). The hostile character of this enemy is illustrated by the imagery of him launching fiery arrows against the believers. His aim is to take ground away from believers by seducing them to sin (4:27).

6. The "powers" will be brought completely under the headship of Christ (Eph 1:10)

Eph 1:10 affirms that all of creation will be consummated in Christ. This is presented as an essentially future event when all of humanity and all of the spirit world will be brought into complete subjection to the Head. The evil spirit "powers" are included in the phrase τὰ πάντα ... τὰ ἐπὶ τοῖς οὐρανοῖς. We may infer that these "powers" will at the time of the consummation be completely disarmed and no longer able to tyrannize the church (Eph 6:10ff.; 4:7). The verb ἀνακεφαλαιόομαι means "to bring something to a κεφάλαιον," "to sum up" (the only other NT use is by Paul in Rom 13:9). In the context of Ephesians, this "summing up" takes place in the subjection of all things to the Head.⁹²

Andreas Lindemann, however, understands this "summing up" as having already occurred and eliminates any future connotations from the term.⁹³ In a certain sense, this interpretation is also true. Christ has effectively broken the hold of the "powers" on humanity by his resurrection (1:20ff.) and he has already effectively become Head of the church (1:22). The final summing up has in no way taken place, however. The "powers" are still in rebellion against Christ in attacking the church (Eph 6:10–20) and are effectively working in unredeemed humanity.[94]

7. Summary of the "powers" teaching in Ephesians

(1) With a rich variety of descriptive terms, the Epistle to the Ephesians provides us with the most detailed Christian response to the "powers" of all the canonical epistles.

(2) Our analysis of the sources for the various terms for the "powers" demonstrates that the writer of Ephesians reflects the prevailing Jewish and Hellenistic view of a belief in the reality of evil spirit-beings. The fact that many of the terms appear to have been used by both Jewish and Hellenistic groups shows that Jews and pagans in the first century could understand one another when talking about the "powers."

(3) The author does not demythologize the "powers" and make them equivalent to the abstract notions of "flesh" and "sin" or see them as some kind of spiritual "atmosphere."[95] The flesh and the devil (with his "powers") work in confluence leading humanity into disobedience from God.

(4) A very practical aim is attained by the writer in his discussion of the "powers." He is not concerned with esoteric speculation about the origin, hierarchical distinctions, names, and specific functions of the "powers" discussed in detail in the Jewish apocalyptic literature. He has the pastoral intention of explaining (a) where Christ stands in relation to the "powers," and (b) where the believer stands in relation to the "powers," both in terms of the past life and the life now experienced in Christ.

(5) The Epistle to the Ephesians provides a complete response to believers having questions and needing instruction about the "powers." It is therefore quite appropriate to my proposed historical setting for the epistle in western Asia Minor. The epistle would greatly help believers formulate a Christian perspective on magical beliefs and the worship of Artemis and other pagan deities. It would reaffirm the demonic nature of these former practices and beliefs to the readers and would provide them with a very practical insight on how to resist the continuing powerful influence of these evil forces through "spiritual warfare."

4

THE POWER OF GOD FOR BELIEVERS

A literary analysis of the prayer in Eph 1, the prayer in Eph 3, and the doxology of Eph 3 reveals a clear verbal and structural emphasis on the theme of the power of God in the epistle. This emphasis prepares the readers for the paraenesis of the epistle, but especially the final part of the paraenesis − the admonition to appropriate the divine power and resist the evil forces (Eph 6).

1. A prayer for divine enabling power (Eph 1:15−23)

The language of power pervades the prayer of Eph 1. The author uses five terms to express the power of God (δύναμις, ἐνέργεια, κράτος, ἰσχύς, and ἐνεργέω). This power of God is juxtaposed to the "powers" of evil described in four different categories: ἀρχή, ἐξουσία, δύναμις, and κυριότης. Before analyzing specifically how this emphasis on power is developed in the prayer, it will be important to discuss the relationship of the prayer to the prooemium (1:3−14).

The introductory eulogy (1:3−14)

Whether it is a reworked hymn from early Christian tradition or the author's own creation, there is no doubt that the first-century Christian could not read through this majestic piece without it touching his or her emotions. The author endeavors to bring praise to God for his glorious plan of salvation, and thereby edify the readers. Schnackenburg has aptly observed that the author has a pragmatic rhetorical purpose. He stresses that the passage is not merely a hymn of praise, but it has been carefully constructed by the author to evoke a cognitive and emotional response in the readers by reminding them in a fresh way of their redemption in Christ and their experience of salvation.[1] These evoked feelings of joy and gratefulness to God for his abundant bestowal of grace prepare the readers to receive the paraenesis with the proper frame of mind.

A number of interpreters have suggested that the themes of the epistle are deliberately announced by the author in his introductory eulogy.[2] P. T. O'Brien has taken a more moderate stance by showing that the eulogy has introduced and prefigured many, though by no means all, the important theological and paraenetic themes of the epistle.[3] For example, he correctly points out that the theme of the body which is very important to Ephesians does not turn up in the introductory eulogy.[4]

There does not appear to be one unifying theme to the eulogy. The author merely gives his readers a rhetorically powerful staccato presentation of the blessings of salvation. These blessings are rooted in the "blessed" God who provides a wide array of spiritual blessings "in Christ." O'Brien mentions three specific groupings of motifs within the epistle which are also evident in the introductory *Berakah*. First, there are the motifs mentioned in the introductory eulogy which are expounded and enlarged upon in the body of the letter. He mentions πλήρωμα in 1:10 (1:23; 3:19; cf. 4:13); γνωρίζω ... μυστήριον at 1:9 (3:3; 6:19; cf. 3:9); et al. He also specifically makes references to God's power and might in 1:11 (1:20; 3:7, 16, 20). Secondly, he cites a theme which is later expanded by way of contrast, i.e. those foreordained to sonship (1:4−5) had once been children of wrath (2:3). Thirdly, he notices the reference to sealing with the Holy Spirit developed in the paraenetic section of Eph 4−6.[5]

The theme of the power of God is therefore introduced in the eulogy (1:11) as an essential theme of the epistle. It is presented in close connection with many of the other blessings, viz. fullness, grace, glory, election, the mystery, redemption, and the Holy Spirit.

The structure, genre, and aim of the prayer

Similar to the introductory eulogy, the prayer of thanksgiving and intercession takes the form of one long sentence. The author approaches God with thankfulness for his readers and then reports to them the nature of his prayer on their behalf. He prays that God would by revelation expand their knowledge and awareness of God himself (vv. 17−19). Specifically, he requests for them a deeper understanding of the divine hope, glory, and power. These are associated with election, inheritance, and faith respectively (vv. 18−19). The final four verses (vv. 20−23) are full of Christological content, emphasizing the resurrection and exaltation of Christ (vv. 20–21), as well as the position of Christ with respect to the church (vv. 22–23). The final section (vv. 20–23) has thematic similarity to other passages in the NT thought to be Christ-hymns, especially the Lordship of Christ over the hostile "powers" (Phil 2:10–11; 1 Pet 3:22; Heb 1:6; see also Col 1:15–22) and the exaltation of Jesus over "all things."[6]

Normally in Paul, the introductory thanksgiving paragraphs fulfill an epistolary function – to introduce and indicate the main theme(s) of the letters.[7] In Ephesians, however, this function appears to have been fulfilled in the introductory eulogy – or has it? O'Brien attempts to solve this question by observing that the prayer takes up and repeats some of the themes of the introductory eulogy. He then concludes that the main thrust of the prayer is for the realization of the blessings of the eulogy in the lives of the readers.[8]

This conclusion is generally correct, in my view, but I would add the following refinements. (1) The power of God, one of the themes of the eulogy, becomes the primary theme of the prayer.[9] (2) The emphasis on the power of God is taken up and stressed throughout the epistle, which makes it one of the central themes of the letter. (3) The power of God does indeed work in and on behalf of believers for the realization of the spiritual blessings (as O'Brien states), but in Ephesians this is presented against the backdrop of hostile spiritual "powers" bent on averting the attainment of this goal. This observation may very well provide the best explanation for the emphasis in this letter on the superior power of God in contrast to other Pauline letters which do not accent this motif as strongly.

The explicit request (1:19)

As his third and consummatory request, the author prays that his readers may be given a special awareness of the incomparably great power of God working in them. Specifically, he calls on God to reveal to them, τί τὸ ὑπερβάλλον μέγεθος τῆς δυνάμεως αὐτοῦ εἰς ἡμᾶς τοὺς πιστεύοντας κατὰ τὴν ἐνέργειαν τοῦ κράτους τῆς ἰσχύος αὐτοῦ.

The writer introduces the power of God in an extremely emphatic fashion. He uses the adjectival participle of ὑπερβάλλω combined with the adjective μέγεθος to emphasize in bold relief the incredibly mighty power of God. Both of these rare terms[10] may have been chosen by the author to communicate especially to those converted from magic in Asia Minor. They both appear in the magical papyri and also in a number of inscriptions from Ephesus.[11] The term ὑπερβάλλω is used in a way very similar to Eph 1:19 in *PGM* XII.284, i.e. as a description of divine power (ὑπερβάλλεις τὴν πᾶσαν δύναμιν).[12] The author has employed this combination to bring out in an additionally emphatic manner the greatness of the power of God toward those who believe.

In referring to the divine power, the writer uses the term δύναμις, the power- denoting term most frequently employed by Paul. He then employs an additional phrase to stress the basis or standard (κατά) of this incomparably great power. The term ἐνέργεια is the object of κατά and it is followed by two genitives providing a further description of the power (κράτος and ἰσχύς). Thus, in v. 19 the author employs four different terms which denote some idea of power! Clearly he places an explicit lexical emphasis on the notion of power.

Δύναμις is by far the most common and important word for power in Greek writings. Its original meaning of "ability" or "capacity" and therefore "power" is fully maintained. Two differing concepts of divine power, however, can be discerned in the first century with a widely held impersonal, "substance" view of power evident in magical-mystical writings as opposed to a non-substance, personal notion of divine power exemplified in the OT and Judaism (where it was not influenced by magic) (see chapter 2, section 8). The term δύναμις was prominent in both traditions, occurring nearly 600 times in the LXX and almost 100 times in Preisendanz's collection of magical papyri. In Eph 1:19 the stress is on the superior power of the one God who imparts his power personally to those who exercise faith in him. In contrast to magic, (1) the power of God alone is sufficient and supreme, and (2) the power of God is personal – it is received through faith in a personal God, not by a recipe or a conjuration using animal viscera or by chanting magical words and names.

The term ἐνέργεια (see also Eph 3:7; 4:16) occurs infrequently in the LXX, with only a few scattered references in Wisdom and 2 and 3 Maccabees. It is found in conjunction with δύναμις only once (Wis 13:4), where the combination is used in describing cosmic "powers."[13] Otherwise the reference is always to the power of God.[14] The meaning is distinguishable from δύναμις, as Walter Grundmann has rightly recognized: "'Ενέργεια is actuality in contrast to δύναμις which expresses potentiality. 'Ενέργεια designates the realization of δύναμις."[15] The same sense is readily discernible in the references to the term throughout the magical papyri. There it invariably refers to a recipe, spell, or charm that has been found to work and is therefore "effective" (ἐνέργεια). For example, *PGM* XII.201–10 describes how to make a small magical ring. Line 210 records, "a similar engraving in gold, too, is equally effective (ἐνέργειαν)."[16] The term never appears in a string of synonyms for power, but is always distinguished as the actualization of the power. This is also its meaning in the seven other occurrences in the NT[17] and in this context. This sense is both confirmed and illustrated in vv. 20ff., where the author employs the verbal form (ἐνεργέω) to describe the realization of the divine power in terms of raising Christ from the dead. It is therefore important to observe that ἐνέργεια stands at the beginning of the phrase.

Both κράτος and ἰσχύς occur in the LXX (see also Philo, Josephus, Test. 12 Patr.) and in the magical papyri.[18] They are more closely linked with δύναμις than ἐνέργεια in the sense that they both express power implied in ability and capacity versus the realization of power. Although some interpreters are inclined toward making a distinction in the meaning of the two terms,[19] they are probably synonymous. The contexts in Ephesians do not demand seeing nuances in their respective meanings and their usage in the literature shows no clear pattern of distinction. In fact, their occasional co-ordination would imply their synonymity (e.g. Job 12:16; Dan 4:30; 11:1; Isa 40:26).

The combination of synonyms for power was popular among Jewish writers. Grundmann cites a number of references to two-fold expressions of power found in the OT. The same stylistic flare is exhibited in the Qumran literature, e.g. 1QH 4:32 refers to "the might (*koach*) of his strength (*gebhurah*)."[20]

The combination of terms for power was also popular in the magical papyri. Three of the terms for power found in Eph 1:19 are clustered together in *PGM* XXXV.15–23, which interestingly is the only place we can find the three terms coordinated outside of Ephesians. After instructing the supplication of fourteen different angels, the recipe reads,

> I conjure you all [i.e. the angels] by the god of Abraham, Isaac, and Jacob, that you obey my authority completely ... and give me (= δίδωμι; cf. Eph 1:17) favor, influence (δυναμίαν), victory, and strength (ἰσχὺν) before all, small men and great, as well as gladiators, soldiers, civilians, women, girls, boys, and everybody, quickly, quickly, because

of the power (ἰσχὺν) of SABAOTH, the clothing of ELOE, the might (κράτος) of ADONAI ...

This papyrus betrays strong Jewish influence and may illustrate the kind of magic practiced by both Jews and Greeks in Ephesus and its environs in the first century. We can observe three decisive differences in comparing this text with the Ephesian passage. (1) There is a different source of power. In the magical papyrus, the angelic powers are called on to obey and accomplish the requests of the one speaking the spell. The God of the Jews is called upon since the author of the recipe has received a tradition that this deity has power over the angels. Indeed, the way the power of God is expressed is similar to the style of the LXX and Ephesians. The power of God is not conceived of as directly providing inner strengthening to the conjurer, rather it is imparted indirectly since it is viewed only as an effective threat to bring certain angels under the authority of the one using the recipe. (2) There is a different means for acquiring power. The angelic powers are brought into submission for manipulation by repeating a set formula, invoking a series of magical names (of which certain Hebrew names for God are a part), and by writing magical symbols (see lines 28ff.). (3) The power is desired for a variant goal. Power is sought in order to influence and gain ascendancy over people rather than for manifesting love to people (cf. Eph 3:17ff.; 5:2) or for living a virtuous life.

In summary, the author of Ephesians has chosen power-denoting terms common both in the Greek versions of Jewish material and in the magical papyri. The terms used are synonymous, with the exception of ἐνέργεια, which refers to the operation or realization of power. The stringing of synonyms for power reflects Jewish influence, but this style has already permeated syncretistic Hellenistic material (viz. the magical papyri), which drew upon Jewish traditions.

The related elements

The introductory portion of the prayer and the first two elements also reveal something of the nature and purpose of the power of God which the author emphasizes in the final part of the prayer. Even this portion of the prayer is particularly appropriate to converts to Christianity from strong magical beliefs.

The author begins the prayer by highlighting the person and power of God. As "the God of our Lord Jesus Christ," he is conceived of as the saving God (see also 1:3, 7). In this title are summarized all of the spiritual blessings God has showered on believers through Christ as they are expressed in the introductory eulogy. As "the Father of glory," God is regarded as omnipotent. A close relationship exists between δόξα and δύναμις, e.g. Paul can attribute the resurrection of Christ on the one hand to the δύναμις of God (1 Cor 6:14), while on the other hand it can be regarded as a manifestation of the δόξα of God (Rom 6:4).[21] As "Father," God is the source of all glory and all power.

The first part of the request (v. 17b) is that God would impart his Spirit to the readers, specifically, the πνεῦμα σοφίας καὶ ἀποκαλύψεως. This characterization of the Spirit is best explained by Paul himself in 1 Cor 2:6–16.[22] In this context Paul teaches that the human spirit (τὸ πνεῦμα τοῦ ἀνθρώπου) is unable to know (γινώσκω) God; only the Spirit of God (τό πνεῦμα τοῦ θεοῦ) can reveal (ἀποκαλύπτω) knowledge about God which is wisdom (σοφία). Behind both 1 Cor 2 and Eph 1 probably stands the influence of the messianic passage in Isa 11:2:[23] καὶ ἀναπαύσεται ἐπ' αὐτὸν πνεῦμα τοῦ θεοῦ, πνεῦμα σοφίας καὶ συνέσεως, πνεῦμα βουλῆς καὶ ἰσχύος, πνεῦμα γνώσεως καὶ εὐσεβείας. The Messianic Spirit thus dispenses knowledge, wisdom, and power. The stress on wisdom imparted by the Spirit may partially be related to faulty notions of wisdom circulating in Asia Minor – a "wisdom" consisting of magical techniques and dealing with the demonic realm purportedly stemming from Moses and Solomon (see chapter 2, section 7). The close connection between the Spirit and power is held in common with Paul. Käsemann observes, "the divine Spirit is for Paul a power ... thus Spirit and power are for Paul interchangeable terms (Rom 15:13, 19; 1 Cor 2:4; 5:3–4; Gal 3:5; 1 Thess 1:5)."[24]

The prayer is continued with a request for the readers' understanding to be illuminated. It is made with the Jewish mode of expression, "[may] the eyes of your heart be enlightened." The first part of the expression, φωτίζω with ὀφθαλμοί, is found in the LXX (Ps 12:4; 18:9). "Heart" is used here with the Hebraic sense of denoting the essential inward being of a person.[25] It is of special significance, however, to note that the word "enlightened" (φωτίζω) was used in the Mystery Religions in a technical sense for the rite of initiation.[26] Scott suggests that it was originally connected with some culminating moment when the initiate suddenly emerged from an unlit chamber into the shrine in a blaze of light. This "illumination" supposedly represented the new condition of his soul.[27] The term is found in a somewhat related sense in the magical papyri (*PGM* II.153; IV.990, 2345). One text in particular gives some insight into the mystery of Apollo at Claros, just north of Ephesus. *PGM* II.119ff. reads, "Hear me, O greatest god, Kommes, who lights up (φωτίζω) the day!" The recipe concludes with (line 140), "I summon you Apollo of Claros." Lines 165 and 170 provide further confirmation of the regional connection by citing one of the Ephesian letters (Δαμναμενεύς). In contrast to the experience of Mystery "enlightenment," the author of Ephesians stresses an enlightenment of the innermost being of man brought about by the Spirit of God and directed toward the true knowledge of God. Paul expresses a similar idea in 2 Cor 4:6 using φωτισμός. The author then delineates three elements of this knowledge of God which demonstrate Christ's sole sufficiency and superiority to all other "powers."

The first of the three requests introduced by τίς is for an expanded awareness of the hope of God's calling. A line of continuity is maintained with the introductory eulogy in this prayer. In v. 11 the author develops the fact of the readers' calling and then provides a guarantee that it will be executed by the divine power (ἐνεργέω). This sequence corresponds with the first and third elements of the prayer. The hope believers possess arises out of the fact of their calling (see also 4:4), but this is not a fully sufficient base as the ground of hope. The writer wants his readers to be fully assured that he who has made these promises has sufficient power and ability to carry them out. The author wants hope to be established as more than a faint wish. He desires it to exist in their lives as a sure foundation. This observation underlines the third element of the prayer as the foundation to the first element. These affirmations about a secure destiny would prove particularly comforting to believers living in a milieu where people experienced great anxiety about their "fate" — a fate thought to have been determined by the stars and the cosmic "powers" (see chapter 6).

As God's inheritance (1:11, 14; cf. Deut 32:9), the saints possess something of the nature of God already — ὁ πλοῦτος τῆς δόξης. This constitutes a clear reference to the power of God which is confirmed by 3:16, where the same phrase is used to denote the resources of God's power imparted to the saints. This creates a strong line of continuity between the second and third elements of the prayer, both emphasizing the access of the believer to the power of God.

The nature of the power

The final request for an increased knowledge of God's incomparably great power leads the author into a Christological excursus extolling the brilliant manifestation of this power in the resurrection (v. 20a) and exaltation (vv. 20b–23) of Christ.

The divine power is made operative (ἐνεργέω) in the resurrection of Christ. The nature of God's power is thereby described as life-giving. This anticipates the author's subsequent discussion of the relevance of this life-giving power to the believer in also being made alive (συνζωοποιέω, Eph 2:5; see also Col 2:12). Paul often refers to the power of God which raised Jesus from the dead as presently functioning as the source of the vitality of the risen Jesus (Phil 3:10; 2 Cor 13:4; Rom 1:4). Fitzmyer eloquently summarizes the significance of this resurrection power:[28]

> It emanates from the Father, raises Jesus from the dead at the resurrection, endows him with a new vitality, and finally proceeds from him as the life-giving, vitalizing force of the "new creation" and of the new life that Christians in union with Christ experience and live.

For Paul, this is a guarantee of the future resurrection of believers (1 Cor 6:14; 15:43; Phil 3:21).

The power of God was also manifested in the exaltation of Christ (vv. 20b–23). In this section, often thought to be either a hymnic quotation or a combination of traditional formulations, the author makes allusion to two different Psalm passages – Psalms 110:1 and 8:6. Both of these Psalms were used extensively in the early Christian preaching.

Christ now possesses the full power and authority of the Father by virtue of his enthronement at the right hand of God (1:20b; see also Ps 110:1).[29] This position is superior to every imaginable hostile power. This supreme position is expressed by the adverb ὑπεράνω (see also 4:8). It is possible that the writer has chosen this rare adverb (a hapax legomenon in Paul) to contrast the position of Christ with that of the "powers" in the "world above" (ὁ ἄνω κόσμος, e.g. *PGM* IV.569) or in the "realm above" (ἡ ἄνω χώρα, e.g. *PGM* XII.256).[30] This adverb was common in the magical papyri to indicate the abode of the "powers." *PGM* IV.569 vividly expresses the common fear of these "powers" in the heavenly region: "So when you see that the world above (ὁ ἄνω κόσμος) is clear and

circling and that none of the gods or angels is threatening you ...
then say ..."

Continuing his description of the power and authority of Christ,
the writer cites Ps 8:6: "and all things he subjected under his feet."
Paul interprets the Psalm Messianically of Christ in 1 Cor 15:25–27
(see also Heb 2:8). The vanquished enemies in this context would
naturally refer to the "powers" of the previous verse.

The source of power for the church

The writer now concentrates on making his exaltation Christology
ecclesiologically relevant in vv. 22b–23 by expanding on the εἰς ὑμᾶς
of v. 19. The nature of the power of God is amplified with regard to
its impartation to the church and its cosmic aim.

(i) The head empowers the body

Christ's subjection of the hostile "powers" leads the author to
describe him as κεφαλή. He is thus "head" over "all things" (ὑπὲρ
πάντα), which includes the "powers." Precisely the same thought
is contained in Col 2:10, but in that context the objects are specifically
referred to as πᾶσα ἀρχή καὶ ἐξουσία. This usage of the term is
derived from the LXX, where κεφαλή is frequently used to translate
ro'sh, where it denotes "superior," "ruler," or "leader."[31] As it is
used in this sense, κεφαλή is closely related in meaning to ἀρχή and
ἄρχων.[32]

Although Christ is superior to the "powers" as their "head" (see
also Col 2:10), the writer appears to stretch more meaning out of the
term when he applies it to the church. In v. 23, the "head" has become
coordinated with a "body" which is the church, or the body of Christ.
Head and body are coordinated in the same manner in Col 1:18 (see
also Eph 5:23; Col 2:19), which some regard as the source of this
conception for Ephesians.[33] This is a notion unique to Ephesians and
Colossians among the epistles attributed to Paul. In 1 Cor 12:12ff.
and Rom 12:3ff. the concept of the church as the body of Christ is
developed, but Christ is not referred to as the head of the church.

Some interpreters think that in contrast to Paul, Ephesians and
Colossians show traces of an earlier Christology (perhaps mediated
through hymns) in which Christ was interpreted cosmically. Σῶμα
would then be understood as the universe, a cosmic body. The
Bultmannian school, here represented chiefly by Heinrich Schlier and
Ernst Käsemann, interpreted σῶμα in this way on the basis of the

so-called Gnostic redeemer myth.[34] Such dependence on the conceptions of this myth have been justly refuted in more recent research in the history of religions, especially by the works of C. Colpe and H.-M. Schenke.[35] These men and others have turned to Hellenistic texts (including Philo) where they have discerned a "macroanthropos" myth in which the cosmos is understood as an ἄνθρωπος or σῶμα and the guiding part of the macroanthropos is conceived of as "head."[36]

The head–body metaphor does occur in the magical papyri. In Preisendanz's collection three references can be found where σῶμα is to be understood in a cosmic sense (*PGM* XII.243; XIII.767–72; XXI.7). All three references are collections of epitaphs to Agathos Daimon having the same content, "Heaven is your head; ether, body; earth, feet; and the water around you, ocean, O Agathos Diamon." I do not dispute that this head–body metaphor could have been current in the first century A.D. and before.[37] I do find it curious that the metaphor is only used three times and always in epitaphs to Agathos Daimon. The actual use of the metaphor betrays a significant qualitative difference to any reconstructed Christian use. First, it includes references to the earth as feet and the environment as water which are not included in the use of the metaphor in Ephesians (and Colossians). "Feet" are mentioned in the context of the use of the metaphor in Eph 1:22–23, but they are clearly part of a Psalm citation and could in no way be construed as the earth. In fact, in Ephesians, those things which are under the feet of the Messiah are the heavenly powers! Secondly, "body" is restricted to ether and not to the whole cosmos, as in the reconstructed "macroanthropos" view.

It is probably best to take the "head–body" correlation as a development of the Pauline concept of the "body of Christ" (1 Cor 12:12–27 and Rom 12:4–5). The idea may have originally been planted in Paul's mind in his encounter with Christ along the Damascus road, where the risen Christ identifies himself with his followers: "Why do you persecute me?" (Acts 9:4; 22:7; 26:14). The Pauline understanding of the "body of Christ" is adequately explained by the OT concept of corporate personality whereby movement between the one and the many can be expressed by the one term with overtones of solidarity.[38] Such a concept is present in Philo (*Spec. Leg.* 3.131) and is quite prominent in the rabbinic texts. For Paul, Christ as the last Adam and second man is the representative of new humanity (Rom 5:12–21; 1 Cor 15:22, 45–49), therefore one can either be "in Adam" or "in Christ." Whereas the body of the first

Adam is animated by the principle of natural life, *nephesh*, the body of the second Adam is animated by the Spirit. One of the main differences between this view and the "macroanthropos" view is that this concept emphasizes "body" as a unified organism, not as a cosmic or universal entity.

If we interpret σῶμα along the Pauline/OT notion of corporate personality, we are left with the difficulty of how to interpret "head." Does it imply more than "representative" of the many? I have already pointed favorably to the OT/Jewish notion of "head" as indicating "ruler" or "superior." We must now ask if this explanation is adequate in view of the apparently intentional juxtaposition of head–body in Ephesians and Colossians.

A plausible answer to this question may be found in combining the OT notions of "head" with that of the Greek medical ideas of the function of the head in relation to the body and its members. J. B. Lightfoot was one of the first to point in this direction by citing passages from Galen.[39] Lightfoot found this background productive in accounting for the dynamic idea given "head" in Colossians (and Ephesians), i.e. the head as "the inspiring, ruling, guiding, combining, sustaining power, the mainspring of its activity, the centre of its unity, and the seat of its life."[40] This view has more recently been taken up and developed by Markus Barth.[41]

Barth leans most heavily on Hippocrates, whose works date between 420 and 360 B.C., and Galen (A.D. 130–200), whose works purportedly sum up the accumulated progress of medical knowledge attained between 300 B.C. and A.D. 100. Both of these ancient writers stress how the brain, or the head, is the strongest power in man, the power animating the body. Barth summarizes the relevance of their writings for understanding the head–body metaphor:[42]

> The evidence offered by the medical parallels is sufficiently strong for concluding thus: by his acquaintance with physiological insights Paul could ascribe to the head more than a representative and dominating function. He could attribute to it the power to perceive, to interpret, to coordinate, and to unify all that went on in the body and its several members. Because the head is the "greatest power" of the body, causation and coordination can be ascribed to nothing else. There is but one source, throne, and acropolis of all members, including their movements and perceptions – the head. In other words, by its power the head is omnipresent

in the whole body; its relation to the body is as a "dynamic presence." Paul mentions emphatically the "power" working in Christ and the congregation (Eph 1:19–20; 3:16; 6:10; cf. 3:18) and he speaks of the "indwelling" of Christ (3:17).

Far from dividing Christ from his body, the head is now shown to be the cohesive and enabling factor for the body.[43] In contrast to the Hellenistic "substance" notion of power which compared power to a fluid, Ephesians (and Colossians) highlights the personal presence of a powerful one who strengthens the individual through the concept of Christ as "head."

This interpretation also has the advantage of providing the best explanation for Eph 4:16 and Col 2:19, which reads, "from it [the head] the whole body grows." This background is also consistent with the thought of the head "nourishing" (ἐκτρέφω) the body (Eph 5:29).

One may wonder how the writer of Ephesians (or Colossians) would have been familiar with contemporary medical thought. Those who are inclined toward Pauline authorship of the two epistles have pointed to the likely influence of "Luke the beloved physician" (Col 4:14) on Paul's thinking.[44] If Luke himself was the author of Ephesians (R. P. Martin, et al.), the possibility of his medical insight here would of course still pertain.

(ii) The church shares the divine "fullness"

The final clause of v. 23 — τὸ πλήρωμα τοῦ τὰ πάντα ἐν πᾶσιν πληρουμένου — presents one of the most complex interpretational difficulties of the entire epistle. The first difficulty surrounds the interpretation of πλήρωμα in the context — does it have an active meaning, "that which fills", or a passive meaning, "that which is filled"? Secondly, how is the voice of πληρουμένου to be understood — is it passive, middle, or middle with an active significance? Finally, does the phrase τὰ πάντα ἐν πᾶσιν bear an adverbial or an adjectival sense? These grammatical and linguistic problems need to be solved in order that this very significant Christological statement may be understood properly.

Two primary views can be discerned among the many treatments of this verse:

(1) πλήρωμα = active (complement); Christ is filled.
πληρουμένου = passive
τὰ πάντα ἐν πᾶσιν = adverb

Proponents of this view would give the clause roughly the following translation: "[the church is] the fullness (complement) of the one [Christ] who is being completely filled." The Christological implication is that the church is the completion of Christ.[45]

(2) πλήρωμα = passive; church is filled
πληρουμένου = active significance
τὰ πάντα ἐν πᾶσιν = adjective

The translation of the clause by the advocates of this view would approximate the following: "[the church is] the fullness, (full, or filled) of the one [Christ] who fills all things totally (or, in every part, member)." The Christological implication is that Christ provides for the church and fills all things.[46]

This problem warrants a more detailed examination of the three elements, not only for the purpose of making a decision for one of the two views, but also for revealing the rich implications of the concepts for further illuminating the power-motif.

The term πλήρωμα occurs a total of four times in Ephesians and twice in Colossians (Eph 1:10, 23; 3:19; 4:13; see also Col 1:19; 2:9) while also occurring six times in Paul (Rom 11:12, 25; 13:10; 15:29; 1 Cor 10:26; Gal 4:4). The Pauline usage does not bear a technical significance whereas the usage in Ephesians and Colossians (except Eph 1:10) does in relation to Christ or God. Paul's usage seems invariably to denote a passive sense – a filled receptacle versus a filling substance or entity.[47] This is particularly clear in the statements about "the fullness of time" (Gal 4:4; Eph 1:10), where the term must indicate completeness.

This question of the active/passive significance of πλήρωμα cannot be discussed without simultaneously treating the mood of the participle. The middle/passive form itself is not decisive since the middle form can commonly have an active meaning in the Koine.[48] The fact that only Christ (4:10) and the Spirit (5:18) are viewed elsewhere in the epistle as the active powers of filling would tilt the balance in favor of the same role attributed to Christ in this passage.[49] This conclusion is corroborated by Col 2:10, where again the church is the recipient of the divine filling. The idea of the church filling or completing Christ is entirely foreign to the rest of the ecclesiological thought of Ephesians and Colossians and also to the rest of the NT.

In contrast to Valentinian Gnosticism[50] or Stoicism,[51] the concept of πλήρωμα in this epistle most likely reflects OT influence. The writer has taken up an OT concept used to express the divine presence and manifestation. In this way the noun denotes something similar to the OT idea of "Shekina" — the essence, glory, power, and presence of God. Although the noun never appears in the LXX in this sense related to God, the verb and the cognate πλήρης frequently appear with this idea, e.g. "behold, the house of the Lord is 'full' of his glory" (Ezek 44:4; see also 43:5; Isa 6:1; Hag 2:7).[52] In this sense, the term may also serve in Ephesians and Colossians as a circumlocution for the Holy Spirit.[53]

If πλήρωμα therefore refers to the divine power, essence, glory, and presence, this fully explains the Ephesian references to the "fullness of God" (Eph 3:19) and "the fullness of Christ" (Eph 4:13; see also Col 1:19; 2:9). But how do we account for the equation τὸ σῶμα = τὸ πλήρωμα in Eph 1:23? It is highly significant to notice that the concern of the immediate context is to convey to the readers that they now share in the divine power: (1) God's inheritance in the saints consists of a wealth of glory, (2) the incomparably great divine power is directed εἰς ἡμᾶς, and (3) the body is empowered and guided by their head, Christ. In the following context the writer will stress that the readers are so closely identified with Christ that they can be said to have been resurrected already and exalted with him. Now in Eph 1:23 the writer affirms that believers are already sharers in the divine πλήρωμα. Lightfoot was therefore correct a hundred years ago when he wrote, "All the Divine graces which reside in Him are imparted to her [the church]; His 'fullness' is communicated to her: and thus she may be said to be His pleroma."[54] This is the ideal church, or what the church can potentially come to possess. The historical church must seek to attain this ideal by, in a paradoxical manner, appropriating what is already hers (πλήρωμα) to attain what she does not yet possess (πλήρωμα). This is the balance the author seeks to communicate when he prays in 3:19 that the hearers "might be filled with all the fullness of God" (see below). It corresponds precisely with the Pauline eschatological tension between the "now — not yet."

Christ is said not only to fill the church but also τὰ πάντα. The filling takes on a qualitative difference dependent on the objects to which it refers. Here τὰ πάντα is used in its most expansive sense to indicate all of creation, earthly or heavenly. It therefore refers to all of humanity as well as to the entire angelic realm, but especially the rebellious "powers." The nature of the filling is not to be explained in a spatial sense,[55] but in terms of a dynamic with Christ (1) assuming his function as ruler vis-à-vis the "powers" (1:21), and (2) imparting grace and power to the church (4:13, 15–16).[56] The ἐν πᾶσιν could then be understood either adverbially = "totally"[57] or as a neuter noun = "in all parts."[58]

The emphasis of the context is upon *Christ* filling "all things" (so also 4:10). The passage does not espouse an ecclesiastical triumphalism in which the church is presented as the agent of the cosmic lordship of Christ. On the other hand, the church is involved in filling all things through preaching the gospel (so R.P. Meyer) and through the prophetic message its existence imparts to the "powers" (3:10).

Summary

Throughout this prayer, the writer carefully chooses words and concepts which can best convey to the readers the wealth of their resources in Christ. He speaks of the readers possessing glory (1:18), having access to the resurrection–exaltation power (1:19ff.), being linked to a powerful and ruling "head" (1:22), and as sharing in the divine "fullness" (1:23). Far from consisting of a string of unrelated requests, the prayer seems to be held together by this underlying motif of the superiority of the divine power working on behalf of believers. The comparison of the divine power to the power of the hostile principalities and authorities relates this passage to the admonition to engage in spiritual warfare against the "powers" in 6:10ff. This build-up of power-denoting ideas anticipates the prayer of 3:14–19 and the doxology of 3:20–21. It also introduces the author's presentation of the nature of their salvation as a transfer from one dominion of power and authority to another dominion of superior power and authority (2:1ff.).

2. The prayer for divine power repeated and developed (Eph 3:14–19)

In the prayer of 3:14–19 the writer solemnly prays for inner divine strengthening on behalf of his readers. Just as the prayer of 1:15–23, this entire prayer is loaded with power-denoting terms and concepts. The writer employs one hapax legomenon (ἐξισχύω) as well as the terms δύναμις and κραταιόω. In addition, the term πλήρωμα appears again and also a series of dimensional terminology to express the power of God.

The genre, setting, structure, and aim of the prayer

In contrast to part of the prayer in Eph 1 (vv. 20–23), form-critical research has not uncovered an alleged hymnic or traditional *Vorlage* in this prayer. This does not mean that the author has not made use of smaller units of tradition. The prayer is a free composition of the author expressing his concern for the readers.

The explicit motive and basis for this prayer (τούτου χάριν) is not only the Spirit-directed growth of believers into a holy temple (2:19–22), but is based on the whole of Eph 2.[59] One must realize that even Eph 2, however, is a development arising out of the prayer and thanksgiving of 1:15–23. The prayer in some sense takes up again the burden of the first prayer by developing and supplementing it. We will seek to determine precisely how this is done below. The introductory τούτου χάριν thus does not refer to the contents of 3:2–13, but has the same reference as its counterpart (τούτου χάριν) in 3:1. In 3:1, however, the author interrupts himself to establish his apostolic credentials (vv. 2–13) before resuming the prayer (vv. 14ff.).

The prayer itself appears to contain two distinct requests after the initial address and a final summarizing request. The general structure of the prayer may be discerned by noticing the three occurrences of ἵνα at the head of each petition.

    I. ἵνα
       a. κραταιωθῆναι (v. 16)
       b. κατοικῆσαι (v. 17)
    II. ἵνα
       a. καταλαβέσθαι (v. 18)
       b. γνῶναι (v. 19a)
    Summarizing request introduced by ἵνα (v. 19b)

This prayer is constructed on the basis of these two mutually dependent and essential components which taken together appear to form the fulfillment of v. 19b. The essence of this prayer can then be summarized as a prayer (1) for inner strengthening through the Holy Spirit and through the indwelling Christ who roots the life of a believer in love, and (2) for a personal knowledge of both the power and love of Christ. These petitions are presented as the two components of attaining the fullness of God. The prayer thus consists of two interrelated and mutually dependent requests with a summarizing statement.[60]

Whereas the prayer of Eph 1 sought for the readers an increased knowledge of the vastness of the divine power working on their behalf, the prayer of Eph 3 goes beyond knowledge to the experience of actual inner divine strengthening. The author repeats his prayerful concern for their growth in the knowledge of the vastness of the divine power, but he also prays for an increasingly greater awareness of the vast love of Christ, a new development on the prayer of Eph 1. The author intimates that divine strength is required to acquire this kind of knowledge.

The explicit request (3:16–17a)

The first petition may be summarized as a request for inner strengthening. It consists of two conceptually parallel infinitival clauses followed by an anacoluthic participial expression. A graphic layout of the syntactical relations should help to clarify the structure.

ἵνα δῷ ὑμῖν:

Source	κατὰ τὸ πλοῦτος	
	τῆς δόξης αὐτοῦ	
Request	δυνάμει κραταιωθῆναι	
Agent	διὰ τοῦ πνεύματος	κατοικῆσαι τὸν
	αὐτοῦ	Χριστὸν
Receptor	εἰς τὸν ἔσω	ἐν ταῖς καρδίαις
	ἄνθρωπον	ὑμῶν
Prerequisite		διὰ τῆς πίστεως

RESULT: ἐν ἀγάπῃ ἐρριζωμένοι καὶ τεθελιωμένοι (v. 17b)

The heart of the request is that the readers would be strengthened with power (δυνάμει κραταιωθῆναι). This is the only occurrence of κραταιόω in Ephesians and it only occurs four other times in the whole of the NT. On all four of these occasions it appears in the passive voice. It is used twice by Luke, both times in combination with αὐξάνω to summarize the growth of the boy Jesus (Luke 1:80; 2:40). Paul uses it once in his final exhortations in 1 Corinthians, where it occurs in the imperative mood (1 Cor 16:13). It is highly significant to note that in this exhortation to the Corinthians to be strong, Paul immediately exhorts them to exercise love (1 Cor 16:14). This bears a strong resemblance to the logic of our epistle, "be strengthened" – "love" (compare 3:16–17 with 4:2; 4:15–16; 5:2; 5:25ff.). The passive voice of the verb in 1 Corinthians can almost certainly be taken as a divine passive, especially in view of the express source of δύναμις in the epistle (cf. 1 Cor 1:18; 1:24; 2:5; et al.).

The author here petitions God for strengthening "with power" (δυνάμει). The combination of these two power terms reflects a Semitic manner of expression (see above).[61] This is not to say that the terminology would have been unfamiliar to Gentile readers, especially those coming from a background of strong magical beliefs. A common epithet of the underworld goddess Hekate was κραταιή, "powerful one" (e.g. *PGM* IV.2614, 2831).[62] She was attributed with wielding compelling authority over the underworld, gods, and men. The fact that this title was current in western Asia Minor is confirmed by a magical table found in Pergamum which extols Hekate as πασικράτεια ("all powerful") and πασιμεδέουσα ("ruler of all").[63]

The source of the power with which the author requests the readers to be strengthened has its basis in "the riches of his glory." Here again the power-character of δόξα is unmistakably brought to the foreground. We have seen in 1:18 that the saints already share in the πλοῦτος τῆς δόξης of God since they comprise the inheritance of God himself. Here the essence of God as consisting of δόξα is viewed by the author as the storehouse of power available to the saints.

Whereas in Eph 1 the Holy Spirit is presented as the mediator of the knowledge of the divine power, the Spirit is here made the explicit agent in the dispensing of divine power. This is certainly in line with the NT teaching concerning the Spirit and power (Acts 1:8, Rom 1:4; 15:19; 1 Cor 2:4; 1 Thess 1:5).

The inner self (τὸν ἔσω ἄνθρωπον) is said in v. 16 to be the object of strengthening through the Holy Spirit. In one of the two other occurrences of the "inner self" in the NT, Paul sets the "inner self" over and against the "outer self," which is the physical or material frame of being (2 Cor 4:16). This inner self requires renewal which it undergoes day by day and is not synonomous with the "new self" (Eph 4:24; Col 3:9ff.). The relationship is better understood by seeing the inner self strengthened to approximate the new self more closely. In the other occurrence of "inner self," Paul uses ὁ ἔσω as that part of self which is in conflict with the law of sin (Rom 7:22; cf. 7:23). If the author is following the Pauline use of these two occurrences of "inner self," the meaning appears to align itself very closely with the biblical significance of "heart" (see below). This would provide further justification to the juxtaposition of "inner self" and "heart" in this context.

A further definition of the divine strengthening sought for the readers is given in v. 17a.[64] In this verse, Christ himself is regarded as the agent of the strengthening. "Christ in you" is a prominent thought in Colossians (see 1:27) as well as in Paul (Rom 8:10; see also Gal 2:20; 4:19). The indwelling of the Spirit is also affirmed in the same context where the indwelling of Christ is mentioned in the Romans passage (Rom 8:9).[65]

The object of the indwelling is the heart. The author of Ephesians does seem to follow the general NT significance of "heart" here and throughout the epistle.[66] J. Behm summarizes the NT use of "heart" as "supremely the one centre in man to which God turns, in which the religious life is rooted, which determines moral conduct."[67] This notion of "heart" corresponds precisely with the summary of the significance of "inner self" as seen above.[68] The inner self/heart is presented as the sphere of strengthening in this context. The inner self indeed stands in need of strengthening in view of its struggle against the principle of sin (Rom 7:22) and for its daily renewing (2 Cor 4:16).

Faith is here presented as the prerequisite to the indwelling of Christ. Schnackenburg describes it as the "condition" to indwelling[69] and Dibelius as "the means" of the indwelling of Christ.[70] Faith thereby also becomes the prerequisite to the inner strengthening wrought by the Holy Spirit (cf. the parallel phrase in 3:16). Faith has already been presented by our author as the prerequisite to the effectual exercise of the divine power toward the readers (1:15, 19).

The indwelling of Christ and divine strengthening are also closely related to the ethical obligation of manifesting love after the pattern of Christ. This I will develop in more detail below.

The request for knowledge of the divine power repeated

The appearance of ἵνα (v. 18) marks the beginning of the second request. This is essentially a request for knowledge with two different yet interrelated objects of knowledge expressed − (1) the four dimensions (expressed without an explicit object), and (2) the love of Christ. In the present section, we will make an attempt to discern the precise meaning of the four dimensions in this context.

When the author here prays that his readers might "know" (καταλαμβάνω), he implies that divine enablement is essential by prefacing his request with the verb ἐξισχύω. The verb ἐξισχύω, belonging to the language of power, is a hapax legomenon in the NT meaning "be able, be strong enough, be in a position."[71] The particular term for knowing seems to have been employed to emphasize the difficulty of comprehending the vastness and magnitude of the intended object. It belongs to the vocabulary describing a fight against a strong opponent or sacking an acropolis; strength is required to accomplish both tasks.[72] This context thus bears similarity to the prayer in Eph 1 where the goal of the prayer is for knowledge of the divine power, but it is prefaced with the request that the Holy Spirit might impart that knowledge (Eph 1:17, 19). It is also significant that the preceding petition sought inner strengthening for the readers. Perhaps the author is viewing this request as another aim of the inner strengthening.

A very close parallel expression can be found in *PGM* XIII.226, which uses the phrase ἴσχυσαν καταλαβέσθαι with the only difference that the auxiliary verb is not compounded with the preposition ἐκ. The phrase is used after the revelation of a certain magical formula to convey the thought that "not even kings have sufficient power or authority to grasp the significance of the solution found in the given formula." The fact that this phrase, as the closest parallel to the expression in Eph 3:18, occurs in a magical papyrus, will strengthen my interpretation of the four dimensions (see below).

The author then asks that his readers might comprehend "with all the saints" what is "the breadth, length, height, and depth" (πλάτος, μῆκος, ὕψος, and βάθος, v. 18b). He makes this request without explicitly stating an object of these four dimensions. A great deal of controversy has shrouded the discussion of the source and significance of these terms. It is my contention that the recognition of the power-motif in this epistle helps to illuminate the contextual meaning of this enigmatic phrase. Specifically, I propose that the phrase would convey to the readers some notion of the power of God. I will first discuss whether this interpretation is evident in the religions-historical provenance of the phrase and then examine the context to see if it confirms or denies my supposition.

A number of alleged parallels to this expression have been found in a variety of sources including the Jewish Wisdom Literature,[73] Jewish–Hellenistic cosmic speculation,[74] Gnosticism,[75] other Jewish texts identifying the heavenly cubic form of Jerusalem,[76] and Stoic writings.[77]

Throughout this volume I have been suggesting that the magical papyri provide a helpful background not only for understanding the background of the readers addressed, but also in explaining some of the difficult and rare expressions occurring in the epistle. Here again, the Greek magical papyri provide the most helpful background for interpreting the phrase.

In contrast to *all* of the above cited religions-historical parallels (except Plutarch and the later Christian texts influenced by Ephesians), the same four dimensional terms appearing in Eph 3:18 never occur in succession except for their appearance in *PGM* IV.965ff. This text twice uses the *four* dimensions – and appears to use the combination as an expression of supernatural power. The expression occurs in the context of a magical formula for the obtaining of a vision while awake. The formula takes the form of an incantation/prayer which is to be repeated seven times. The magician is instructed to call on a certain god (magical names in text) and request his power (σθένος) so that the secrets of the power of the god Albalal might be made known (*PGM* IV.964–74):

> Give your strength, rouse your daimon, enter into this fire, fill it with a divine spirit, and show me your might (ἀλκή)! Let there be opened for me the house of the all-powerful (παντοκράτωρ) god Albalal, who is in this light! Let there be light, breadth, depth, length, height, brightness (καὶ γενέσθω φῶς, πλάτος, βάθος, μῆκος, ὕψος, αὐγή), and let him who is inside shine through, the lord Bouel ... (magical words) ... now, now; immediately, immediately; quickly, quickly!

The suppliant wants to know the secrets of Albalal and thereby gain access to his power. Albalal is known as παντοκράτωρ and the magician seeks illumination into all aspects of his power, expressed by the dimensional terminology. This is made clear by the introductory portion of the spell: "give your strength ... show me your might!" We could paraphrase the latter part of the spell in the following way: "let it become clear to me, in all its dimensions, what are the secrets of your power!"

The dimensional terminology occurs again a few lines later in the same text (*PGM* IV.979–85). Here the spell is introduced as a recipe for gaining access to "light magic" which the conjurer can possess for a given length of time:

> I conjure you, holy light, holy brightness, breadth, depth, length, height (πλάτος, βάθος, μῆκος, ὕψος), brightness,

by the holy names which I have spoken and am now going to speak. By ... (magical names) ... remain by me in the present hour, until I pray to the god and learn about the things I desire!

The dimensional terms seem to appear as spiritual hypostases, but this is uncertain. It is difficult to determine in the magical papyri when an expression for power actually fades into a personalized power. The overriding emphasis on the fact of power is certain, however. The suppliant seeks to find out secrets, i.e. "until I ... learn about the things I desire." The formula records the necessity of gaining access to supernatural power ("remain with me" = παραμεινόν μοι) in order for these secrets to be unlocked.

I am not the first to cite the relevance of these magical texts for understanding the four dimensions of Eph 3:18. The Bauer–Arndt–Gingrich lexicon lists the *PGM* passages as the closest parallels.[78] Nils Dahl has rightly observed: "Commentators have taken account of the similarity between the magical spells and Eph 3:18 but have not quite known what to do with it."[79] Most of the commentators have been influenced by Reitzenstein's interpretation of the dimensions in the magical texts as "spatial" (*raümlich*), as opposed to my interpretation, which stresses a dynamic meaning.[80] As a spatial expression, Reitzenstein thinks the dimensional terminology refers to the creation of a house in which the deity will appear and respond.[81] This interpretation ignores the second occurrence of the terms (*PGM* IV.979–85), in which they are in no way capable of a spatial interpretation and must be taken as spiritual hypostases or as expressions for power. Further, I have attempted to show that the four dimensions as an expression of power is the most plausible interpretation for their first occurrence in the magical text (*PGM* IV.964–74).

It is doubtful that the Ephesian passage influenced the magical texts I have cited.[82] The two spells betray no sign of Christian influence, much less any influence by the Ephesian epistle. I can only tentatively suggest that the author of Ephesians may have been familiar with a similar magical tradition which could use this combination of four dimensions as an expression of supernatural power. If the recipients of the epistle had come from a background of magical practices it is likely that the dynamic significance of the four dimensions would be readily intelligible to them. They would not be stumped by the author's failure to provide a corresponding object; they would recognize the terms as a rhetorical expression of supernatural power.

It is interesting to note that in the history of the interpretation of the four dimensions in Eph 3:18, almost all interpreters have sought an object to the dimensions. The most popular view has been to see the love of Christ as the object.[83] Others have referred to the "mystery" of salvation revealed by God,[84] the manifold wisdom of God,[85] the heavenly inheritance (thought of as a cube, like the heavenly Jerusalem in Rev 21:16),[86] the cross of Christ which embraces the world in all its dimensions,[87] and the *immensitas Dei*.[88] Only recently has someone suggested that there is not an explicit object in view. Nils Dahl has set forth the thesis that Eph 3:18 must be understood as a rhetorical preamble to Eph 3:19, i.e. knowing the vastness of the love of Christ.[89] The thesis has much to commend it, but I would observe that among all of the passages he cites each of the terms invariably has an object to which it refers, be it heaven, earth, sea, or Hades.[90] He cites no passage where the terms are listed without an expressed object as a rhetorical preamble. For this reason, the *PGM* IV passages still appear to be the closest parallels.

I will now turn to an analysis of 3:18 in the context of Ephesians and in relation to the Pauline corpus to discern whether the magical papyri do give us an insight into the author's use of the four dimensions. The following five points would seem to confirm my impression that the four dimensions are to be understood as an expression of power.

(1) There is a very close correspondence between the prayers of Eph 1 and Eph 3. If Eph 3:18 consists of a request for knowledge of the divine power, it is certainly not inconsistent or illogical to conceive of the author reiterating his prayer of ch. 1 in different terms, especially in a way which would freshly depict the incredible vastness of the divine power. This would also be consistent with the tendency of the author to refer to the power of God with a wide variety of expressions. The vastness of this power was described in extraordinarily emphatic terms in 1:19 (ὑπερβάλλον μέγεθος); in 3:18 it appears that the author has taken up a new way of expressing this vastness by employing these four dimensional terms. Both prayers stress the role of the Holy Spirit, first in mediating knowledge of the power of God (ch. 1) and secondly as the agent of divine strengthening (ch. 3).[91] Faith and love are coordinated in the prayer in ch. 1; faith and love are also coordinated in the prayer of ch. 3; however, love takes on an increasingly prominent goal as one aim of the strengthening and as an object of knowledge. Finally, both prayers are concluded with a statement concerning the relationship of the church

to the πλήρωμα. The high degree of correspondence in the two prayers and the manner in which the power theme is continued confirm that the prayer in 3:14−19 is both a detailed reiteration and a development of the prayer in 1:15−23.

(2) There is a close parallel structure in each of the two petitions of the prayer in 3:14−19. Power and love are coordinated in the first petition (3:16−17). A balance in the prayer is achieved by seeing a coordination of power and love in the second petition (vv. 18−19). Specifically, the first petition contains a request for inner strengthening which leads to a request for an establishment in love (see below); the second petition contains a request for a greater comprehension of the vastness of the divine power and for an increased comprehension of the greatness of the divine love. As J. Gnilka has noticed, the petition loses this balance when both objects of knowledge are taken as love in the second petition.[92]

(3) The emphatic extolling of the power of God in the doxology makes this interpretation more likely (3:20−21). God is extolled as the one who has the inherent ability to accomplish "exceedingly more than all we ask or imagine" (3:20). This is in accordance with the standard of his power (δύναμιν), which is made effective (ἐνεργουμένην) in the saints. Here again the potency of God on behalf of the readers is emphasized in a new and fresh manner. Just as the power of God is sufficiently capable of accomplishing far beyond the limited dimensions of what our minds can comprehend (3:20), so also can the power of God be described by a set of dimensions that go beyond the normal manner of perceiving things (3:18), i.e. no longer three dimensions but four dimensions!

(4) Eph 3:18 has a significant point of contact with Rom 8:39, the only Pauline passage which uses one or more of the dimensional terms without an expressed object.[93] Paul employs both ὕψωμα and βάθος in Rom 8:39 in an absolute sense. There are two prominent views concerning the nature of the "height" and "depth" in the Romans passage. Most interpreters take these terms as metaphors of spiritual hypostases, members of the angelic realm.[94] Others see the two dimensions in the literal sense of "height" and "depth," which would convey that no distance which appears to separate one from the love of Christ can actually do so.[95] With either interpretation the important aspect to notice is that height and depth are treated as something bearing sufficient (or apparently sufficient) ability to separate one from the love of Christ. It is also significant that "height" and "depth" are juxtaposed to "angels," "principalities," and "powers."

The point of the passage stresses that there is no power of any type or magnitude sufficiently capable of separating a believer from the love of Christ. Here then is a Pauline context where "height" and "depth" are employed by Paul in their absolute sense solely through the fact that they can communicate to the readers a certain sense of power or might. It is surprising that many of the commentators merely cite this passage and do not analyze the manner in which these dimensional terms are employed by Paul. For example, Dahl fails even to cite this important Pauline text.[96]

(5) Phil 3:10 brings additional confirmation to my hypothesis. Schlier has rightly pointed out that Phil 3:10, 12 is the only other text in the Pauline corpus where the verbs καταλαμβάνω ... γινώσκω are found in the same context (cf. Eph 3:18, 19).[97] It is highly significant to note that Phil 3:10 is a text where Paul is expressing his ambition of coming to know (γνῶναι) Christ *and the power of his resurrection*. In v. 12 Paul refers back to his desire to know these things — Christ, the power of the resurrection, the fellowship of his sufferings — and states that he presses on to take hold (καταλάβω) of that for which Christ Jesus took hold (κατελήμφθην) of him. The implication of this is important for 3:18. It is a clear use of the verb καταλαμβάνω to refer to divine power, thereby rendering it conceivable for Paul, or one familiar with Paul, to designate the divine power as an object of the verb in another context.

The context of Eph 3:18 does reaffirm my hypothesis that the magical papyri provide the most informative background to the four dimensions. The four dimensions therefore function in the prayer as a dynamic, rhetorical expression for the vastness of the power of God. This absolute use of the terms in succession does not require an expressed object. The readers would have readily understood it to be the divine power. I would therefore suggest the following paraphrase of Eph 3:18—19: "[I pray] that you might be able to grasp with all the saints what is the incredible vastness of the power of God and that you might be able to know the love of Christ which surpasses knowledge." This view has the advantage of providing a more coherent structure and meaning to the prayer. It is furthermore consistent with the prayer of 1:15—23 and the role of the two prayers in the structure of the epistle.

It is important to reaffirm the rationale of the author of Ephesians for placing such paramount emphasis on the knowledge of the magnitude and vastness of the divine power. The author is certainly not extolling a god who possesses power for himself, but a god who exercises power from his vast resources for the benefit of those who have faith in him. This power is sufficiently able to effectualize all the promised spiritual benefits (Eph 1:3–14) regardless of the strength and might of the hostile spiritual "powers" opposing believers (Eph 1:19, 21; 2:2; 4:25; 6:10ff.). This power is also sufficiently able and effective toward the believer to root this new-found life in the love of Christ and empower it to live a life of love (e.g. 5:2) which is quite contrary to its original nature (Eph 2:1–3) under the influence of the "powers" and the "flesh."

The related elements

Both the introductory address of the prayer (3:14–15) and the summarizing request (3:19b) contribute to and help define the emphasis on power in the prayer. It is significant to notice the manner in which God is qualified in the introductory address (3:14–15). God is humbly addressed as "Father" and is then identified as the one "from whom every family in heaven and on earth derives its name." This statement is loaded with meaning, unequivocally extolling God as all-powerful in relation to the angelic "powers" and men. The bestowing of a name (ὀνομάζω) and the reception of a name would suggest to the reader certain notions about power and authority. The act of granting a name signifies much more than the granting of a verbal symbol as a means of identification: it amounts to the exertion of power and the conveyance of an authority.[98] Conversely, the reception of a name constitutes the reception of authority and power (cf. 1:21). The fact of this naming extending to πᾶσα πατριά in heaven and on earth, stressing the expansive universal power of God, brings the hostile "powers" back into focus (3:10). This description of the Father would then serve to provide further reassurance to the readers fearing the threat of the hostile "powers" – a reassurance that God is indeed capable of fulfilling the requests presently brought to him in prayer.

The reference to God as Father in this context is suggestive of the quality of his nature as creator, the source of all life. Not only is he the fountainhead of all life ("the creator of all things" in 3:9), but he is the source of all power and authority (cf. "the Father of glory" in 1:17).

Divine power is again brought into perspective with the occurrence of πλήρωμα/πληρόω in the summarizing request of the prayer (3:19b). In praying that the readers might be filled with all the fullness of God, the writer is thinking of the realization of the contents of his two prayer wishes, viz. that the readers would be filled with divine power and that they would be filled with the love of Christ.

We have already seen how the background and usage of the term πλήρωμα is tied inextricably with divine power expressing the OT idea of the presence and power of God (see above). This connotation of the term is clearly indicated in the prayer of Eph 3 but is now also expanded to include the divine love manifested in Christ.

The author is not inconsistent when on the one hand he prays that the readers might be filled with the πλήρωμα (3:19b) and on the other equates σῶμα and πλήρωμα (1:23; see also Col 2:10: πεπληρωμένοι). It can be explained by the Pauline eschatological tension between the "already" and the "not yet."[99] This tension can be seen in Eph 2:19ff., where the saints are described as already constituting an edifice built upon the foundation of the apostles and the prophets with Jesus Christ as the chief cornerstone (2:20) but at the same time as progressively growing into a holy temple in the Lord (2:21–22; cf. 4:15–16; Col 2:19). The situation of the now – not yet for the believer is also maintained in the paraenesis following the prayer. The saints are held in a tension between the "new self" and the "old self." They retain characteristics of the "old self" (4:22) but they are urged to put on the things of the "new self" (4:23–24), the new life which they already possess but not to its full degree. Divine enablement is presented as indispensable for the lives of the saints who are in the midst of this tension.

By virtue of its union with the resurrected and exalted Christ who possesses πᾶν τὸ πλήρωμα (cf. Col 1:19; 2:9), the church also possesses the divine πλήρωμα. This still needs to become the experience of believers, however, through the process of taking off the old self and putting on the new. This perspective is also helpful in explaining the request for the indwelling of Christ (3:17). The author is not praying for the inaugural indwelling of Christ, since his prayer is on behalf of believers. Furthermore, the writer has previously affirmed their union with Christ in his death and resurrection (2:5–6). Therefore, just as the author can pray for their filling with the divine πλήρωμα, he can also pray for the filling, or indwelling, of Christ. The author desires for his readers a fuller existential realization of their divine status. He wants them to be strengthened through the Spirit and to experience the effects of the indwelling of Christ and the filling of the divine πλήρωμα to a greater degree.

The relationship of power and love in the prayer and in the epistle

We have already observed that a major development in this prayer in relation to the prayer of Eph 1 is the stress on love. It is highlighted in both requests of the prayer and closely coordinated with the divine power. Love is therefore also included as a constituent element of the πλήρωμα of God with which the believers are to be filled. It remains to examine the precise nature of the relationship between power and love in the prayer. I will then make some observations regarding the nature and relationship of the two concepts throughout the epistle.

In the latter part of the first request, the author prays that his readers might be "rooted and founded in love" (ἐν ἀγάπῃ ἐρριζωμένοι καὶ τεθεμελιωμένοι).[100] This clause functions as a prayer-wish of the writer flowing out of the previous request for the indwelling of Christ (and strengthening of the Spirit). The two coordinated participles break the pattern of the finite verb followed by two infinitives (cf. vv.16, 17a, 18, 19) and also stand in a syntactically irregular connection to the context by appearing in the nominative case. They are best understood in an optative sense, as a prayer-wish or request, rather than an exhortation.[101] Because of the anacoluthic construction which links the phrase so closely with the request for the indwelling of Christ and strengthening through the Spirit, it can therefore be regarded as an aim or function of the indwelling/strengthening. One of the goals of the indwelling of Christ is then to establish believers in a foundation of love. This provides the enablement requisite for the expression of love in the life of the community, thereby anticipating the paraenesis of the following chapters (e.g. 4:2; 5:2).

In the second request (3:18–19), the writer prays for knowledge for his readers − knowledge of the vast power of God and knowledge of the vast love of Christ. As a way of expressing the vastness of the divine love in Christ, the author intentionally puts the statement in a paradoxical form, viz. to know that which cannot be known. The love of Christ is described as that which surpasses (ὑπερβάλλουσαν) knowledge. This request has a number of affinities with Rom 8:37–39. We saw above that the Romans pericope employs dimensional terminology as an expression of power. In that passage, however, the Roman Christians are comforted by the declaration that the divine love is so great that no conceivable power can separate believers from that love. This can be asserted on the presupposition of an omnipotent God who is sufficiently capable of keeping all his people under the umbrella of his love regardless of the nature and strength of entities that could conceivably sever believers from that love. In Eph 3, the vastness of the divine love is again asserted but in a context magnifying the magnitude of the divine power. The readers of Ephesians would also be comforted to realize in a fresh and rhetorically powerful manner that God is indeed capable of maintaining his people in the sphere of his love in spite of the strength and number of hostile "powers" working toward the opposite end. In addition, the tremendous love of Christ as presented in this prayer would have provided incentive and motivation for the readers to manifest love toward others.

Love holds an exceedingly prominent place in the entire epistle as well as in this prayer. Some form of the term ἀγάπη appears nineteen times in the epistle. The occurrences can loosely be placed into two categories: references to the status of the believer as beloved and admonitions to love. It is interesting to note that no commands or instructions to love appear in the first three chapters. This section solely reveals the great love of the Father for the Son (1:6) and for believers, especially in Christ (1:4; 2:4; 3:17, 19; and then in 5:2, 25; 6:23). The first section culminates with this prayer for establishment in the love of Christ and for an expanded awareness of the magnitude of this divine love. The second section (chs. 4−6) contains a series of instructions to love (4:2, 15, 16; 5:2, 25, 28, 33; 6:24) summarized best by the statement of 5:2, "Walk in love just as Christ loved us and gave himself for us."

This prayer in Ephesians 3 plays an important role as preparatory to the subsequent admonitions to love. The author has carefully interwoven this prayer concerning love with requests regarding divine power. In this prayer, power and love are related in such a way that the divine power becomes the source of ethical enablement, the basis for the exercise of Christian love.

"Power" for the author of Ephesians is then the inherent or received ability to accomplish a given end. "Love" is a powerful virtue, but it is an ineffective virtue unless there is the capacity for it to be manifested in a tangible way. The love of God would have been much less meaningful for mankind if God had not possessed the power to procure salvation for his people despite strong opposition (be it Pharaoh or the devil). The author of Ephesians has therefore not only given his readers a definition of love (the example of Christ), but informs them of their access to the divine empowering essential to manifesting that love. He affirms that they possess the received ability (divine power) to accomplish a given end (love) — in spite of opposition!

This perspective on power and love stands in stark contrast to the attitude of the pagan world. In magic, many of the recipes and spells were used for the purpose of gaining advantage over people — winning a chariot race, attracting a lover, winning at dice, etc. God's power enables the believer *to love* after the pattern of Christ. The seemingly impossible demands of this kind of love require divine enablement in order for them to be fulfilled. Scholem has rightly observed that the language of the theurgist is "dominated by the attributes of power and sublimity, not love or tenderness."[102] Christ, however, roots and establishes the believer in his own love and strengthens the believer to follow the pattern of that love (3:16–17).

Summary

The prayer of Eph 3 takes up and repeats the main theme of the prayer of Eph 1 — that the readers would come to know the vastness of the power of God working on their behalf. The author makes two important developments on this theme: (1) he now prays that the readers themselves will actually be strengthened by this power, and (2) he links this power with the love of Christ. The writer thereby lays the foundation for the ensuing paraenesis by stressing that divine enablement is required in order to fulfill the primary ethical imperative — manifesting love according to Christ's own example. The author has not lost sight of the evil "powers" as is evident in the way in which he addresses the Father. In fact, it is precisely because God is the source of all power, even the power wielded by the evil forces, that he can grant believers sufficient strength to love after the pattern of Christ despite all opposition.

3. The divine power is praised (Eph 3:20–21)

The superabundant power of God working for the benefit of the people of God is now extolled in doxological praise in 3:20–21. The doxology forms a fitting and moving conclusion to the prayers and the entire first half of the epistle, which brings the power of God into bold relief.

This paragraph is amply attested as "doxological."[103] R. Deich-gräber has discerned what he considers to be the ground-form of the

many doxologies created and employed by early Christian writers.[104]
He sees doxologies as most frequently consisting of the following three
parts:

ᾧ/τῷ/αὐτῷ/σοὶ   ἡ δόξα   εἰς τοὺς αἰῶνας.   (ἀμήν)

These three elements are sometimes varied or expanded for a number
of reasons. The background for these short exclamations of praise
in early Christian literature may be decisively rooted in the Jewish
manner of prayer. Similar doxologies can be found in the OT, but
especially in late Jewish texts.[105] This form of praise probably found
its way to the early Christians through its presence in the LXX and
through the common employment of doxologies in the synagogue
worship of Hellenistic Judaism.[106]

It becomes readily apparent that the doxology of 3:20−21 is far
more expansive than the hypothetical ground-form given by Deichgräber, particularly with regard to the first element. It would be
instructive to note what expansions have been made and pose the
question of a possible motive behind the expansions.

The most remarkable aspect of the content of the doxology of
3:20−21 is the emphasis on divine power seen in the employment of
three power denoting terms − δύναμαι, δύναμις, and ἐνεργέω. The
doxology begins with an ascription of power to God in the appellation
Τῷ δὲ δυναμένῳ.[107] Because God possesses power, he is able to
accomplish exceedingly incredible (ὑπερεκπερισσοῦ) deeds on behalf
of his people. Perhaps the author is here thinking of the Father
bringing "every spiritual blessing in the heavenly places" (1:3) to
realization among believers. Indeed, he presents the Almighty as
capable of accomplishing even more than the readers may ask or even
imagine. This is a fitting praise to the God whom the author has
already described in his prayers as possessing "incomparably great"
power, a power that exceeds all dimensions.

"The Powerful One" is presented as acting according to the power
(δύναμιν) which is given to and actualized within (ἐνεργουμένην)
believers.[108] The author thereby praises the fact that God does indeed
bestow strength on his people (3:17). This context also bears considerable similarity to Phil 4:13, where the Apostle is so aware of God's
presence and strengthening in his life he can confidently assert, "I can
do all things in the one who strengthens me" (ἐν τῷ ἐνδυναμοῦντί με).

The second element of the ground-form of the doxology is
then expressed in the usual manner: "(To him [be]) ἡ δόξα."
This element customarily brings divine power into view, according

to Deichgräber.[109] Here the dynamic element is present in the word δόξα. The locus and the basis of the glory ascribed to God is "in the church and in Christ Jesus."

The doxology thus exclaims the almighty power of God. This doxology especially praises the fact that the divine power works on behalf of the church, that the power is in fact actualized within the lives of believers. Because of the emphatic praise of the gracious divine omnipotence, this doxology is the perfect capstone not only to the prayer of 3:14–19, but also to the entire first half of the epistle.

4. Conclusions

(1) The prayer of Eph 1 and the prayer and doxology of Eph 3 clearly establish the power of God as a key theme of the epistle.

(2) The power provides salvation which the author understands as a release from the bondage of death and the dominion of the devil and his "powers." The power of God also provides enablement to love after the pattern of Christ, the primary ethical injunction. It is a personal power in the sense that it is imparted through union with Christ, or conversely, his indwelling in the lives of his people. Therefore, in both aim and nature it qualitatively differs from Hellenistic notions of power.

(3) The emphasis on the saving and enabling power of God in the first half of the epistle sets the stage for the ensuing paraenesis in the latter half of the epistle. In particular, it anticipates the admonition to resist the hostile spiritual "powers" (6:10–20). The readers need to appropriate the power of God in order successfully to resist the powerful evil influence of these mighty forces. These evil "powers" as the opponents of the spiritual advancement of the readers weigh heavily on the author's mind not only in the two prayers and in the first half of the epistle, but throughout the entire letter.

(4) The extraordinary structural and verbal emphasis on power in the two prayers and the doxology is made in the context of perceived conflict with evil "powers." I would suggest that this explicit emphasis on the enabling power of God has come to expression because the author is addressing a group of believers on the nature of the Christian life in light of the continuing presence and hostility of the evil "powers." This was a deep concern for Christians in Ephesus and western Asia Minor because of the widespread influence of magic, the mysteries of the underworld deities, and astrology.

5

THE CONFLICT WITH THE "POWERS"

1. Introduction

The call to acquire divine strengthening for the purpose of engaging the spirit-forces of evil (Eph 6:10–20) is not an irrelevant appendix to the epistle. It is a crucial part of the paraenesis to which the rest of the epistle has been pointing. In the present chapter we will seek to discover the meaning and significance of the author's concept of "spiritual warfare."

The unique emphasis on spiritual warfare and power

This is the only place in the Pauline corpus where believers are explicitly called upon to struggle against the "principalities and powers." The "struggle" is not merely mentioned as a parenthetical aside. It is taken up by the author and elaborated on in ten verses integrally connected with the foregoing paraenesis of the epistle (4:1–6:9). The enemy is listed by a collection of appellations (vv. 11, 12, 17), some of which occur nowhere else in Paul or in the NT. As a further expression of the divine strength needed for the "struggle," a list of "spiritual armor" is delineated by the author (vv. 14–17).

The author underlines the need for divine power in vv. 10, 11, 13, and 16. In no other single passage in the epistles attributed to Paul is there such a number and variety of terms for power: nine terms in all encompasing six different word groups. The author begins with the imperative form of ἐνδυναμόω (v. 10). Three cognates of this term are then employed in vv. 11, 13, and 16. The author also uses both κράτος and ἰσχύς (v. 10), which are quite rare in the NT. Finally, the author takes up three different power terms as appellations for the categories of demonic "powers": ἀρχή, ἐξουσία, and κοσμοκράτωρ (v. 12).

Clearly there is a significant emphasis on power which is brought about by the author's perception of a "spiritual warfare" in which the readers are already engaged. This concept is present in Paul, but it is never elaborated to the degree that it is here.

The problem: why is there an extended discussion on "spiritual warfare"?

In approaching this passage an adequate explanation needs to be sought for the elaboration on the topic of "spiritual warfare." What gave rise to this emphasis? Was there a crisis or some kind of situation that motivated this presentation? This question has been sorely neglected by interpreters of Ephesians. A good number of the commentators simply avoid the question, neither postulating a situation nor giving a rationale for the unusual emphasis and elaboration on the theme of spiritual warfare.

Only a few writers take Eph 6:10−20 into account in attempting to uncover the setting of the epistle. A. Lindemann, for example, takes the spiritual warfare passage as evidence of a concrete situation of persecution the readers would be facing under Domitian in A.D. 96, although still explaining the nature and style of Ephesians as a "theological tractate."[1] R.P. Martin sees the epistle as directed to a situation in the Gentile churches in Asia Minor where gnosticizing and antinomian tendencies were being felt. The writer (for Martin it is Luke) calls the readers to engage in combat with the demonic agencies (also called aeons) who held mens' lives and destinies in thrall under a relentless "Fate" (Eph 6:10ff.).[2] This may be the general direction E. Käsemann and H. Conzelmann would argue if they were pressed with the question of the author's motive for this emphasis on divine power and spiritual warfare. Unfortunately, they, as many other interpreters, neglect the passage when they discuss the occasion and purpose of Ephesians. Others, such as R. Schnackenburg and K.M. Fischer, envision a fairly specific situation in western Asia Minor, yet neither use Eph 6:10−20 as evidence for formulating their impressions regarding the situation.[3] Partly on the basis of Eph 6, Horacio Lona has suggested that the Ephesian author is addressing an atmosphere of *Weltangst*, or a fear of the influence of evil forces.[4] His discussion of the setting has much to be said for it, as I will make clear in the following chapter.

There is still one further question of importance: what place does this passage have in relation to the rest of the epistle, and what relevance does it have for an understanding of the theology of the epistle? In considering these questions, one notices a conspicuous neglect of Eph 6:10–20 in formulating an understanding of the theology of the epistle among the monographs written on Ephesians in the past twenty years.[5] This neglect is inexcusable since the passage must be taken into account in arriving at the overall purpose and theme of the epistle and by virtue of the fact that it does contribute to an understanding of the theology of the letter (especially Christology, eschatology, and ecclesiology).

2. The structure and genre of the passage

The structure

The section begins with the phrase τοῦ λοιποῦ, which introduces the conclusion to the paraenesis of 4:1–6:20.[6] This phrase is immediately followed by three imperatives: ἐνδυναμοῦσθε (v. 10); ἐνδύσασθε (v. 11); and ἀναλάβετε (v. 13). By asyndeton, the writer clarifies how the strengthening is to be acquired in v. 11, viz. by putting on the armor of God.[7] The third imperative, ἀναλάβετε (v. 13), continues the same sense as the ἐνδύσασθε of v. 11. All three of these phrases are then similar in meaning and emphasize the need for divine strength in order to resist the enemy.

The conjunction οὖν introduces the main admonition in v. 14 by making a general reference to the need for divine power because of (cf. ὅτι in v. 12) the supernatural, powerful, and cunning nature of the adversaries. Verse 12 functions as an explication of the nature of the enemy and not as the central element in the development of 6:10–20 as R. Wild suggests.[8] Because of the ominously threatening nature of the enemy, the readers need the power of God in order to stand. The imperative στῆτε (v. 14) has been accurately described as the chief admonition of the passage.[9] The admonition to acquire divine strengthening and enablement has not been given by the author as an end in itself. The strength is required for a particular purpose — that the believer might be enabled to stand against the evil "powers" and successfully resist them (vv. 11, 13, 14).

Four participles follow the finite verb of v. 14, all acquiring its imperative force: περιζωσάμενοι (v. 14); ἐνδυσάμενοι (v. 14); ὑποδησάμενοι (v. 15); and ἀναλαβόντες (v. 16). These are followed by the imperative verb δέξασθε (v. 17), which does not introduce a new and independent admonition,[10] but is dependent on στῆτε (v. 14) and is thereby parallel to the participles in the armor section.[11]

The pattern of employing participles is broken here for stylistic variation,[12] presumably to avoid the monotony of six consecutive participles. One final participial phrase (προσευχόμενοι, v. 18) is mentioned which is still dependent on the main admonition of v. 14.

The whole of vv. 14–20, then, is dependent on the main thought of v. 14 – "stand!" All other thoughts are subservient to this ultimate aim. The divine armor and power are provided for the attainment of this goal. The opponents are carefully delineated so that the reader may know the nature of the enemies to be withstood. Even prayer is given with the goal of resistance in mind.

The genre

A number of interpreters have regarded 6:10–20 as an integral part of an early Christian catechetical pattern of teaching connected with baptism. A 1940 monograph by Philip Carrington has wielded a significant influence on subsequent scholarship in this regard.[13] He traces a specific pattern which he finds present in Colossians, Ephesians, 1 Peter, and James, where a given set of topics are covered using a particular vocabulary: "put off" (ἀποτίθημι), "be subject" (ὑποτάσσομαι), "watch" (γρηγορέω; ἀγρυπνέω; νήφω), and "resist" (ἀνθίστήμι; ἵστημι).[14] The common vocabulary points to a shared reservoir of baptismal hortatory material, probably oral, on which the writers could draw. This method of catechizing baptized Christians follows the procedure of Jewish proselyte baptism in which the initiate was instructed in the Torah, wisdom, and walking.[15]

The greatest difficulty with relying too heavily on this explanation is that the distinctive presentation of each of the epistles may be too easily neglected. In introducing Eph 4:25–6:20, Schlier (who at this point acknowledges indebtedness to Carrington) remarks, "They are typical admonitions which are not tailored for a particular congregation but for Gentile Christians in general."[16] I would observe, however, that Eph 6:10–20 only bears slight similarity to the other NT passages which speak of "resisting." Carrington finds the themes of "resisting" present in 1 Pet 5:8–9 and Jas 4:7b while he must concede that Colossians lacks this "standard" catechetical theme. The only commonalities between these two passages and Eph 6:10ff., however, are the words "resist" and "devil." Ephesians is far more expansive and detailed in its call to engage in "spiritual warfare." Ephesians not only mentions the devil, but delineates a list of pernicious "powers" working in collaboration with the devil; neither

1 Peter nor James mentions these. Ephesians repeatedly stresses the need for divine δύναμις and embarks on a lengthy presentation of metaphorical weaponry which the believer is to don; these aspects are also lacking in 1 Peter and James.

I am not intending to deny the presence and influence of a set catechetical pattern with stock phraseology. I am seeking to pay special attention to the unique and expansive development of the theme of "resistance" in Eph 6:10–20 as opposed to explaining its significance as general instruction and exhortation for new believers (*Neophytenparänese*). One needs to ask: why are the "powers" stressed? Indeed, why is the whole concept of a "spiritual warfare" emphasized here more than anywhere else in the NT?

3. The acquisition of divine power for the battle

The admonition: "be strengthened"

Upon concluding his instructions to the various members of the Christian household (5:22–6:9), the author exhorts his readers to "be strong" (ἐνδυναμοῦσθε) in the Lord. The verb is best understood as a passive voice with the sense of "be made strong in the Lord."[17] This accords well with the strictly passive use of δύναμαι in the rest of the passage (vv. 11, 13, 16) and also the passive sense of κραταιόω in 3:16: "be strengthened with power through his Spirit."[18]

The reader is unavoidably struck by the frequency of the verb δύναμαι throughout the passage. The power of God will enable the reader to "stand against the wiles of the devil" (v. 11), "resist on the evil day" (v. 13), and "quench the flaming arrows of the evil one" (v. 16). The verb is not used in this context in the less forceful sense of an auxiliary verb, but bears the full significance of δύναμις – the presence and exercise of sufficient power.[19] The writer wants his readers to know that their chances of success are more than possible or even probable: victory will be a reality given their dependence upon the divine power.

The explicit admonition to "be strong" occurs only two other times in the Pauline corpus. Paul urged the Corinthians to "be strong" (κραταιοῦσθε) in 1 Cor 16:13. This verse contains a number of other thoughts in common with our passage. The Corinthians are exhorted to "watchfulness" (cf. 6:18) and "to stand" (cf. 6:11, 13, 14) in the faith (cf. 6:16). Timothy is admonished to "be strong" (ἐνδυναμοῦ) in 2 Tim 2:1. The source of the strength is "in the grace that is in Christ

Jesus." The passage then employs the imagery of warfare (2 Tim
2:3–5): "Endure hardship with us like a good soldier of Christ
Jesus."

The source of the power in Eph 6:10 is "in the Lord." This phrase
not only describes the person with whom the readers have been
brought into union, but also refers to the sphere or new set of
conditions in which they live. The readers have been transferred from
the domain of darkness into the domain of light (5:8ff.); they are no
longer subjected to the tyranny of life under the control of the prince
of the authority of the air (2:2), but now live under the loving headship
of Christ who is Lord. Grundmann has fittingly commented, "This
place [in Christ] is to a great extent charged with the superior power
which belongs to Christ."[20] For this reason the readers can be
admonished to "be strong."

The source of the strength is more specifically defined as existing
in "the strength of the Lord's might" (ἐν τῷ κράτει τῆς ἰσχύος
αὐτοῦ). These are the same terms the author used to describe the
divine power which brought about the resurrection and exaltation of
Christ (1:19–20). The writer affirms that believers have access to this
vast divine power which has already proved itself sufficient to overcome powerful diabolic opposition. The terms κράτος and ἰσχύς are
linked in one place in Isaiah (40:26), which the author may have been
thinking of as he penned 6:10.[21] He appears to be significantly
indebted to Isaiah for many of his terms and metaphors, particularly
with respect to the armor.

There is one OT passage in particular that stands out as having
a significant correspondence to Eph 6:10ff. The Ephesian author cites
Isa 52:7 in his delineation of the weapons, but the broader context
of that passage is worth closer examination. (1) The prophecy begins
with the rousing call to awake (ἐξεγείρω) because redemption is
drawing near (v. 1); Ephesians stresses the importance of watchfulness as a necessary prerequisite together with prayer for putting
on the divine strength (Eph 6:18). (2) The prophecy continues with
an exhortation to "clothe yourself with strength" (ἔνδυσαι τήν ἰσχύν
σου); this finds a very close parallel with "put on (ἐνδύσασθε) the
armor" (Eph 6:11), which is a further definition of the summons to
"be strong" in his power (ἰσχύς) (Eph 6:10). (3) Jerusalem is urged
by the prophet to "rise up" (ἀνάστηθι) and "sit enthroned"
(κάθισον); this appears quite similar to what the Ephesian author says
in Eph 2:6, "you have been raised with Christ (συνήγειρεν) and seated
(συνεκάθισεν) with him in the heavenly places" as a consequence of

their release from captivity. (4) Jerusalem is described as a captive
in bonds (52:2) but is exhorted to free herself; similarly, Paul is
described in 6:20 as "in chains" while he exhorts his readers to withstand their common enemies. (5) Isa 52:3 speaks of future redemption
(λυτρόω) and so does Ephesians (ἀπολύτρωσις, Eph 1:14 and 4:30).
(6) Most importantly, the Ephesian author cites Isa 52:7 in the
delineation of the weapons. Thus, the extended similarity of ideas
throughout the wider context of Isa 52 with Ephesians (especially
ch. 6) suggests that our author thought of the entire Isaianic passage
as he wrote. The primary contact point is the theme of the "new
exodus," with Israel's experience of redemption from foreign
bondage similar to the experience of Christians liberated from the
bondage of the devil. This is also consistent with the author's tendency
to use Isaiah to a large degree.[22]

The armor of God as a manifestation of strength

The delineation of the armor is given by the author as an elaboration
of the divine strength upon which the readers are to depend. This is
made clear by the juxtaposition of the two verbs in vv. 10−11:
ἐνδυναμοῦσθε ... ἐνδύσασθε. The might of the Lord is thus made
parallel with the armor of God. By clothing themselves with the
πανοπλία of God the readers will be enabled (πρὸς τὸ δύνασθαι,
v. 11; ἵνα δυνηθῆτε, v. 13; ἐν ᾧ δυνήσεσθε, v. 16) to resist the crafty
maneuvers of the devil and his host. We can therefore gain a deeper
appreciation of the author's conception of the nature of the divine
strength by considering his explication of the armor of God.

The book of Isaiah appears to be the author's primary source for
his presentation of the metaphorical weaponry (especially Isa 11:5;
52:7; 59:17).[23] It is possible that the author was also thinking of Wis
5:17−20, particularly because of the common use of πανοπλία
(absent from Isaiah).[24] It is unlikely that the author was influenced
by the Qumran War Scroll (1QM) either for his terminology or for
his concept of spiritual warfare for two reasons.[25] First, there are too
many differences in the forms of expression to maintain a direct
connection.[26] The Qumran documents know nothing of putting on
armor and neither does the literature speak of spiritual counterparts
to the weapons it does mention. The weapons mentioned are
qualitatively different − viz. lances, darts, throwing spears, slings
− with the shield being the only implement held in common.
Secondly, the nature of the warfare described is entirely distinct.

In the Qumran documents an actual warfare was expected to take place with men fighting against men on one plane and with God vanquishing Belial on another plane. The Qumran community itself did not anticipate a direct struggle with the "powers" in heaven. In addition, the Ephesian author states emphatically that the Christian warfare is not against "blood and flesh" (v. 12). Perhaps the most we can say is that the esteem accorded Isaiah by the Qumranites stimulated the author of Ephesians, if he knew of 1QM at all, to return to the more ancient source which inspired the Qumran community, i.e. the scroll of Isaiah. Finally, it is much too speculative to see the war imagery mediated to the author through early Christian baptismal tradition.[27] In his elaboration of the weapons of God, the author mentions the material metaphor and then the spiritual counterpart. Six of these physical arms are listed together with their spiritual counterparts. A seventh spiritual weapon is mentioned without a physical counterpart.

The author presents the armor of God as the strength of believers which enables them to resist the diabolic "powers" of darkness. Each of the material weapons used as metaphors depicts some aspect of divine strength. For example, "loins" can be a metaphor of strength and "girding oneself" is frequently used as a symbol for displaying power and courage (Ps 18:32; 65:6; 93:1; Isa 45:5; Job 38:3; 40:7; Prov 31:17; Nahum 2:1).[28] The various spiritual counterparts to the material arms can also be seen to a certain degree as expressions of spiritual power and strength in this epistle and in the Pauline tradition.

"Truth" (v. 14), the first weapon, has been used by the author as a description of the gospel (1:13). Paul conceived of the gospel as the δύναμις of God for salvation (Rom 1:16). Insofar as "truth" is a circumlocution for the gospel it can be considered as divine power. Those who practice the truth are assumed to be under the influence of the sphere of divine power since the character of the realm of the devil, his "powers," and all who are under his control consists of lies, deceit, and falsehood. The very name διάβολος (6:11; 4:27) would conjure up to the readers the notion of an adversary who misrepresents, deceives, and gives false information.[29] He is described as employing μεθοδεία (v. 11), which implies cunning and trickery. Those who live under the influence of the powerful gospel and "walk in the light" will live by the truth and speak truth (4:25; 5:9) and thereby resist the devil, not giving him a place (4:27).

If the author of Ephesians reflects anything of Pauline tradition in his use of "righteousness," the concept of divine power is clearly present. Paul writes that the reason the gospel can be described as the power of God has to do with the fact that it reveals the righteousness of God (Rom 1:16). The righteousness of God is therefore construed as divine power. Regarding all the occurrences of the expression δικαιοσύνη θεοῦ in Paul, Käsemann aptly concludes that, "Paul has kept to the aspect of righteousness as power, implicit in the formulation itself and supported by the various parallel expressions."[30]

The motif of the gospel is picked up again in the sixth spiritual weapon – the ῥῆμα θεοῦ given by the Spirit (v. 17). There should be no doubt that ῥῆμα here refers to the gospel (cf. Rom 10:8). In this instance, the author goes beyond the "readiness" of the Christian warrior to make known the gospel (v. 15) to a mention of the dynamic which makes the gospel successful – the Spirit. This is the same Spirit which the author characterizes as the mediator of divine power to the believer (3:16). Paul sees the gospel as having successfully penetrated Thessalonica because it came ἐν δυνάμει καὶ ἐν πνεύματι ἁγίῳ (1 Thess 1:5). The gospel thus proves to be a key implement in the church's resistance against the kingdom of the devil.

"Faith," the fourth weapon (v. 16), has already been presented by our author as the *means* to acquiring divine strength (3:16–17; 1:19). Consequently, it follows that the author would here present it as essential to gaining access to the power of God in order to engage in spiritual warfare.

Ephesians unquestionably emphasizes the present aspect of "salvation" to a greater degree than any of the other epistles attributed to Paul. The Ephesian author's use of "salvation" in 6:17 is no exception. He expects his readers to think immediately of what their salvation means to them – they have been resurrected with Christ to a position of power and authority in the heavenly places. This position equips them with a greater power than that possessed by their mighty supernatural enemies.

In summary, the author has given his readers a vivid picture of all that is essential to maintaining a successful resistance against the devil and his "powers." Just as any soldier needs to be outfitted with the proper equipment to engage in combat, so also the Christian. The author could undoubtedly have mentioned other "spiritual weapons" (e.g. love), but he has chosen those which have an OT metaphorical counterpart. Many of the concepts overlap as in the three-fold mention of the gospel (v. 14 as "truth"; v. 15, "the gospel"; and v. 17, "the word of God"). This emphasis on the gospel undoubtedly highlights the importance of the gospel in opposing the evil "powers."[31] "Righteousness" is intimately connected with the gospel and is an expression of the power of God in itself. The readers also need to realize that the nature of their salvation entails a high position of power and authority and this can be appropriated through faith and prayer.

Prayer as the prerequisite and means of acquiring divine enablement

In 6:18–20, prayer is seen as essential to the arming of believers with the power of God in order to resist the diabolic "powers" who would seek to prevent them from living according to Christian ethics. With his summons to prayer the author completes his presentation of the spiritual weaponry. The author appears to give prayer a more prominent place than merely the seventh among a list of spiritual weapons.[32] Prayer here seems to serve as a partial basis for the deployment of the other arms. The author maintains a structural continuity with the foregoing delineation of the weapons by employing a participle (προσευχόμενοι) still in dependence on the main verb "stand" in v. 14. Conversely, the author seems to highlight the importance of prayer by a two-fold departure from the pattern of the preceding manner of listing the weapons. First, he does not employ a material metaphor to correspond to prayer and secondly, he elaborates on prayer, emphasizing its importance by using the adjective πᾶς four times in v. 18. This emphasis on prayer is extended even further when in v. 19 the author requests prayer for himself to the end that he himself might have an effective use of one of the spiritual weapons, i.e. the gospel.

The writer thus wants his readers to understand prayer as an essential spiritual weapon, but more than a weapon, it is foundational for the deployment of all the other weapons. Indeed, the author has modeled this to the readers already. He prayed that the readers would gain an expanded awareness of the divine power available to them (1:15–23) and he has also directly prayed for the divine strengthening of the readers (3:14–21). In very general terms, the author has prayed for divine power on behalf of his readers in the first section of the epistle (chs. 1–3) in order that they may be able to conduct themselves according to the ethical demands of the latter half of the epistle (chs. 4–6).

4. The time of the battle

The time coordinates of the battle reveal a continuity with the Pauline eschatological schema. The key expression in this regard is "on the evil day" (ἐν τῇ ἡμέρᾳ τῇ πονηρᾷ, v. 13b). The phrase has end-time connotations. This precise Greek phrase is found in three prophetic passages in the LXX (Jer 17:17, 18; Obad 13). Dan 12:1 speaks of a "day of tribulation" (ἡ Ἡμέρα θλίψεως; Theodotion = καιρὸς θλίψεως). This then became an important theme of apocalyptic Judaism, which spoke frequently of the evil character of the last day(s).[33]

The phrase does not occur in Paul, but Paul does speak of "the present *evil* age" in Gal 1:4 (ὁ αἰών τοῦ ἐνεστῶτος πονηροῦ). The fact that the "evil days" are occurring in the *present* is brought out by Eph 5:16, where the readers are urged to redeem the time because the days are evil (note the present tense of εἰμί). "The evil day(s)" concept may be quite similar to the idea of "the present evil age" in Galatians.[34] If this is so, the author of Ephesians is underlining the character of the days prior to the final "day of redemption." These days are particularly treacherous because of the Satanic proliferation of evil which poses a significant threat to the believer (for similar ideas, cf. 2 Tim 3:1; Jas 5:3; Heb 3:8ff.). The "evil day(s)" are not an Ephesian substitution for or equivalent to the Pauline "day of the Lord" (1 Cor 1:8; 5:5; 2 Cor 1:14; et al.). The "eschatological" character of the present evil days anticipates the intensification of evil prior to the parousia (as Dibelius has rightly recognized), when Christ shall return for the day of wrath and judgment upon unbelievers and evildoers (cf. Rom 2:5, 16) and simultaneously consummate the salvation of the elect (1 Thess 5:9).[35] Both ideas, i.e. impending wrath for unbelievers and final salvation for believers, are present in Ephesians (wrath: 5:5–6; 6:8–9; future redemption 1:14; 4:30). The Ephesian author can still refer to this consummation of salvation as the "hope" of the believer (1:15–18; 4:4), which he places beside "faith" and "love."

The idea of "redeeming the time" in 5:16 strongly suggests that the author did not seek to eliminate the eschatological implications of the "evil day" sayings. On the contrary, the author stresses urgency in view of an implicit speedy end (i.e. parousia).[36] G. Harder comments, "The days are evil in Eph 5:16 because they are part of the last time, threatened by the approaching last judgment and darkened by the woes of the end time."[37]

In light of this evidence, a strictly ethical or individualized interpretation of this phrase must be ruled out.[38] We may be in error, however, if we deny any ethical sense to the phrase. The fact that the author refers to an "evil day" (singular) in 6:13 and "evil days" (plural) in 5:16 may mean that he intends his readers to think in terms of specific times of attack, when the power of the attack comes with extraordinary power and the temptation to yield is strong. The sense of v. 13a could then be rendered: "Put on the armor of God so that you may be divinely enabled to resist diabolic attack during this age preceding the parousia which is particularly treacherous because of the active forces of evil, but especially that you may be able to resist on those occasions when the diabolic hostility against you seems at its strongest."

The fact that Eph 6:10−20 employs military terminology has far-reaching implications for the understanding of the eschatology of the epistle. Paul's use of military terminology is consistently placed in the context of an expectation of the end-time (see chapter 6).[39] Rom 13:11−14 in particular may provide perspective on this eschatological question when one recognizes the similarity of presentation to Eph 6:10−20. (1) Paul employs light−darkness imagery to describe his readers' present situation (cf. "this darkness" in Eph 6:12; the light−darkness imagery is more fully developed in Eph 5:6−14). (2) Putting on the armor of light is set parallel to the putting on of the Lord Jesus (cf. Eph 6:10−11: "Be strong in the Lord" is explicated by "put on the armor of God"). The fact that Paul can say that the readers have access now to the weapons of light reveals a partially realized eschatology even in Romans! Hall has correctly recognized this: "The weapons of light belong to the Day; Christians therefore have available to them the power of the future ... they have the weapons of the future with which to fight."[40] (3) Both passages employ military imagery and utilize it for a similar common goal − ethical Christian living. (4) More important for our understanding of the time of the warfare is the parallel emphasis on wakefulness (Rom 13:11b: "the time has come for you to wake from your slumber"). The wakefulness in Romans is clearly based on the nearness of salvation and the approaching of the day − the parousia of the Lord Jesus Christ. With regard to Rom 13:11ff., E. Lövestam concludes that, "The eschatological orientation of the idea of wakefulness is central. The enjoined awakening from sleep is oriented to the approaching day, and the designed wakefulness implies letting oneself be determined by the (light) character of the day to come, and thus being prepared for its arrival.''[41] The similarity of thought between Ephesians and Romans in this regard implies a shared eschatological understanding. The Ephesian author makes no attempt to omit or reinterpret the eschatological connotations of "watchfulness." Conversely, the author of Romans betrays a realized understanding of eschatology.

My review of the statements having a bearing on the time of the battle demonstrates a view of the end-time similar to that found in Paul. The "already – not yet" has not been displaced by a "once – now" (ποτέ – νῦν) schema in Ephesians. The "already" has rather received a fresh emphasis by the highlighting of the present aspect of salvation for the purpose of gaining victory in the engagement with the evil "powers." The "already" can be described in terms of a "once – now" transformation without losing the "not yet" aspect of salvation. The Achilles' heel of those who have seen an elimination of the "not yet" in Ephesians has been in explaining a continuing engagement with the forces of evil (6:10–20). If salvation has been thoroughly realized and the parousia is no longer in view, no adequate explanation has been provided for believers' continuing struggle with the "powers" of evil. To say that this passage affirms that a believer will never succumb to demonic attack and temptation (Lindemann) fails to recognize the paraenetic significance of the passage. The ultimate redemption of the believers has not yet been gained (cf. 1:14; 4:30). Darkness, evil days, and demonic activity still persist.

5. The nature of the warfare

We have already gained some indication of the nature of the battle through analyzing the weaponry, the enemies, and the time of the engagement. A more precise understanding of the nature of the warfare can be ascertained by looking at the unique term used for "struggle," determining the mode of enemy attack, and by considering the expressed goal of the battle, "to stand."

πάλη

The readers are called to stand opposed to the wiles of the devil (v. 11). This conflict against the powers of darkness is described by the author as ἡ πάλη (v. 12). The term is a hapax legomenon in the NT and does not occur at all in the LXX, necessitating the view that the author has taken it from Hellenistic use.

Some have argued that the author has borrowed the term from Stoic usage (e.g. Epict., *Diss.* 3.25.2) and that it still retains the notion of self-sufficiency in the midst of the struggle.[42] The broader context of the passage, however, emphasizes complete and total dependence on the resources only God can supply.

It is more probable that the author has taken πάλη from the context of sport, i.e. wrestling.[43] The LXX does employ the verbal cognate παλαίω in the sense of "wrestling" (Gen 32:24; Judg 20:33; Esther 1:1). Pfitzner suggests that there are two possible interpretations of the word in this context. It can either be interpreted by the colorless meaning of "struggle" (the view taken by most of the commentators), or conditioned by the following phrase, "against blood and flesh" (thereby retaining the war/sport idea), in which case the meaning would be, "Our battle against the powers of darkness is not like the contest of the wrestler, for he can easily come to grips with his opponent."[44]

Either explanation leaves us with the difficulty of trying to understand why in a context of armor and military preparedness, the author would choose to use a term with wrestling connotations, especially when he could have used the seemingly more appropriate στρατεία, which Paul had employed on occasion (cf. 2 Cor 10:4; also 1 Tim 1:18). It may have something to do with the fact that wrestling was a popular event in the games held in Asia Minor, particularly in Ephesus, Smyrna, and Pergamum. These games included the κοινὸν ᾿Ασίας in Ephesus (initiated by Augustus),[45] the "Epheseia," which were also held in Ephesus,[46] and the Balbilleia, named after Nero's astrologer Balbillus. The Balbilleia were held in Smyrna and perhaps also in Pergamum. During the reign of Vespasian, Ephesus was granted permission for the "sacred contest" to be established there.[47] Wrestling was one of the main attractions in all the games, and it is most commonly referred to in the inscriptions by the term πάλη.[48] This is well illustrated by an inscription from Ephesus:[49]

> The council and the People honour Alexandros son of Menodoros grandson of Dionysios, an Ephesian who won the wrestling (πάλην) at the Isthmian games, the common games of Asia (κοινὸν ᾿Ασίας) at Ephesus and the great Epheseia and the wrestling (πάλην) in the common games of Asia, the Balbilleia, in Smyrna as well as the Pankratia in the common games of Asia at Smyrna, [in addition to] the wrestling (πάλην) in the common games of Galatia, the

Pankratia in the common games of Lycia in Myra, the wrestling (πάλην) in the common games of Asia in Sardis, and very many other games – πάλην πανκράτιον.

The popularity of wrestling in the games of western Asia Minor may account for the Ephesian author's use of the term πάλη instead of στρατεία in his discussion of the engagement of believers with the forces of evil. In contrast to the flesh-and-blood wrestling, with which the readers of Ephesians would have been quite familiar, the true struggle of believers is a spiritual power encounter which requires spiritual weaponry.

There is an interesting and perhaps relevant parable related by Pausanias of an Ephesian wrestler who was unbeatable in his event at Olympia until the Ephesia Grammata he wore around his ankle were discovered by the officials.[50] They were subsequently removed and his Milesian opponent then proceeded to win three consecutive victories over him because of his loss of magical power. Pausanias twice uses the verb παλαίω, the verbal cognate of the noun πάλη, in referring to the wrestling. The account probably served as a good piece of popular propaganda for wearing the Ephesia Grammata. It is impossible for us, however, to determine the source of this anecdote or when it arose or whether it was well known throughout western Asia Minor. If it was the kind of proverbial account which was well known in first-century Asia Minor, it is conceivable that the author of Ephesians may have made a subtle allusion to it in his instructions on engaging in spiritual warfare. Consequently, it may explain why the author chose πάλη instead of στρατεία. The allusion could have proved an effective way of communicating to the converts that they should no longer "put on" the Ephesia Grammata as an amulet (i.e. turn to magic), but should now "put on" the armor of God (i.e. the power of God). Furthermore, they would also understand in a fresh way that the struggle in which they have been enlisted as Christians is against supernatural "powers" – in fact, the very supernatural "powers" who were summoned to their aid by the Ephesia Grammata are now the attacking opponents which they need to resist! I mention this as an interesting possibility for understanding the author's choice of the word πάλη in the context of spiritual warfare, but the evidence is somewhat late. Furthermore, if we could be certain that the account was known in the first century, it might be too speculative to assume that a sufficient number of readers would have been familiar with the proverbial account for the author to make such a subtle allusion to it.

In light of this "struggle," the author strongly encourages the readers to equip themselves with God's "full armor" (πανοπλία: vv. 11, 13). Paul is fond of the simpler ὅπλα, using it in Rom 6:13; 13:12; 2 Cor 6:7; and 10:4. The presence of the fuller term can best be explained as a collective for representing the substantial number of arms listed in the context. Simultaneously, it could highlight the danger and seriousness of the threat facing the readers and therefore more strongly emphasize the importance of total dependence on God's strength. The cognate term ὅπλα is used by Paul in a way similar to the present context. It fundamentally points to "the transcendental conflict between God and satanic powers, in which man is both passively and actively involved."[51]

The opposition

No human opposition is mentioned in this context. On the contrary, the author expresses that the true nature of the struggle is not against "blood and flesh" (v. 12).[52] By means of this expression the author highlights the spiritual character of the believers' struggle.

The expressed opposition of the believers is the "devil" (v. 11), the various "powers" (v. 12), and "the evil one" (v. 16). The believer needs divine strength to resist the devil not only because of his supernatural nature and power, but also because he employs many "insidious wiles" (μεθοδεία). The term is invariably used in a bad sense and carries the notion of attacks that are constantly repeated or have an incalculable variety.[53] This would include the usual function of Satan as tempting the believer to do evil deeds, but would also involve any effective method in the overall goal of hindering the progress of the gospel and the cause of Christ.

The manner of diabolic attack is expressed in a different way in 6:16, where the aggressor bears the appellation, "the evil one," and launches "flaming arrows" at the saints. This probably involves more than just inner temptations to evil (or, concupiscence: cf. Thomas Aquinas), but extends to "every kind of attack and assault of the 'evil one.'"[54]

The "devil" is mentioned only at one other point in Ephesians (4:27), where he stands ready to take "ground" (τόπος) from those who would surrender it by sinning. The immediate reference is to uncontrolled anger (v. 26), but there is no reason to limit the reference solely to anger. Practicing falsehood (v. 25), stealing (v. 28), and presumably any other conduct characteristic of the "old self" (v. 22) is viewed by the author as surrendering territory to the devil and grieving the Holy Spirit (v.30).

The author goes far beyond the mention of the devil as the opposition: various kinds of spiritual "powers" are set forth as the opponents of the believers (6:12). The writer does not now establish a different strategy for resisting these evil "powers" in contrast to how they would resist the devil. Neither does he ascribe varying functions or differing strategies of attack to each of the different categories of spiritual forces. The author works from the assumption that the "powers" operate in precisely the same fashion as the διάβολος. The "powers" suddenly appear in connection with the διάβολος and are assumed to have a common nature, objective, and method of attack, which necessitates the believer to depend on the power of God to resist them.

The expressed goal: "to stand"

The objective of the warfare for the readers is expressly stated by the author in vv. 11, 13, and 14. The readers are called to "stand." This involves resisting (ἀνθίστημι, v. 13) the evil "powers." There is difficulty in deciding on all that is entailed by the concept of "standing" as presented here. Is it static or dynamic? Is the reader called upon solely to resist the attacks of the evil "powers" in whatever manner they come and thus not fall into sin? Or, is the reader also called upon to take more "offensive" action such as in proclaiming the redemptive message of the gospel to humanity held in bondage by the devil?

There is a strong ethical emphasis in this passage. The readers are essentially enjoined to resist temptation. The author has closely related the work of the devil to the ethical conduct of believers (cf. 4:27). There thus appears to be a continuance of the Pauline idea of "Satan" as tempter and seducer of individuals.

Victory is not necessarily assured in this struggle.[55] R. Schnackenburg is correct in differentiating the promise of victory from the promise of the prospect of victory in the struggle.[56] This is consistent with the author's posing the possibility of the readers' giving "a place to the devil" (4:27). It is also consistent with the need for the readers to "put on" and "take up" the armor of God (6:11, 13; see also "put on" the new man in 4:24). Resisting the evil one's temptations to sin is a thoroughgoing Pauline (and NT) idea that is taken up here. Equipped with "the armor of God," the believer is enabled to resist enemy aggression and maintain the ground which rightfully belongs to one who is in Christ. Without appropriating the armor of God, the believer is not equipped to resist the influence of the "powers."

The flow of the context also reveals that the author conceives of "standing" in offensive terms. The author does not explicitly state that the readers need to regain old ground given to the enemy (cf. 4:27) and capture new ground currently held by the enemy, but this is the implication of the context. The offensive aspects of the resistance can be summarized as developing conduct governed by Christian ethics and maintaining the mission which Paul himself had inaugurated.

Resisting the temptation to unholy anger, for example, logically entails both a defensive and an offensive aspect in the struggle against the tempter. On the one hand, new ground is taken from the control of the enemy. On the other hand, the continuing temptations of the evil one have been successfully resisted. The ethical objective of the Christian as presented by the author of Ephesians is to develop a pattern of life which is appropriate to one who has become a child of God (5:2). This involves laying aside the old self and putting on the new (4:17–24) and walking no longer in the darkness under the control of the enemy (2:6–14; cf. 2:2), but walking in the light.

In addition to the ethical obligations, the author passes on to his readers the importance of continuing the mission as part of their resistance movement against the forces of evil. This is set forth in vv. 15, 17b, and 19. Specifically, the author calls on his readers to make known the εὐαγγέλιον.

The feet of the believer are to be fitted with the preparation of the εὐαγγέλιον of peace (6:15). The gospel is that which announces and brings peace to those who receive it, not only peace with God (2:16) but also peace with men formerly at enmity (2:14, 15; 4:3). This peace should be exhibited in the interpersonal relationships of the readers because it is an inherent characteristic of the gospel message itself. Perhaps the author is subtly suggesting that unity and peace within the community are part of the "readiness" (ἑτοιμασία) requisite to proclaiming the gospel of peace.[57]

This task of mission is picked up again by the author in v. 17. Here the preaching of the gospel is depicted as the most aggressive maneuver against the realm of the devil and his hosts by the employment of the use of the sword as the final weapon in the enumeration. The believer is admonished to take up the sword not merely for the self defense but also "to go on the attack and make new conquests in God's cause.''[58] The sword is given by the Spirit. The readers have already been sealed with the Holy Spirit of promise (1:13) and are being strengthened by the Spirit (3:16). The "sword of the Spirit" in one sense could be considered a circumlocution for the power of God.[59] The metaphor of the sword is not expressly identified with the Spirit, however, but with the word ($\dot{\rho}\tilde{\eta}\mu\alpha$) of God. This word is nothing other than the Christian message, the gospel (cf. Rom 10:8: "... the word ($\dot{\rho}\tilde{\eta}\mu\alpha$) of faith which we are proclaiming"). In spite of the fact that the readers will encounter substantial diabolic opposition to their proclamation of the gospel, they have no reason to fear or give up. They have been endowed by God with a divinely empowered weapon to overcome all resistance intending to hinder the progress of the gospel.

Not only have the readers received their own commission and enablement to proclaim the gospel, they are also requested to support the apostolic proclamation of the gospel (v. 19). Their prayer and petition is solicited as the apostle makes known the mystery of the gospel in his imprisonment.

Summary

The goal of the "spiritual warfare" in this passage bears an overall striking resemblance to the goal of the "agon motif" in Paul. Pfitzner summarizes the essence of the agon motif in the following way: "to strive for the extension of the Gospel and to strive to deepen its gifts in one's personal life are aspects of the one task given to man, to seek the goal of God Himself and His rule of righteousness."[60] The struggle/ warfare can best be described in terms of an offensive aspect (making known the gospel) and a defensive aspect (resisting temptation; endurance). The demonic "powers" are bent on regaining their control in the lives of believers. Through a variety of means they attempt to block the progress of the gospel and cause believers to walk according to the pattern of their former manner of life. Victory over the "powers" is not assured apart from the appropriation of the power of God. Failure to resist allows the devil to reassert his dominion.

6. Conclusions

(1) The emphasis on the power of God in Ephesians reaches its zenith in 6:10−20, exhibited both in the array of power-denoting terms and in the concept of the armor of God. The divine power is provided

to the believer for a specific purpose — that the influence and attacks of the evil forces might be successfully resisted.

(2) Spiritual warfare is fought in the context of the church existing in two ages and in two spheres of power. The work of Christ has given believers access to some of the blessings of the age to come, but the age of this world has not ended; the days are evil until Christ pours out his wrath on the world and consummates the salvation of believers. Hence, Christians are engaged in a conflict with the demonic "powers" but with access to the more powerful provisions of God. The passage shows no sign of influence by the fully realized eschatology of Gnosis. On the contrary, the present engagement with the "powers" of evil demonstrates that the church awaits its complete redemption.

(3) The passage may reflect a standard catechetical pattern known throughout the early church, but this section is far more expansive than any of its NT counterparts and strongly emphasizes the role of the host of evil "powers," which none of the other passages mention. These distinctive traits require an explanation based on the purpose and occasion of the epistle.

(4) The situation we have envisioned in the churches in western Asia Minor corresponds with these data perfectly. Many converts were streaming into the churches — converts who were formerly affiliated with the Artemis cult, practiced magic, consulted astrologers, and participated in various mysteries. Underlying the former beliefs and manner of life of all these converts was a common and deepset fear of the demonic "powers." Ephesians addresses that fear directly and instructs the new and older believers alike on how to resist the powerful influence of these evil forces. The author gives them instruction based on OT teaching (Isaiah) in light of the work of Christ who provides the church with access to the power of God.

(5) The passage brings the power-motif in Ephesians to a climax by highlighting the power of God working on behalf of believers as juxtaposed to the might of the "powers" of evil working against believers. An understanding of this power-motif helps to make the structure of the epistle more intelligible.

6

FEATURES OF THE THEOLOGY OF
EPHESIANS IN LIGHT OF ITS BACKGROUND

In the present chapter I will elucidate a variety of theological con-
structions the author employs to emphasize divine power and
enablement. Conversely, I will draw out the implications of the power-
motif to some of the aspects of the theology of the epistle. First, I
will begin the chapter by making some tentative conclusions about
the epistolary situation.

1. Tentative conclusions regarding the situation behind Ephesians

A multiplicity of sources attest to the pervasive influence of magic,
the Phrygian mystery religions (including the worship of the Ephesian
Artemis), and astrology not only among the pagans of Ephesus and
western Asia Minor, but also among the Jews. The common feature
in all of these religious and/or magical traditions is an acute and
thriving belief in and fear of evil spiritual "powers." The influx of
Christianity into this region brought numerous individuals into the
churches from this milieu. It cannot be assumed that the fears of these
converts about the evil spiritual realm were immediately allayed by
their new-found faith. It would also be erroneous to assume that their
conversion to Christianity would have brought about a complete
forsaking of all their former means of protection from the hostile
"powers." Even if many (or the majority) of Christians did totally
turn aside from their former apotropaic practices, some at least would
have faced a great temptation to combine their Christian faith with
magical techniques.

The most pressing question facing the believers at Ephesus and
throughout western Asia Minor was, where does Christ stand in
relation to the hostile "powers"? Or more specifically, is Christ alone
sufficient, or do we need additional protection from the attacks and
influence of these "powers"? These questions receive an eloquent

and thorough response in Ephesians. The epistle provides answers to other implicit questions in the minds of the readers: how can we gain access to Christ's power for protection from the "powers"? and how does a Christian resist the attacks of the "powers" without the help of the former methods?

Ephesians provides by far the fullest teaching about the "powers" of all the epistles attributed to Paul. This fact alone suggests that the "powers" were a concern to the readers, but an understanding of the spiritual milieu of western Asia Minor illuminates why this should be so. Numerous sources verify the tremendous fear of the "powers" by the people of the region. That is not to say that this same concern was unknown elsewhere, such as at Corinth or Rome, but this region was similar to Egypt in having a reputation for prolific magical practices. Perhaps the majority of the converts in the churches in Asia had come from a background of magical practices and involvement in the cult of the Ephesian Artemis, as Luke seems to imply in Acts 19. This could conceivably have provided the occasion for the author to address the issue of the "powers." This setting, which I refer to as "the situation," may explain why the "powers" are given more attention in Ephesians than in any of the other epistles attributed to Paul.

2. Christology

The superiority of Christ

Ephesians has aptly been described by numerous interpreters as presenting a "cosmic Christology." Christ is portrayed in numerous ways as superior to "all things." Most significant, for our concern, is the fact that Christ is juxtaposed to the "powers" and declared to be superior to them.

The idea of the ascension/exaltation of Christ receives a strong emphasis in Ephesians.[1] A. van Roon remarks, "The exalted kurios is central to this epistle."[2] It forms an important part of the author's intention to establish firmly the lordship of Christ in the understanding of the readers. Taking up a traditional conflation of Ps 110:1 and Ps 8:6 emphasizing both an enthronement and a cosmic Christology, the writer gives a prominent place to the expression of this theme in the summary of his prayer for the readers in Eph 1:20–22. One of the most conspicuous aspects of his handling of the theme in this context is the expansive list of enemies conquered at the resurrection (1:21). The exaltation theme is then taken up again in 2:6, where the author affirms the identification of believers with Christ in his ascension. In quite different terms, he refers to it yet again in 4:8–10 in the preface to his description of Christ as the giver of gifts to the church. This strongly suggests that the relationship of Christ to the "powers" was a live issue to the readers of the epistle.

It is significant to note that in his discussion of the religions-historical source of κύριος, Wilhelm Bousset points out that Artemis of Ephesus bears this title and that it also appears to have been a customary title of the Magna Mater (Cybele), and Hekate.[3] In contrast to these western Asia Minor deities claiming to possess power over the underworld and the cosmos, Ephesians declares the sole and supreme lordship of Christ.

The idea of the exaltation of Christ as having significant implications to Christ's relationship to the "powers" is not new to Paul (1 Cor 15:24, 27; Phil 2:9) or other parts of the NT (1 Pet 3:21–22). The author of Colossians eloquently acclaims Christ as Lord, not the least by describing the effect of his resurrection with respect to the "powers" (2:12–15). He has "stripped" them of their power and dignity, publicly "exposed" them and disgraced them, and finally has "led them in a triumphal" parade as his vanquished enemies (2:15). This victory took place in the cross–resurrection event, which necessarily encompasses the ascension–exaltation of Christ (3:1). On this basis, the author can then polemicize against the aberrant teaching of the "philosophy." The Philippian "hymn" conveys the same thought as Ephesians in a condensed form: "God has highly exalted him and bestowed on him the name which is above every name" (ὄνομα; cf. the use of ὄνομα in Eph 1:21). 1 Peter also is quite explicit: "[Christ] has gone into heaven and is at the right hand of God, with ἀγγέλοι καὶ ἐξουσίαι καὶ δυνάμεις subjected to him." It is likely that this "exaltation theology" was a well-known part of early Christian tradition with a set of stock phrases which may have included lists of "powers" and which also transmitted the conflated Psalm citations as an essential ingredient of the tradition.[4] If such a tradition did exist as a part of the confession of the early church, Ephesians stands in the mainstream of that tradition. Ephesians takes up this tradition, elaborates on it, and stresses its immediate relevance to the readers.

An assortment of other expressions have already been discussed at length in prior chapters which make significant contributions to the one overriding concept of the superiority of Christ. The author's use of the term πλήρωμα reflects the power and supremacy of Christ as derived from the Father. Similarly, the author's use of the term κεφαλή highlights the ruling authority of Christ over all "powers." Finally, Ephesians refers to the future gathering of all things under the headship of Christ (ἀνακεφαλαιόω, 1:10). Special reference is made in this context to the "powers" (τὰ ἐπὶ τοῖς οὐρανοῖς) implying the future subjugation and pacification of these hostile forces (cf. in Paul, 1 Cor 15:24). Christ is specifically named as God's agent in bringing about this consummation. There is therefore no question of the "powers" gaining any ascendancy in the future. They are part of the creation of God (Eph 3:9) and, in spite of their current rebellion and hostility, they are under the sovereign control of Christ and will be brought into subjection at the consummation.

In summary, we must ask why the author has underscored this aspect of Christology in the letter. I would suggest that the Ephesian author desired to reaffirm the supremacy of Christ over the "powers" in a variety of ways to his readers – Christians living in a socio-cultural milieu where the spirit-"powers" were acknowledged and feared. The author wanted his readers to be assured beyond any doubt that Christ is superior to these malignant "powers." He has therefore taken up and contextualized not only Pauline theology, but the early Christian understanding of the ascension–exaltation, to the life situation of the churches in Asia Minor.

Christ as the μυστήριον

The Ephesian "mystery" has clear cosmic coordinates with the "powers" in view. The aim of the "mystery" is revealed in 1:9–10 to be the consummation (ἀνακεφαλαιόω) of all things in Christ. This includes the subjugation of the hostile "powers" to Christ. Christ is the one who will consummate all things by providing ultimate redemption for believers and by pacifying the opposing forces. The fact that the church exists is said by our author to bear witness to God's administration of the mystery (ἡ οἰκονομία τοῦ μυστηρίου), which further implies the defeat and ultimate fate of the "powers" (3:9–10).[5]

The situation of perceived demonic hostility in western Asia Minor may have provided a partial motivation for the author's emphasis on the cosmic aspect of this concept of "mystery." The "mystery" spoken of in Ephesians may very well provide a contrast to the Lydian–Phrygian "mysteries" which were so popular.[6] In this way the author could have employed it as a polemic against the influence of the ideas of the "mysteries" in the churches. Ephesians presents an entirely new "mystery" — a mystery understood along OT lines with Christ himself as the content. This mystery is superior to the mystery religions in that it implies their impending doom when Christ will bring "all things" under his headship, including the so-called deities invoked in the mystery religions and magic.

It is clear that the author's concept of "mystery" has not been shaped by pagan religion, viz. the mystery religions or magic.[7] In fact, the content of a pagan mystery was precisely the opposite of the mystery revealed in Ephesians. In *PGM* I.128–32, the mystery initiation involves, among other things, receiving ὁ κύριος τοῦ ἀέρος (cf. Eph 2:2) as the indwelling deity![8]

The Ephesian author's notion of the "mystery" reflects a Semitic background.[9] More specifically, it corresponds precisely to the use of "mystery" (*raz*) in the book of Daniel.[10] There it is used to describe the hiddenness, or secrecy, of the redemptive plan of God.

The writer of Colossians applies the concept of mystery in a way that brings out the divine power and enablement available to the believer in and through Christ. He characterizes the mystery as: "Christ in you, the hope and glory" (Col 1:27). The indwelling of Christ in the lives of the Colossian believers would strengthen them for living according to Christian ethics which, in specific terms for them, meant a refusal of the dogma promulgated by the "philosophy." The Ephesian author also brings out an enabling significance to the mystery in 5:32, where he uses the term to describe the relationship of Christ to the church. Part of this relationship entails Christ "nourishing" the church (5:29). On the basis of the extended context of this epistle we may be sure that part of this "nourishing" is the provision of power and enablement to believers. Certainly this strengthening proceeds out of the union of Christ with his church.

It is too restrictive to hold that the content of the mystery in Ephesians is defined solely as God's acceptance of the Gentiles and the unification of the Jews and Gentiles in Christ (Eph 3:3, 4).[11] If we seek a precise definition of "mystery," it is best found in the proposition found in Colossians: "the mystery of God is Christ" (cf. Col 2:2). The mystery is also identified with Christ in the phrase τὸ μυστήριον τοῦ Χριστοῦ (Col 4:3), where the genitive is best described as appositional.[12] In Ephesians, Christ is the content of the gospel message, termed a "mystery" (6:19). Christ is the starting point for an

accurate understanding of the concept of "mystery." Thus, there are
not a number of "mysteries" with limited applications, but one
supreme "mystery" with a number of applications.[13]

Election in Christ

The theme of election in Christ occurs just as frequently in Ephesians
as it does in Romans (especially Rom 9–11 and in the latter part of
Rom 8). The distinctive contribution of Ephesians is the emphasis laid
on election. The fullest expression of this election occurs at the
beginning of the prooemium (1:4): "He chose (ἐξελέξατο) us in him
before the foundation of the world." Election is then stressed
throughout the remainder of the prooemium and again in chapter 3.
It was "in Christ" that believers were foreordained (προορίζω) in
accordance with the purpose (πρόθεσις) of God (Eph 1:11). This was
in fact carried out according to the counsel (βουλή) of the will
(θέλημα) of God (Eph 1:11). The phrase, "the will of God" (θέλημα
τοῦ θεοῦ), clearly a Pauline phrase,[14] is more frequent in Ephesians
than in any other epistle attributed to Paul (Eph 1:1, 5, 9; 5:17; 6:6).
It was "through Jesus Christ" that believers were foreordained
(προορίζω) to adoption for God (Eph 1:5).[15] This action was in
accordance with the good pleasure of God (εὐδοκία), or his divine
decree or desire. Even the good works of believers were "prepared
beforehand" (προετοιμάζω,[16] Eph 2:10) by God.

This concept of election is closely linked with the foregoing
discussion of the "mystery." God has purposed (προτίθημι:[17] Eph
1:9; πρόθεσις: Eph 3:11) to consummate the μυστήριον "in Christ
Jesus," that is, the "mystery" which was originally conceived in
Christ.

The Ephesian author presents Christ as integrally involved in the
process of electing and also as the object or sphere in which believers
have been chosen. It only remains for us to ask why election in Christ
is stressed in Ephesians to such a degree. It is true that the statements
regarding election are made in the context of positive praise and
adoration of Christ as opposed to a context of polemic. One must
therefore exercise caution in tying them too closely to a situation
facing the readers.

We may safely say, however, that the author's concept of election
in Christ would provide a comforting and instructive counter to the
fears of Christians formerly under the influence of magic, the
mysteries, and astrological beliefs. Christians who before their

conversion received false comfort from Artemis by viewing the zodiacal signs so prominently depicted on her cultic image and assuming that their goddess held sway over the "powers" controlling fate would now experience true and profound comfort knowing that they had been chosen by God before the foundation of the world. There would be no reason for these converts to consult either Artemis or any other pagan deity for oracular advice. Their fate does not rest in the whims of hostile spiritual "powers." Their future is secure and blessed by virtue of their election in Christ.

Summary

The supremacy of the Lord Jesus Christ to "all things" and the powerful rule of the Lord are repeatedly asserted throughout the whole of the epistle in a variety of ways. The author leaves no doubt whatsoever in the minds of the readers that any conceivable hostile "power" is outside and independent of Christ's dominion.

The instruction appears to be especially designed to bolster and encourage the faith of believers fearing the power and influence of malignant forces. The place of Christ in relation to the "powers" is vividly depicted. By virtue of his resurrection and exaltation, our "Lord" and "Christ" has triumphed over the "powers" and now exercises his reign as ruler, or "head," preparing for the time when he will completely and finally subjugate all hostile "powers." Christ can exercise such authority because of his filial relationship to God, with whom he shares all power, or "fullness." The depths and riches of God's plan, a "mystery," consisting of Christ in all his power and authority, have now been revealed along with the fact that believers are not in the grip of cosmic fate, but have been chosen by God to be in Christ, even prior to the creation of the cosmic "powers."

3. The "cosmic powers" and anthropology

I have been using the expression "cosmic powers" as a synonym for "powers," "demons," evil spirits and hostile angels, i.e. as personalized forces of evil. For some theologians this may appear to be an unnecessarily restrictive use of the expression. There is a trend in recent scholarship to see Paul himself as already demythologizing this so-called apocalyptic terminology. J. C. Beker contends that for Paul, these apocalyptic forces have been interpreted anthropologically, with the result that the human situation is not influenced by the mythological demons and angels, but rather by the ontological powers of death, sin, the law, and the flesh.[18] He refers to the personalized sense this field of forces is given in Paul with each having a specific reign or dominion (e.g. sin and death "reign," Rom 5:21; 6:9; death is "the last enemy," 1 Cor 15:26; the flesh "desires," Gal 5:17).[19] Beker's intepretation has been substantively taken up and developed with regard to the Pauline "principalities, powers, and authorities" by W. Wink in his recent work, *Naming the Powers*.[20] Wink concurs that Paul had already moved a considerable distance toward demythologizing the "powers" and that the author of Ephesians (not Paul) carried it still further.

Their observations raise two issues compelling our attention and comment. First, has Paul himself "demythologized" the apocalyptic "powers" terminology? Secondly, has the author of Ephesians done the same, and if not, how does he view the "powers" in relation to the categories of death, sin, the law, and flesh?

Beker's principal argument for the anthropological reinterpretation of the demons and angels hinges on his observation that,[21]

> Paul uses traditional apocalyptic terminology sparingly and interprets it anthropologically, so that words such as "powers," "rulers," "lordships," "thrones," "world rulers of darkness," "the spiritual forces of darkness in the heavens" (cf. Eph 6:12; Col 1:16) are primarily restricted to the apocalyptic sections of 1 Cor 15:24−28 and Rom 8:38−39 (cf. 1 Cor 2:6−9).

Because of this he can assume that Paul employs the apocalyptic "powers" terminology only when he is constrained to do so by an apocalyptic context. This observation manifestly ignores a substantial amount of references placing the more personalized evil "powers" in an ethical context. Ironically, he unwittingly concedes this point by an earlier remark that "mythological personification abounds in the NT." He correctly observes,[22]

> Apocalyptic thought lends a new dimension to the historical fabric of life. Human agents, historical entities, and natural phenomena are dominated and pervaded by transcendent spiritual forces ... Spiritual forces "blind" (2 Cor 4:4) and "deceive" (Rom 7:10), just "as the serpent deceived Eve by its cunning" (2 Cor 11:3); they "tempt" (1 Thess 3:5) or "hinder" ("Satan hindered us," 1 Thess 2:18) ... Paul can

speak about Satan as "the god of this world" (2 Cor 4:4) or about "the rulers of this world" (1 Cor 2:8), "forces in heaven and on earth and under the earth" (Phil 2:10) and about "the elemental *spirits* [my italics] of the universe" (Gal 4:3, 9).

We could also add to this other Pauline references to the figures of Beliar (2 Cor 6:15) and Satan, who can destroy the flesh (1 Cor 5:4−5), and who tempts (1 Cor 7:5), taking advantage of persons by his scheming (2 Cor 2:11) and deception through appearing as an angel of light (2 Cor 11:14). Paul also speaks of "demons" and expresses the dreadful potential of Christians becoming partners with them by participating in pagan sacrifice (1 Cor 10:19−21). These demons are the so-called "gods" and "lords" (1 Cor 8:4−6). Paul can even conceive of an "angel of Satan" buffeting him (2 Cor 12:7). These particular references all occur in the context of important ethical decisions facing the respective readership, not in the context of God's final apocalyptic triumph. He has therefore not been obligated to employ "mythological" imagery in these passages because of the constraints of an apocalyptic context.

In the face of such "mythological personification" it simply does not follow that Paul would have understood the apocalyptic "powers" (δυνάμεις, ἀρχαί, ἐξουσίαι, κ.τ.λ.) as representing a different ontological category than "Satan," "Beliar," angels, and demons. Beker furthermore argues for Paul's anthropological reinterpretation of these "powers" by observing that the apostle does not elaborate on apocalyptic timetables, descriptions of the architecture of heaven, or accounts of angels and demons.[23] This observation proves nothing for Beker. Paul could have believed in the reality of these beings without being transfixed with useless speculation about them. The fact that the "mythological" imagery occurs in a number of ethical contexts would suggest that Paul's concern was focused more on responding to the forces he believed to exist.

Finally, I have argued earlier that in light of the magical tradition, which entertained no skepticism about the reality and harmful influence of the "powers," Paul would have run the risk of being severely misunderstood by his readers if he was reinterpreting the "powers" terminology anthropologically. Beker has failed to treat the question of how Paul would have been understood by his first-century readers in this regard.

It would be more accurate to state that Paul prefers the categories of sin, law, flesh, and death (particularly in Romans), but he can simultaneously speak of personalized forces of evil. There is not a necessary contradiction in Paul's mind between the two general categories of "cosmic powers."

When one comes to Ephesians a significant increase in the so-called mythological language is readily discernible, with abundant references to "principalities and powers" and a lengthy admonition to engage these forces in a struggle. Wink, however, sees Ephesians as having traveled further down the road of demythologization.[24] This appears inconsistent with his appeal to Beker. Beker seems to be saying that Paul has reduced the number of his references to apocalyptic powers terminology (i.e. "principalities and powers," etc.) in favor of a demythologized terminological field of ontological powers (i.e. sin, the law, flesh, and death). Precisely the opposite has happened in Ephesians, where there is only one reference to "sin" (2:1), one reference to "law" (2:15), and no reference to "death," although there are a number of references to "flesh," but not all having Pauline theological significance. In contrast, there are numerous references to the "personal" or "mythical" powers. If anything, Ephesians has been "remythologized"! Wink's alleged "clue" for interpreting Eph 1:20ff. has turned out to be of no help at all. In fact, the above evidence would lead us to conclude that the Ephesian author should reflect an increase in non-apocalyptic "powers" terminology.

Wink is actually attempting to build a case for seeing an implicit demythologization within the apocalyptic terms themselves for the "powers." The above line of evidence does not support this thesis and I attempted to demonstrate earlier[25] that the terms for the "powers" in Ephesians and Colossians are not multi-referential, but refer to angelic forces.

The fact that the apocalyptic "powers" terms refer to angelic beings does not imply that these have no relationship to the more abstract category of "powers," viz. sin, the law, flesh, and death. On the contrary, the two categories should be seen not only to coexist, but as a mutually interdependent composite group of powers constituting the present age. Eph 2:2−3 is the most decisive passage in demonstrating the confluence of these two different categories in Ephesians. Here the author gives a three-fold description of life in the former sphere of power:

ποτέ
1. TEMPORAL κατὰ τὸν αἰῶνα τοῦ κόσμου
τούτου
2. DEMONIC κατὰ τὸν ἄρχοντα τῆς ἐξουσίας
τοῦ ἀέρος

τοῦ πνεύματος τοῦ νῦν ἐνεργοῦντος
ἐν τοῖς υἱοῖς τῆς ἀπειθείας

ποτέ
3. FLESHLY ἡμεῖς πάντες ἀνεστράφημέν ποτε ἐν
ταῖς ἐπιθυμίαις τῆς
σαρκὸς ἡμῶν ποιοῦντες τὰ
θελήματα τῆς σαρκὸς καὶ
τῶν διανοιῶν

The "flesh" holds a significant place in the Pauline anthropology to describe the power which leads man away from God and is opposed to the working of the Spirit. It is distinguished from the demonic "powers" in so far as it is not just a power alien to man, but it belongs to man himself.[26] Here in Eph 2:2, 3 the influence of the flesh is coordinated with the influence of the "authority of the air," viz. the devil as head of a troop of spiritual forces. They conduct their operation in the present age. "Flesh" does not function in this passage as an explanation or definition of what the author means by "the authority of the air" or "spirit." The author is here describing two different kinds of "powers," one internal with respect to man and the other external, but both intent on exerting their dominion over man in this present age.[27] This reference to "flesh" is the only occurrence of the term in Ephesians with the Pauline anthropological sense of σάρξ as the subject of sin (but cf. Col 2:13, 18, 23).

As we noted earlier, the term "death" never occurs in Ephesians. The only reference to "sin" appears in Eph 2:1 (cf. Col 1:14), where the author uses the unusual (for Paul) plural of ἁμαρτία. Here the meaning in connection with the plural of παράπτωμα probably indicates the fullness and variety of concrete acts of sin versus the meaning of sin as a compelling power. Finally, there is only a single mention of "law" in Ephesians. Christ is attributed with abolishing the law only in so far as it consists of statutes and ordinances dividing the Gentiles from the Jews (2:15).[28] This would include the ceremonial aspects of the law together with the ever-expanding oral explications and applications. It is insightful at this point to examine a concept of "law" presented in Colossians. Although νόμος is not mentioned in that epistle, "law" in the general sense of ἐντολαί and δόγματα takes on special significance in relation to the angelic "powers." The Colossian author portrays all of the aberrant dogma of the errorists as only indirectly coming from men (2:22) and having its ultimate derivation from the στοιχεῖα τοῦ κόσμου (2:8, 20).[29] Here the ordinances and statutes function as part of a loosely organized religious institution or "philosophy," but are regarded by the author of Colossians as being directly inspired and animated by the hostile angelic "powers."

It is precisely at this point that the question of structures of existence, institutions, and -isms should come into the discussion. Ephesians (and Colossians) betrays a belief in the reality and existence of personified evil spiritual "powers." Simultaneously, the epistle affirms the influence of another category of powers – the flesh and law. One power is internal to man, the other is external. Man is capable of creating laws, philosophies, and institutions, but this does not necessitate an absolute identification with the "principalities, powers, and authorities." The angelic "powers" may have worked together with the flesh of man in order to create these entities. Nevertheless, these created entities can be considered "demonic" since they have been inspired by the spirit "powers." At this juncture I have broached a hermeneutical topic extending beyond the scope of my purpose. It is necessary, however, to give this indication of where the exegetical evidence of my research would suggest as a starting point for future discussion of the "principalities and powers" in their relationship to structures.

One may wonder why the spirit "powers" in Ephesians receive the greater emphasis when the non-personal "powers" in the accepted Paulines are referred to more frequently. This question can best be answered by referring to my overall thesis regarding the prominence of the demonic realm as an issue for the readers. The author is indeed addressing a group of readers who are keenly aware of demonic "powers" at work and who are also in need of instruction about the place of these hostile angelic "powers" with regard to Christ.

4. New life in Christ

The new life of the believer in union with Christ is summarized by a distinctive word used both in Ephesians and Colossians – συνζωοποιέω. Believers have been "made alive with" Christ.

The transfer of dominions

Ephesians stresses the contrast between two opposing dominions and their lords. This two-dominions thought is also foundational to Pauline theology.[30] Tannehill finds that for Paul, "everything depends on the reality of release from the powers of the old world and incorporation in a new world."[31] This is especially true of Ephesians, which stresses the role of the hostile spirit "powers" to a much greater degree than Paul. The two dominions are distinguished by a number of contrasting metaphors, esp. light–darkness and death–life. The Ephesian author emphasizes the nature of life in each realm under the "once–now" schema (Eph 2).

This fundamental structure of transfer of dominions in addition to a number of alleged liturgical elements in Ephesians together with the lack of explicit indicators of a situation has led a number of scholars to conclude that the setting of Ephesians has a connection with baptism. Specifically, some suggest that Ephesians was a letter written to provide instruction to members of new Gentile churches on the meaning of their baptism.[32] Others see a more formal purpose behind the "letter" and would rather describe it as a "baptismal homily"[33] or as a "wisdom discourse" (*Weisheitsrede*) to the newly baptized Christians.[34]

There are a few features of Ephesians which cause me to approach the "baptismal homily" view with some skepticism. First, C. Caragounis has aptly observed that it seems curious and inexplicable that an epistle devoted to baptism should make only a single mention of the term (4:5), not for the sake of baptism itself but as one of a number of points that constitute the Christian faith.[35] Secondly, the rite must be inferred from a number of metaphors scattered throughout the epistle. The difficulty is that the alleged baptismal reference behind many of these metaphors is quite subtle and therefore highly debatable. For example, a key metaphor is the "sealing" by the Holy Spirit of promise in 1:13 (see also 4:30), which is taken to be a direct reference to the reception of the Spirit on the occasion of baptism.[36] One must object, however, that any hint of baptism is extraneous to the context. The seal is the Holy Spirit, not baptism, and the occasion for the reception of the Spirit is not linked by our author with baptism.[37] It is certainly possible that the Ephesian author does not link the Spirit with baptism in a sacramental sense, in line with the Pauline view.[38] Thirdly, the advocates of the baptismal background point to the similarity of expression between Eph 2:5–6 and Col 2:12–13 where baptism is explicitly mentioned: "and you were buried with him in baptism." An additional line of continuity is then drawn with the baptismal context of Rom 6. The difficulty with this line of argument is that the Ephesian author not only leaves out the explicit reference to baptism, but also omits any reference to burial with Christ (συνθάπτω; Rom 6:4; Col 2:12). Again, it is odd that in a literary work allegedly constructed as a "baptismal homily" the author would omit this expressive metaphor unambiguously linked with baptism in the Pauline tradition.

This evidence does cast doubt on the theory of the overall intention and purpose of the epistle as being a "baptismal homily," but it by no means disproves that the Ephesian author was making tacit allusion to the baptism of the readers and elaborating on its significance. On the contrary, it would be entirely fitting and appropriate for a writer in addressing a group of believers perceiving themselves as still threatened by the influence of the hostile "powers" to develop the relevance of the events depicted in baptism for their embattled situation.

Incorporation into Christ

The Ephesian author brings into bold relief the identification of his believing readers with Christ – particularly through the phrases "in Christ" and "with Christ" in addition to the concept of "Christ in you." This identification with Christ not only provides hope for the future, but provides divine enablement to believers for the present deportment of their lives.

There is a relatively greater number of occurrences of the phrase "in Christ" and its equivalents in Ephesians than in the accepted Paulines. J. A. Allan counts 34 occurrences in Ephesians as compared with 164 in the accepted Paulines (including 2 Thessalonians).[39]

The phrase and its equivalents were popular with Paul and designate the incorporation of the believer into Christ. The background of the concept comes from the Hebrew idea of corporate personality or solidarity according to which the head of a family or tribe is the representative of all his members. For Paul, Adam and Christ are the representative figures of old and new humanity (1 Cor 15:22; Rom 5:12–21). Both a spatial-local sense and an instrumental sense can be discerned in Paul's use of the phrase.[40] The Ephesian author reflects Pauline tradition in this regard.[41]

The frequency of the phrase likely relates to the desire of the author to emphasize the identification of the Christians with their victorious Lord. By virtue of being "in Christ" believers have access to his power for engaging in spiritual warfare and living lives of obedience. Believers enjoy an intimate union with their risen Lord, who nourishes and provides for them, bestowing salvation upon them.

Ephesians also uses the language of "with Christ" to express the solidarity of believers with the new life of Christ in death and resurrection (Eph 2:4–6; see also Col 2:12, 13, 20; 3:1). This concept closely resembles "in Christ" since they both express the incorporation motif, which is also true of the accepted Paulines. The "with Christ" language of Ephesians (and Colossians) has been indicted as being discontinuous with Paul because it appears to have lost its future apocalyptic moorings – resurrection is experienced by the believer in the present.[42] I will attempt to show below (see section 5) that the epistle has not lost sight of a future hope. It is true that the "with Christ" concept is not used explicitly for the future resurrection, but this does not necessarily imply that the future resurrection has been displaced. The one-sided presentation of the "with Christ" statements is consistent with the author's desire to stress the present identity of believers with Christ. Why this emphasis? The readers need reassurance of their secure position and certain access to God's power in order to face the hostile world filled with evil "powers."

Finally, the Ephesian author can also speak of Christ indwelling the lives of believers (Eph 3:17; see also Col 1:27). In this context, the author closely links the indwelling of Christ with the indwelling of the Holy Spirit in empowering believers.

The language of incorporation/participation/indwelling has been stressed in Ephesians because of the situation facing the readers. Their perceived weakness and vulnerability before the cosmic "powers" needs to be supplanted by the confidence which comes from knowing that they are intimately identified with their risen and victorious Lord. His victory over the "powers" is their victory. His present authority over the "powers" is their authority.

Access to divine power

Clearly one of the central themes of the Epistle to the Ephesians is that believers have access to divine power. This is not portrayed as substantive power that can be manipulated through magical means, but it is a power that comes from an intimate relationship and identification with the Lord Jesus Christ. It is power for a purpose – resistance of the evil angelic "powers," ethical Christian conduct, and mission.

The very structure of the epistle itself highlights the thematic importance of the power of God, as I have sought to demonstrate in chapters 4 and 5. Ephesians is also filled with a range of concepts and terms chosen to affirm to the readers that divine help and strengthening is within their reach. It begins with the reference to the reception of "every spiritual blessing" (1:3) and the numerous benefits, including enablement, from receiving God's grace (1:6; see also 2:5, 7, 8; 3:2, 7, 8; 4:7; 6:24). Believers may now also experience a foretaste of God's glory (Eph 3:16; see also Eph 1:6, 17, 18; 3:21). As the chosen and elect people of God, believers possess an invulnerability to the perceived "powers" of fate (1:4). Believers now also share in the brilliance of God's "light" (Eph 5:8, 9) and share also in the "fullness" of God (Eph 1:23) in increasing measure (Eph 3:19; 4:13).

Beyond these direct statements and expressions encouraging the readers as to the strength available to them from God are four theological emphases stressing the accessibility to divine power. (1) The *cosmic Christology* of Ephesians highlights the supremacy of the Lord Jesus Christ to "all things," especially the malignant angelic "powers." The epistle stresses the close identification of the believer with this cosmic Christ, with the result that they now share in the power and authority of Christ over the hostile "powers." Their lives are no longer held in thrall by these forces. (2) The emphasis on *realized eschatology* stresses the significance of the identification of the believer with the resurrection and exaltation of Christ (see the next section). This denotes divine enablement to the readers and power for resisting the evil forces. The spatial emphasis within the eschatology communicates to the readers their transfer from one sphere of power to another.

(3) Ephesians reflects a two-fold development in *ecclesiology*, first by setting forth the metaphor of the head–body to depict the relationship between Christ and his church and secondly by employing the concept of "fullness" to describe the resources with which the church has been divinely endowed. In Eph 1:23 the church is explicitly described as the "fullness" (τὸ σῶμα = τὸ πλήρωμα). This is true of the church because it constitutes the body of Christ himself. The church thus shares in his divine power. The πλήρωμα properly belongs to Christ (Eph 4:13), however, and ultimately belongs to God the Father (Eph 3:19). When Christ is called the "head" of the church

(his body), his role as its leader and sustainer is prominent. As we noted before, when the author coordinates κεφαλή and σῶμα, he is using an analogy based not only on the OT notion of corporate personality, but also on the common medical understanding of his day, which regarded the head as the control center and enabling force of the body. Kōshi Usami rightly thinks that one of the main concerns of Ephesians is to "somatize" the awareness of the power of God.[43] The church as the πλήρωμα and as the "body" linked with the "head" is the agent of the one who is endeavoring to fill all things completely (Eph 1:23), viz. by the divinely empowered and directed church fulfilling its mission to the lost world. The concept of πλήρωμα also signifies the dynamic for spiritual growth (Eph 3:19). With this in mind, Cerfaux rightly describes πλήρωμα in these two epistles as "the concentration of the sanctifying power of God."[44]

(4) Ephesians also has a distinct *pneumatological accent*. For Paul, the Holy Spirit functions as the power of God in the present Messianic age. The Spirit is the agent of God conveying to believers the results of Christ's work on the cross in its redemptive presence and power. Paul can therefore say to the Thessalonians that the gospel came to them "in power" and "in the Holy Spirit" (1:5). In Ephesians, the Holy Spirit is in fact explicitly presented as the agent of divine enablement for the believer (3:16).[45] The Spirit's function here is also intimately connected with the indwelling of Christ as the agent of power (3:17). The Spirit is also presented in Ephesians as illuminating to believers their access to the power of God (1:17–19) and as being their strength for engaging in spiritual warfare (6:17). Giving a place to the devil, the ruler of the kingdom of darkness, and falling into sin grieves the Holy Spirit (4:30), who has been granted to believers as the power to prevent them from falling and to help them resist the evil one. The Holy Spirit has been given as a seal and "down payment" of the divine inheritance of the believer (1:13–14; 4:30; cf. Rom 8:23; 2 Cor 1:22; 5:5).

A theology of glory?

With the distinct emphasis on the believer's access to divine power in Ephesians it is important to ask whether the epistle is arguing for a triumphalism and therefore forsaking "the word of the cross" with its attendant suffering as part of discipleship. This question acquires more significance when one realizes that Ephesians never mentions "weakness" (ἀσθένεια), a concept important to Paul in a number of contexts where he simultaneously speaks of experiencing the enabling power of God.[46]

Martin Luther stressed a "theology of the cross" which became an important focal point in the theology of the Reformation — the Christian's "progress" is to be a "regress" to the foot of the cross. The "theology of the cross" emphasized that suffering and weakness are an inherent part of discipleship exemplified in Jesus' own suffering and patterned also in the life of the apostle Paul. Divine power is experienced within this context of suffering and distress. The importance of a "theology of the cross" is being reasserted by German theologians as an essential part of the NT teaching.[47] Work has also been done by German NT scholars on arriving at a more precise definition on what constitutes the Pauline "theology of the cross" (*Kreuzestheologie*).[48] Apart from the references to the atoning death of Jesus, Paul, according to P. Stuhlmacher, sees the crucified Christ as the pattern for the church in his obedience through suffering. Paul identifies himself closely with the suffering of Christ so that his own suffering existence becomes the primary and living commentary on his "theology of the cross."[49] Suffering becomes an integral part of discipleship not only through imitating the pattern of Christ and Paul, but by continuing the ministry of Jesus through the "body of Christ" and by bearing the burdens of the weak in manifesting Christ's love.[50] It is in this suffering estate that the church will experience the Spirit as the power and the presence of the resurrected one.[51]

Some interpreters have objected to this picture of Paul's alleged "theology of the cross" as too one-sided. H. Nielsen has recently argued the most effectively against the apparent myopic tendency in *Kreuzestheologie*.[52] She concedes that it should not be doubted that believers should live in the sphere of the cross with the consequential weakness, suffering, and distresses as, for example, Paul's catalogs of hardships make plain. She objects, however, that *Kreuzestheologie* has too exclusive a character in so far as the cross, weakness, and suffering receive such a one-sided emphasis that other aspects of Pauline thought are discriminated against.[53] Specifically, she denies the claim that the power and glory of God only come to expression in suffering and distress as a signature of the cross.[54] She adequately defends her thesis by assessing Paul's δύναμις statements in combination with his concept of glory, kingdom, and Spirit with their present relevance for the Christian life. For example, passages such as 1 Cor 2:4–5, 1 Thess 1:5, and Gal 3:5 can speak of the visible display of the power of God without any indication, implicit or explicit, that it is concealed in weakness.[55] She also concludes that the Pauline references to δύναμις and ἀσθένεια (e.g. 2 Cor 12:10) should not be construed as a paradox, but more in terms of a dialectic. Weakness should be viewed as an emptiness, a part of the experience of man in a transitory and sinful world which the power of God can fill.[56] Paul is not saying that the power of God only comes to expression in an exceptional time of weakness and distress, although this would be the case as well, but that the power of God is received by man, who is inherently weak. J.C. Beker independently reaches a similar conclusion with regard to the Pauline epistles:[57]

> I therefore conclude that Paul often speaks of the Spirit in an inherently triumphant manner that prevents its integral relation with the weakness and suffering of the crucified Christ. In the context of the Pauline hermeneutic of the Spirit, it is questionable whether the risen Christ "at the right hand of God" remains the crucified one (vs. Moltmann).

If one accepts the conclusions of Nielsen in terms of a modified "theology of the cross," the incessant references to the power of God available to the believer become more palatable as part of a truly Pauline "theology of the cross." Ephesians has certainly not forsaken references to the "cross" and allusions to suffering. It was the suffering work of Christ on the cross and the shedding of his blood that has brought about the reconciliation of Jews and Gentiles into one body to God (Eph 2:16). Christ had to experience death (νεκρός) before he could be raised and exalted above the "powers" (1:20). As in the accepted epistles, Paul is presented in Ephesians as the suffering minister experiencing tribulations (Eph 3:13; 4:1; 6:20), but carried along by the power of God (Eph 3:7). Paul's life is exemplary for the readers.

It can safely be assumed that the readers of Ephesians suffered because of the fact that they were still a part of the present world. As such, they were still susceptible to the vicious attacks of the demonic "powers," they still possessed flesh and blood, and they were still encumbered by their "old self" even though they were in the midst of the painful process of removing it. Because of these influences, they retained a penchant to commit sin and could therefore experience the distressful consequences of their actions which included grieving the Holy Spirit of God. Above all, if my hypothesis of the situation behind the epistle holds true, the readers perceived themselves as truly weak and helpless in front of the very powerful and seemingly compelling influences of the evil spirits. Although the author never mentions weakness, it is clearly in the background as the realistic experience of the readers. The power of God is then presented by our author as available to the believers to fill this vacuum and void. The author is therefore not arguing for an ecclesiastical triumphalism. He is writing to encourage believers who are losing altitude in their holding pattern of "resisting" the evil forces.

Ethics

Ephesians has traditionally been described in terms of two overall sections, a doctrinal section spanning the first half of the epistle (chs. 1–3) and an ethical section constituting the latter half of the epistle (chs. 4–6). In spite of its oversimplification, this schema correctly implies the presence of numerous admonitions in the latter half of the epistle including a lengthy household-code (5:21–6:9). This section of the epistle together with the ethical teaching of chs. 1–3 needs to be discussed in relation to the setting I am postulating as behind the epistle.

(i) *Resisting the demonic "powers."* I have already discussed at length the fact that Ephesians places a very significant stress on equipping believers to resist the influence of demonic forces (6:10–20). This section on "spiritual warfare," while constituting the concluding section to the paraenesis, is actually the apex of the paraenesis. The whole of the epistle is moving in this direction. It focuses on the unseen dimension of Christian existence, envisioning a host of evil spiritual forces under the leadership of the devil continuing to assail believers and causing them to fall. Granted that believers have experienced a transfer out of the compelling influence of this dark dominion, they are still susceptible to its influence and can only resist it by appropriating the power of God. Surely such a message would be applicable to all Christians living within the Hellenistic world in the first century, but Paul or the other NT epistolary writers never discuss this dimension of life at such length and with such forcefulness. This emphasis, as I have been suggesting, is best explained by the writer of Ephesians explicitly addressing himself to this issue having been motivated by the exigency of a group of readers perceiving themselves as facing intense demonic hostility.

(ii) *Living by the pattern of Christ.* Conducting oneself on the basis of love is the foundational ethical command of Ephesians (and Colossians).[58] This love is patterned on the ultimate example of

Christ himself: "and walk in love, as Christ loved us and gave himself up for us" (Eph 5:2). This is the same love that impelled God to provide Christ as the sacrifice (Eph 5:1) which believers are likewise admonished to imitate. The power of God is not only intended to help believers resist the evil forces, but also to enable them to love in accordance with this pattern. If the readers are strengthened by the Holy Spirit, which means that Christ is dwelling in their hearts, the result is a rooting and founding in love (Eph 3:17). The prayer of 3:14ff. is expressly for divine inner strengthening in order that the believers might be established in love (3:17, 19) and ultimately that they might express their love in the life of the community (4:2, 15, 16; 5:2, 25, 28, 33).

(iii) *Taking off the old self – putting on the new self.* Now that believers have experienced a change of rule by being transferred into the domain of Christ's rule (perhaps illustrated by baptism), their conduct needs to be made consistent with their new status and position. The Ephesian author writes, "put off your old self which belongs to your former manner of life ... and put on the new self, created after the likeness of God in true righteousness and holiness" (Eph 4:24). This tension between the old order and the new corresponds to Paul's use of the indicative-imperative.[59] As in the accepted epistles, the imperative urges the believer to remain in the lordship of Christ and not to allow him to be enslaved again by the former powers.[60]

The fact that the imperative is still operative in Ephesians combined with the additional fact that the hostile spiritual "powers" are still assailing the church should warn one against assuming that the author has displaced the apocalyptic future glory in favor of the universal dominion of the church as the body of Christ.[61] In fact, the extra emphasis on the "powers" of evil in Ephesians and on the two dominions structure heightens the reality of the believers' continued existence in the old order and consequently stresses the need to appropriate the resources of the new order – the power of God through the indwelling Christ and his Spirit.

(iv) *Faith.* The power of God can only be appropriated to resist the evil forces, to put on the new self, and to continue Christ's redemptive mission by the exercise of faith. Thus the author writes that the empowering Christ can only indwell their hearts "through faith" (3:17). It is only to those who exercise faith that the Spirit can make known the incomparably great power of God (1:19). Faith functions as a shield by which "all the flaming darts of the evil one" can be quenched (6:16). Their faith had been an essential part of securing their transfer of dominions, viz. their salvation (2:8), and is now a prerequisite for further spiritual progress. One of the clearest expressions of faith in God is through prayer. The Ephesian author thus prays for his readers to understand the vastness of the divine power available to them (1:15ff.) and to experience inner strengthening through the power of the indwelling Christ and Spirit (3:14ff.). He finally presents prayer as the prerequisite and means of gaining access to the power of God (6:18–19).

(v) *The household-code.* The household-code of 5:21–6:9 demonstrates that the sovereign rule of Christ is relevant and essential to every area of life of the believers in western Asia Minor. The power of God has not been provided to them merely to alleviate their dread of the hostile "powers," but to enable them to conduct themselves according to proper Christian ethics in the household.

The Ephesian household-code distinguishes itself from others (e.g. Colossians & 1 Peter) by an elongated section on the relationship of the husband and wife in marriage (5:21–33). In the passage, the husband is called upon to love his wife sacrificially and the woman is enjoined to subordinate herself to the leadership of her husband as κεφαλή. Markus Barth has recently made the novel suggestion that this passage may contain a factual though critical dialogue with the Cybele–Artemis tradition (see chapter 2).[62] If Barth's observation is true, it further supports my contention that the pervasive influence of the cult of the Ephesian Artemis is a concern to the author of Ephesians.

Mission

Ephesians stands in the center of Pauline tradition with regard to the missionary task of the church.[63] Mission is a definite implication of the head–body imagery where the readers are presented with a dynamic picture of a body empowered and directed by its head to penetrate the world with the gospel. The growth of the body in Ephesians is not only to be understood in an intensive sense but also in an extensive sense through the world-wide mission.[64] Paul is still represented as the servant of God with the commission to preach the gospel to every creature (Eph 3:7–10).

One of the most striking ways the mission of the church is presented is as an offensive maneuver against the kingdom of evil in the warfare in which the saints are engaged (Eph 6:10–20). The military imagery describes both the task of mission and the divine enabling power for fulfilling the task. The author depicts the mission in the context of spiritual warfare to heighten the expectation of the readers for encountering demonic opposition and their need to continue the mission with the power God will supply. The concept of divine enablement for the task of mission is brought into strong relief in the head–body imagery.

5. Eschatology and salvation

Realized eschatology in Ephesians

Interpreters of Ephesians have discerningly noticed an apparent stress on "realized eschatology" in the epistle. In attempting to understand the author's motive, many have argued that he must have been heavily influenced by Gnostic or Hellenistic categories of thought. They detect in Ephesians a noticeable shift away from Jewish apocalyptic categories and a salvation-historical framework; the Pauline emphasis on the imminent return of Christ has given way to the new accent on the present rule of Christ.[65] It is true that in many of the Gnostic texts one encounters a spiritualized significance imparted to the apocalyptic resurrection terminology.[66] The main problems facing the interpreter in using this Gnostic material as part of the religions-historical background of Ephesians are the late date of the Gnostic texts and, more importantly, the uncertainty as to whether these texts portray a widespread de-apocalypticizing process occurring in Pauline and pre-Pauline times. In the discussion of Gnosis in chapter 2, I brought forth evidence casting doubt on the existence of "Gnosticism" as a viable system in the first century and before. The catalyst for the development of the anti-cosmic dualism probably postdated the composition of Ephesians. This does not exclude the possibility of early forms of Gnosis developing. I suggested, however, that a more accurate approach would be to refer to religious traditions *known* to be in existence and known to have been contributing factors to Gnosis, rather than reading the texts of the fully developed Gnostic systems back into the first century. One further complicating factor is the clear later Christian influence discernible in passages in Gnostic texts where there is also an adaptation of apocalyptic ideas.[67]

Other interpreters attempt to demonstrate that there is an authentic "parousia" expectation present in Ephesians with apocalyptic coordinates. Most of these interpreters would regard Ephesians as Pauline and describe the eschatology of Ephesians more in terms of emphasis rather than discontinuity with the accepted Paulines.[68] A weakness of this approach is that it does not give an adequate explanation for the emphasis on "realized eschatology" in Ephesians.

In his recent monograph on the eschatology of Ephesians and Colossians, Horacio Lona has attempted to find an answer to the question of authorial intent concerning the unique accents of the eschatology of Ephesians. He contends that future expectation was not consumed by the present experience of salvation in Ephesians.[69] He agrees with Lindemann, however, that there is not a "concrete eschatology" in Ephesians in the sense that it employs the common Pauline expressions, but he affirms that there is indeed a future eschatology. Although he does not see the author of Ephesians as Paul, he argues that the eschatological outlook is essentially Pauline.[70] Of special interest to us is how he makes a serious attempt to relate the eschatology of the epistle to a general situation, or crisis, facing the churches in western Asia Minor.[71] As part of the essential backdrop to the epistle, he points to the pervasive influence of a general crisis affecting the entire Hellenistic world as it was being integrated into the universal political rule of Rome.[72] In spite of the apparent unity Rome was bringing to the empire, individuals felt lonely and estranged. The once ordered cosmos was now viewed as the embodiment of evil and full of demonic "powers." Lona characterizes the period as a time of "world-anxiety" (*Weltangst*) induced by the realization that the world is unstable and under the influence of evil demonic powers easily capable of causing chaos.[73] Lona characterizes the Hellenistic world as finding new answers to these fresh problems through: (1) religious experience in the mystical cults (Lona cites the Ephesian Artemis as a prominent example) which could bring escape from the world and deliverance, and (2) worship of the "elemental spirits" for protection from the sinister "powers."[74] The church faced the danger of responding to this *Weltangst* in the same way as the heathen world. It is to this overwhelming concern that Lona finds the author of Ephesians tailoring his eschatological statements.[75] The result, according to Lona, is that the Ephesian author emphasized the presence of salvation in history to strengthen Christians facing the mounting threats of their environment.

Lona's analysis has brought us a long way in better understanding the author's motive for highlighting the presence of the future for those who are in Christ. I will now examine some specific aspects of the eschatology of Ephesians in light of the setting I propose for the epistle – a setting which corresponds in a general way to that suggested by Lona. My remarks will go beyond those of Lona by specifically anchoring the epistle to the religious climate of western Asia Minor.

Resurrection and exaltation with Christ (Eph 2:4–10)

The crux for discerning the author's understanding of eschatology and salvation is Eph 2:4–10. In this passage, the power of God brilliantly shines forth as the power bringing life out of the dead. Believers are said to have been made alive together with Christ, raised up with him, and made to sit with him in the heavenly places in Christ Jesus. This powerful work of God on behalf of the believer is set forth in a series of three σύν-compounds – συνεζωοποίησεν, συνήγειρεν, and συνεκάθισεν. The writer summarizes this status of the believer with the phrase, "you have been saved" (ἔστε σεσῳσμένοι, vv. 5, 8).

There is surely no doubt that the author has emphasized the present aspect of salvation to a degree unparalleled in Paul. Is there an explanation for this emphasis? Apart from the work of Lona there has been no serious attempt to treat this question of motivation.

J. T. Sanders takes a large first step in answering the question of authorial motive when he observes that, "these verses [2:4–7] set salvation over against the cosmic "powers," who are described in 2:1–3 as ruling over the pre-Christian person."[76] Salvation is thus described as deliverance from the power and influence of the cosmic "powers."

A similar argument was employed by the author of Colossians to affirm the secure position of the believer in his identification with Christ in relation to the hostile "powers" (Col 2:12ff.). In fact, two of the σύν- compounds are also found in Colossians (συνεγείρω: 2:12; 3:1; συνζωοποιέω: 2:13). It is important to recognize that the Colossian author gives this particular explanation of their baptism to assure them of their complete identification with Christ – including co-resurrection – as the basis of their freedom from the tyranny of the hostile forces. Resurrection has only been "realized" insofar as the believer has been identified with the resurrection of Christ as depicted in baptism. This does not exclude or contradict the possibility of an actual future resurrection of the believer. Indeed, this future resurrection is implicit in Col 3:4:

"when Christ who is our life appears, then you also will appear with him in glory."

Because of the hostile role of the "powers" as presented in the larger context of Ephesians (2:1–2; 1:20–22), it is probable that Eph 2:4–7 also seeks to stress the salvation of believers from the spiritual "powers." This theological purpose holds true whether one sees Eph 2:4–7 as having its source in a Christian hymn also used by Colossians,[77] or whether one sees this section as a reworking of Col 2:10–13.[78]

It appears that the author of Ephesians has taken the terminology of 1:20ff. concerning the resurrection and exaltation of Christ and has applied it to the Christian in 2:4ff.[79] As the reader of Ephesians would digest the significance of 2:5–6, he would first, and most importantly, realize that he has been resurrected and exalted with Christ to a position of power and authority far superior to the hostile cosmic "powers." Because of the presence of salvation, the believer no longer lives under the authority and compulsion of the "prince of the authority of the air" (2:2).

The Ephesian author stresses the notion of "co-seating" (συνκαθίζω), an expression foreign to the accepted Paulines and even Colossians. It should simultaneously be observed that there is no other theological construct which could so effectively and vividly communicate to the readers their access to the authority and power of the risen Lord. The thought is not substantially different than what is expressed in Col 3:1–2. Since believers have been raised with Christ, they have the right to seek the things at the right hand of God where Christ is seated. Neither is the concept of co-seating at variance with Pauline thought, where the idea of a present experience of heaven can be found (cf. Gal 4:26; 1 Cor 15:47–49; 2 Cor 12:2, 3; Phil 3:20).[80]

It is important to note that the resurrection and ascension of the believer are not described by the author as having realistically occurred; these events are qualified by "*in* Christ Jesus" (2:6). It is only through identification with the death and resurrection of Christ that the believer experiences the benefits of these events. The door has thus not been closed to a future resurrection of the believer; the Pauline baptismal identification (Rom 6) has merely been expressed in different terms. The fact that the author can refer to a "coming age"(1:21; 2:7) confirms that a future eschatology has not been entirely displaced by the author's emphasis on the presence of salvation.[81]

God intends to lavish the full abundance of his grace upon believers in the coming age. This grace has only partially been manifested to believers in the present age by procuring their salvation. By divine grace (2:5, 8), the believer has now been saved from entrapment in the kingdom of the prince of the authority of the air.

The writer of Ephesians is not advocating an ecclesiastical triumphalism when he proclaims, "you have been saved" (ἔστε σεσῳσμένοι); rather he is portraying salvation as a "rescue act" accomplished on behalf of believers through their inclusion in what God accomplished for Christ (cf. 1:20, 21).[82] The author probably used the perfect tense of σῴζω instead of justification language for two additional reasons. (1) He does not appear to be engaged with Judaizing opponents who are making an issue out of obedience to the law; therefore, the more general concept of "salvation" rather than the juridical justification terminology is more appropriate (e.g. Gal 2:16: "by works of the law shall no one be justified"). The author asserts that no one is saved by works (2:9), but he does not refer to "works of the law." Lincoln may therefore be correct in assuming a predominantly Gentile readership and arguing that the works of the *law* are not primarily in view, especially since the only reference to ὁ νόμος occurs in a passage which reminds Gentiles of what God did in the past to allow them access to the God of Israel (2:15).[83] "You have been justified" would not be an accurate summary of the three σύν compounds, whereas "you have been saved" does accurately tie together the inherent meaning of the propositions. The overriding issue for the readers is the dread of demonic influence, not a threat from Jewish legalists. (2) The perfect tense more accurately depicts the significance of the transfer of dominions procured for the believer by the work of God through Christ. The perfect tense, denoting a condition or state as a result of a past action, as used of σῴζω in Ephesians, refers to the temporal work of Christ (resurrection-exaltation) with which the believer has been temporally identified (in baptism) and which inaugurated for the believer a new and continuing mode of existence ("made alive with Christ").

The author of Ephesians in no way conceives of salvation as fully realized. He can speak of a coming age, a future consummation (1:10), and an upcoming "day of redemption" (4:30). Believers do not yet live in a perfect world free from the influence of sin and the devil. On the contrary, believers live in a time in which spiritual warfare is essential (6:10–20) and they face the dangerous threat of an opponent who launches fiery arrows (6:16), intending to cause them to fall into sin (4:27). These same believers have not yet attained perfect knowledge (4:13) and have not experientially reached the fullness of God (3:19). Since these believers still live in the world and have not experienced the full installment of their salvation, they need to be admonished and encouraged to live by Christian ethics (Eph 4–6). Since this world is controlled by an evil prince surrounded by a host of hostile minions bent on destroying Christians, believers need to be reminded of the power and authority that is theirs in Christ.

The "once–now" schema

In addition to the statements about co-resurrection and co-ascension, some contemporary exegetes have detected a more extensive shift away from the Jewish linear time concept in the epistle. This evidence has led H. Conzelmann to conclude, "In Ephesians the spatial idea has nearly displaced the time concept which was characteristic of Paul."[84] H. Merklein concurs: "The contrast is no longer present versus future, but under versus above. The Eschaton is no longer in the future, but above."[85] As evidence, interpreters point chiefly to two aspects of the worldview presented in the epistle which are at the apex of the controversy: (1) the "once–now" (ποτέ–νῦν) schema, and (2) the heavenly dimension – "ἐν τοῖς ἐπουρανίοις."

Past and present are brought into focus and contrasted in the "once–now" schema. The idea of ποτέ–νῦν as being part of a "schema" has been advocated by P. Tachau.[86] This so-called schema does occur a number of times in Ephesians and appears to be integral to the argument of the epistle. A clear example of its use can be found in Eph 5:8: "for 'once' you were darkness, but 'now' you are light in the Lord." It is also found throughout Eph 2:1–22 (cf. the use of ποτέ in vv. 2, 3, 11, 13). The schema is not unique to Ephesians, however, but occurs in Colossians, Paul, and other epistles.

Tachau regards Eph 2 as representing the high point in the history of the ποτέ–νῦν schema because of its prominence and also because of its development.[87] He contends that, in contrast to its use in Paul (and elsewhere in the NT), there is no historical development of the "once–now" schema in Ephesians. The past serves exclusively to qualify the present. "Once–now" serves only to make plain the "having been taken out of existence" (*Herausgenommen-Sein*) of the Christian from his sphere of bondage. The implication of the "once–now" schema for 2:11–22, as Tachua and Lindemann[88] see it, is the elimination of a *heilsgeschichtlich* point to the passage.

A time antithesis (*Zeitantithetik*) has been collapsed into a space antithesis (*Raumantithetik*).

These results need to be tempered to some degree. The "once–now" schema must be interpreted by the way it is used by the author of the epistle. I have already demonstrated that our author does employ the Jewish two-age concept. In his most complete contrast between the "once" and the "now" (2:1–7), the author includes the temporal coordinate of the present age (2:2)[89] alongside a reference to the future age (2:7). The Jewish concept of time has thus not been totally displaced, but it is indisputably over-shadowed by the stress on the present aspects of the future. We can thus completely agree with the statement of Tachau, "the full effectiveness of salvation in the present cannot be emphasized more strongly."[90]

I would suggest that the writer of Ephesians employed this schema extensively to emphasize the absolute transfer of dominions experienced by the believer. The concern of the author was to demonstrate the decisive break with their pagan past which the readers experienced when they turned to Christ. The spatial emphasis helps the author to communicate to the readers that they are no longer under the power and compelling influence of the hostile supernatural "powers," viz. according to the sway of "the prince of the authority of the air [filled with demonic forces], the spirit now 'energizing' the sons of disobedience."

The heavenly dimension

The author has consistently used the expression ἐν τοῖς ἐπουρανίοις in very close connection with the statements regarding divine power and the "powers" of evil in Ephesians. The "powers" of evil are in the immediate context of its use in all passages except 1:3. Correspondingly, either an explicit or an implicit reference to the divine power is present in conjunction with all of its occurrences in Ephesians. The nature and significance of this correspondence needs to be explored.

There is general agreement that the expression maintains a consistent meaning in its five appearances in the epistle (1:3, 20; 2:6; 3:10; 6:12) and that it should be taken as local in significance.[91] The overarching issue continues to be whether the author has been influenced by Hellenistic thought in his use of the expression or whether he remains in continuity with Paul and Jewish thought.

Have temporal associations given way to a fully spiritualized sense?
Is the expression to be taken literally or figuratively?

Those who argue for the influence of Gnosis on the author of the
epistle obviously explain the references along mythological or
spiritualized lines.[92] H. Schlier, seeing Gnostic influence, interprets
the phrase existentially as the transcendental dimension of human
existence.[93] "Heaven" thus becomes the possibility of life under the
rule of Christ as juxtaposed to life under the rule of the hostile
"powers." Others, following Greek philosophical thought, viz. Plato,
define the expression in terms of eternal timeless reality.[94]

In spite of these efforts, there does not appear to be sufficient
evidence for overruling the Jewish background of the expression in
its use here. There are clear lexical antecedents in Paul, who uses the
adjectival form (1 Cor 15:40, 48, 49; Phil 2:10). It was also familiar
to Matthew (18:35) and the writer of Hebrews (3:1; 6:4; 8:5; 9:23;
11:16; 12:22). The form does occur in the LXX, although it is rare.[95]
According to 2 Macc 3:39 it is the abode of God: ὁ τὴν κατοικίαν
ἐπουράνιον ἔχων. A. T. Lincoln has drawn additional Jewish parallels
which convincingly demonstrate the correspondence of the use of the
expression in Ephesians with Jewish thought.[96] Lincoln develops his
view by affirming the identity of ἐπουρανίοι with οὐρανίοι.[97]

There is an occurrence of the term ἐπουράνιος in a magical
papyrus (*PGM* IV.3042) which some adduce as an example of
its use in Hellenism parallel to its use in Eph 3:10 and 6:12.[98] The
line where it occurs is part of a recipe for exorcism in which the
exorcist is instructed to say to the demon: "So say of what sort
you might be, whether heavenly (ἐπουράνιον) or of the air, whether
upon the earth (ἐπίγειον), under the earth (ὑπόγειον), or under the
world (καταχθόνιον)!" The immediate context of this recipe reveals
a strong Jewish influence, probably from the Solomonic magical
tradition. The text specifically refers to the seal of Solomon (line 3040)
and the God Sabaoth's rescue of Israel through the Jordan and the
Red Sea (lines 3052ff.). It is quite conceivable, but assuredly only
speculative, that the Ephesian author and the readers of the epistle
were familiar with this term from their acquaintance with Solomonic
magical traditions. There is a strong line of evidence linking these
traditions with Ephesus and western Asia Minor (see chapter 2, section
7). If this assumption is correct, it would certainly help to explain the
striking frequency of the compound throughout the epistle in contexts
where it is used of the dwelling place of hostile "powers." It is certain,
however, that the recipe does reflect Jewish thought forms.[99]

Some have attempted to explain the distinctiveness of the compound form (ἐπι + οὐρανίοι) on the basis of the alleged liturgical background of the epistle.[100] It is also possible, as we have seen above, that the author may have used it because of its familiarity to the readers from the magical traditions with which they had formerly been acquainted. The readers may also have known the term from its use in Asia Minor. It occurs on a burial inscription found in Magnesia ad Sipylum in reference to the abode of divine beings: ἀλλὰ ὤλη πανώλη γένοισαν καὶ τοὺς ἐπουρανίους καὶ καταχθονίους θεοὺς κεχολωμένους ἔχοισαν.[101]

As used by the author of Ephesians, the expression places heaven in a Pauline eschatological perspective.[102] Lincoln observes how Paul maintains the Jewish two-age structure with heaven participating in the evil nature of the present age and also in the renewal of the age to come. Paul presents two developments in this idea. First, the two ages are now seen as overlapping as a result of the Christ event. The believer is regarded as involved in two spheres of existence simultaneously.[103] Secondly, Paul speaks not only of a linear aspect of this two-age structure, but now also of a vertical aspect. In this way, Paul (and also Ephesians) can employ *both* spatial and temporal terms since they are bound together as both heaven and earth are involved in the two-age structure.

It is important to note that within this tension between spatial and temporal concepts, circumstances can dictate whether the writer places emphasis on one side or the other.[104] The advocates of the spatial view are correct in affirming the spatial aspect, but their final results are skewed by not recognizing the temporal, two-age aspect of the phrase seen in conjunction with the future statements of the epistle (see figure 1 for an illustration of the worldview of the epistle).

Why, then, the emphasis on the spatial aspect in Ephesians? Lincoln himself points to the author's probable concern about aberrant influences similar to the Colossian syncretism. He rightly points to the author's concern to stress the readers' freedom from hostile cosmic "powers" and access to the fullness of the divine presence.[105] He goes beyond this, however, by suggesting that the epistle subtly polemicizes against a radical cosmic dualism presumably advocated by the Colossian errorists.[106] The evidence for the popularity of such an anti-cosmic dualism in western Asia Minor in the first century is based more on the assumption that the basic forms of Gnosis were already present rather than on traditions known to exist in that locale at that time. On the other hand, fear of the hostile cosmic "powers"

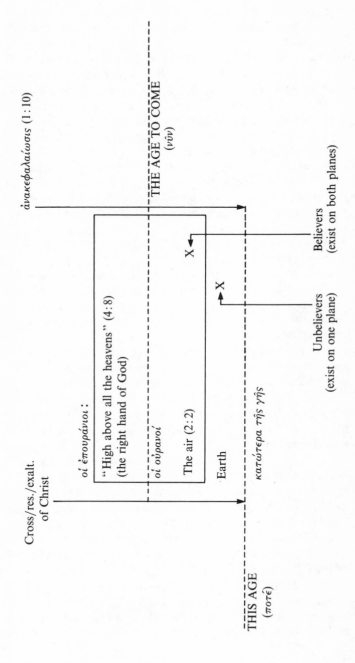

Figure 1 The worldview of Ephesians

was known to exist and the issue likewise appears to be a major concern of the author of Ephesians. The author's emphasis on the heavenly realm and the spatial category is probably closely connected with his concern to address the issue of the "powers."

The author wants to assure his readers that they are not in a weak and vulnerable position with respect to the "powers."[107] On the contrary, they have been co-raised and co-seated with Christ Jesus "in the heavenly places" (2:6). The author categorically declares that this position at the right hand of God "in the heavenly places" is infinitely greater than the power and authority of all the cosmic "powers" (1:20–21; cf. 4:10). This access to divine power and position of authority is undoubtedly one of the spiritual blessings "in the heavenly places" referred to at the outset of the epistle (1:3). Although these "powers" once controlled their conduct and still control that of non-believers (2:2–3), they no longer need to fear the "powers" or live under their dominating control. By virtue of the work of Christ and their union with him, believers now also have a position of power and authority "in the heavenly places" where the "powers" are (3:10; 6:12). Believers can be assured of victorious warfare against the powerful spiritual forces of evil since they occupy a position in the heavenly places with substantially more authority than the "powers" (1:20–21; 4:10). Powerful diabolic assaults are not resisted on the basis of one's own strength or by reliance on magical techniques, but on the basis of the strength that belongs to believers as children of the new age who have access to heavenly power through their union with Christ.

Battle imagery and eschatology

Eph 6:10–20 contains the most extensive use of battle imagery in any of the letters attributed to Paul. The undisputed epistles reveal that Paul himself was quite fond of military terminology; he employed it in his epistles on a number of occasions, with many of the terms found also in Eph 6. In her study of battle imagery in Paul's letters, Barbara Hall found that Paul's use of the terms provides an insight into his understanding of eschatology. She concludes, "Military terminology comes to Paul's mind first of all and repeatedly in the context of thought about the imminent parousia of Christ; that is, when he thinks of the present time under the impact of the Day."[108] According to Hall, Paul employs military terminology to describe the nature of the Christian life as a life of conflict. God has acted decisively in Jesus Christ and the turn of the ages has occurred in some sense, but the Kingdom of God is not yet fully present, it awaits the parousia. Believers have been liberated from the sphere of power controlled by Satan, but their liberation gives them the freedom to fight. They fight with the weapons with which God has endowed them: indeed, the weaponry is the power of God itself.[109]

OT and Jewish thought are seen by Hall to be at the background of Paul's way of thinking here.[110] She also points to the direct influence of the book of Isaiah (e.g. 11:5; 52:7; 59:17) on passages such as 1 Thess 5:8 and 2 Cor 6:7,[111] as well as the passages referring to the day of the Lord as including battle (e.g. Ezek 7:14; Joel 2:1; Zeph 1:16; Zech 9:14).

In a very brief section, Anton Grabner-Haider also discusses the relationship of God's eschatological battle to present Christian experience as presented by Paul.[112] He too affirms that Paul uses battle imagery to describe a present Christian involvement in this final struggle.

Ironically, the discussion on spiritual warfare in Eph 6:10–20 has been largely neglected in the debate on the eschatology of Ephesians. It is also unfortunate that B. Hall has completely omitted any reference to Ephesians in her study, which analyzes only the accepted epistles of Paul. Most of those who explain Ephesians in terms of Hellenistic or Gnostic categories ignore 6:10–20 and do not make an attempt to explain it in terms of a fully realized eschatology.[113]

It is my contention that the passage presents a major, if not insurmountable, difficulty for those advocating a fully realized eschatology in Ephesians (see chapter 5). The fact that the author believes in the existence of a devil and a host of evil "powers" set on assailing believers is not consistent with a fully realized eschatology. If, in some very real sense, Christians have been resurrected and seated in heaven (versus mere identification with Christ), then the author could not think of falling as a very real danger. The notion of "giving a place to the devil" (4:27) and the rigorous paraenesis of chapters 4–6 would not be necessary. Gnostic ideology, harboring a strong antipathy toward the world, has little interest in ethical issues. Its concentration is focused on the world above and the unworldly nucleus of man.[114] Further, those who argue against any temporal coordinates in Ephesians overlook three apocalyptic concepts in 6:10–20: (1) "this darkness," (2) "the evil day," and (3) "watching."

The Pauline idea of eschatological tension expressed by the

"now – not yet" formula better explain the evidence here than an elimination of all temporal coordinates.[115] The strong emphasis on spiritual warfare is particularly appropriate to an area fearing the influence of the hostile "powers." It provides a helpful piece of instruction to the converts of western Asia Minor on how to live "between the ages" while facing intense demonic attack.

A future consummation

The writer explicitly refers to a future consummation at the outset of the epistle (see chapter 3, section 6). He speaks of a "summing up," an ἀνακεφαλαίωσις, a time not yet at hand when everything will be brought effectively under the sovereign headship of Christ (1:10).[116] At this time the hostile "powers" will be brought into complete subjection and will no longer be the tyrannizing opponents of God's plan and his people.[117]

This will also be the "day of redemption" for which believers have been sealed by the Holy Spirit (4:30; 1:13). On this day Christ will present to himself the now glorified church as his holy and purified possession (5:27).[118] God's wrath will also be poured out on the disobedient during this future day (5:8). Christ will then rule as Lord over a world characterized by complete peace and reconciliation.

Summary

(1) It is true that Ephesians lacks some of the specific terms of the future eschatology present in Paul, for example, "the day of the Lord," "parousia," and specific references to a future resurrection. On the other hand, it should be mentioned that Ephesians does refer to "a day of redemption" and an "evil day" as well as a future age.

(2) Ephesians was found to contain a future expectation of a return of Christ. The Ephesian eschatology has not been replaced or reinterpreted according to Hellenistic or Gnostic spatial categories. This is not to deny the presence of spatial categories. Indeed, the author does stress two opposing spheres of power, with the devil, his "powers," and the world on one side and Christ, believers, and a heavenly position laden with the power and authority of God on the other.

(3) My hypothesis regarding the occasion of the epistle was found to provide a key to unlock the motive for the emphasis on spatial thought. One of the primary concerns of the author was to encourage

his readers in light of their perceived fears of the demonic realm. He sought to assure them that by virtue of their identification with Christ they possessed all the resources needed to resist the influence and attacks of the hostile "powers." He believed that an emphasis on spatial thought could effectively communicate the absolute transfer of the believer from the dominion of the devil to the dominion of Christ ("once–now"). He also believed that an emphasis on co-resurrection and co-seating could express the now superior position of the believer to the "powers" and indicate the access of the believer to divine power. These concepts, along with the summary expression "you have been saved," were not intended by the author to imply there would be no future consummation. In fact, the author indicates that there would be a future consummation by using an expression that graphically depicts that the "powers" would one day be finally brought under the headship of Christ.

6. Ecclesiology

The topic of the church has been considered the primary theme of Ephesians by some interpreters.[119] If it is not the chief theme of the epistle, it is certainly very important to the writer. This topic raises a number of difficult theological problems which could lead us far beyond the scope and purpose of this book. I will limit the discussion to assessing the author's desire to communicate the enabling power of God through some of the ecclesial images and draw the implications of our theme to the concept of "early catholicism."

Images of the church

The doctrine of the church is expressed in three images, each of which depicts an inseparable link between ecclesiology and Christology. They also portray (1) the unity of the church, and (2) the divine empowering of the church. Although the prominence of unity in these metaphors has long been recognized, the enablement idea has not been accorded sufficient recognition as part of the message conveyed by the ecclesial metaphors.

The head–body imagery comes to expression a number of times in Ephesians (Eph 1:22–23; 4:15–16; 5:23; see also Col 1:18; 2:19). I have argued against the Hellenistic "macroanthropos" derivation in favor of an OT and Jewish understanding of σῶμα as corporate personality with κεφαλή to be understood as "superior," or "ruler."

I have also found that Ephesians combined this OT view of "head" with contemporary Greek medical ideas to give parallel expression to the dynamic presence of Christ in the body (see chapter 4). As "head" Christ is not only sovereign, but is also the causation of the movement of the body, the dynamic empowering and coordinating the body.

In addition to the theme of unity, the idea of divine enablement is also evident in the picture of the church as the new temple of Eph 2:21−22. The new temple, consisting of both Jews and Gentiles, is said to be indwelt by God's Spirit (2:22). This indwelling denotes God's powerful presence in the new temple.[120] As in the concluding phrase (ἐν κυρίῳ) of the previous verse the addition of ἐν πνεύματι in v. 22 refers to the source from which the new life of believers streams. This is the power of the Spirit which is given to believers from God and now resides in the new holy temple.[121] The similarity of roles between the Spirit and Christ corresponds to the divine strengthening of believers attributed to both the Spirit and Christ in Eph 3:16−17.

Finally, there is a dual message of both unity and empowering in the section of the household-code dealing with husband and wife relationships (5:22−33). The notion of enablement is present in the idea of Christ "nourishing" the church (see above, section 2).

Christ's gifts to the church

The resurrected and ascended Christ is now setting out to "fill" all things (4:10). He is accomplishing this task through the church, which he empowers to fill all things (1:22−23) (see chapter 4, section 1). Part of the equipping which was alluded to in 1:23 is made more explicit in 4:11ff. Christ supplies the church with gifted men; he provides both charisma and office in an inseparable unity. The author then lists five categories of ministers with which he endows the church − apostles, prophets, evangelists, pastors, and teachers (4:11). Without going into extensive discussion on the precise nature and function of these particular ministries, one can observe the general role of these gifted persons in the church. Their responsibilities move in three directions. (1) They are "ministers of the word" in the sense that they provide the church with the true teaching of Christ for the edification of the body (4:12) and for the avoidance of heretical teaching (4:14). (2) They perform an edificatory ministry of facilitating and admonishing all of the members of the body to involve themselves in service with the aim of stimulating the intensive growth of the body in love and unity. (3) Finally, they facilitate the extensive growth of the body through maintaining the vitality of the mission of the church in the proclamation of the gospel to all men (4:12, 15; cf. 4:11).

This section sheds additional light on the power-motif we are tracing by providing additional insight into *how* the resurrected Christ operates within his church and what he aims to accomplish by empowering his church. It is instructive to note how the theme of power looms in the background of this passage. The church receives its gifts as a direct result of Christ's victorious siege against the principalities and "powers" (4:8; cf. 1:19–22). He has ascended to heaven, where he fills the church in order that it might fill "all things." In 'filling all things" the church sets out to complete its task of proclaiming the gospel to all people. It will be remembered that "all things" refers also to the things in heaven, viz. the principalities and "powers." The hostile "powers" are not the beneficiaries of the redemptive message, but the existence of the church testifies to the "powers" of their impending subjugation and doom (3:10) (see chapter 3, section 4).

At the end of the section, the author explicitly attributes the growth of the body to the power of God. Every individual member of the church is enabled to make a contribution to the body's growth because each has been infused with divine power from God (4:16). F.F. Bruce summarizes well the significance of the verse by commenting, "It is from him [God] that the body, in all its parts, derives its life. By his power it is 'fitted together' ... so that through all its joints or ligaments the means necessary for its development flow from the head into every limb and organ."[122] Each joint directly receives divine power (ἐνέργεια).[123] This term has been used twice before in this epistle to describe the operation of God's power (1:19; 3:7; cf. Col 2:12). In fact, Paul is presented as a model of what God's divine enabling power (ἐνέργεια) can accomplish (3:7; cf. Col 1:29). The enabling idea is also brought to expression here through the head–body metaphor. The agency of the head in imparting strength to the members of the body is seen to work in concert with the supply of enabling power from God. In this passage the physiological implications of the head–body imagery come to the fore with the life of the body depicted as proceeding from the head (see also Col 2:19). Barth then fittingly summarizes, "The head's energy does not remain external, it conveys vitality to the body."[124]

The apostle

In this section I will limit my remarks to only one aspect of the image of Paul in Ephesians — the presentation of the divine enablement of the apostle. In Eph 3:7 the apostle is said to have become a servant by (κατά) the gift of the grace of God "that is by the working of his power" (κατὰ τὴν ἐνέργειαν τῆς δυνάμεως αὐτοῦ: see also Col 1:29). What connection does this image of the apostle have with the situation of the epistle, if any, and how does it relate to the emphasis on divine power we have already observed in Ephesians?

This operative power of God in Eph 3:7 is actually a further description of the divine grace granted to the apostle. The second κατά does not coordinate the two clauses, but serves to underline and define "grace," the object of the first κατά.[125] Paul frequently spoke of the grace granted him by God to sustain his ministry (1 Cor 3:10; Rom 1:5; 12:3; 15:15; Gal 2:9; see also Eph 3:2, 8). This grace and power is further described as part of the "unfathomable riches of Christ" which comes from the gospel. This "gospel of salvation" (1:13) is a message of grace to the Gentiles (2:5, 7, 8) which not only provides them with the forgiveness of sins (1:7) but equips and enables them through their identification with Christ (2:6).

The dynamic aspect of the "grace" of God is stressed in Eph 3:7 through its modification by power terminology. A distinction between the two terms is probably in the mind of the author, with the result that ἐνέργεια stresses the operation of power and δύναμις underlines the fact and presence of power, which in this case is divine. Paul himself was well aware of the divine δύναμις enabling him and strengthening him in spite of his self-perception of bodily weakness. The risen Lord declared to Paul, "my grace is sufficient for you, for my power is made perfect in weakness," and Paul responded, "I will all the more gladly boast of my weaknesses, that the power of Christ may rest upon me" (2 Cor 12:9; see also Rom 15:19; 1 Cor 2:4–5; 2 Cor 4:7; 6:7).[126] It should be noted that the concept of "weakness" is also present in Ephesians when the apostle is described as "the least of all the saints" (3:8),[127] a "prisoner" (3:1; 4:1), and an "ambassador in chains" (6:20).

The heaping up of the power terms, a distinctive trait of Ephesians, accentuates the fact that the apostle depends solely on the enabling power of God.[128] The nature of this power is best described as resurrection power.[129] The stress on the divine enabling power in this context contributes to the emphasis on this theme throughout

Ephesians. It is stressed here not only because it is the foundational part of the apostle's existence and ministry, but also because the apostle is held up as a model or pattern to the readers.[130] The beleaguered believers in the churches in the environs of Ephesus share the same access to God's enabling power as the apostle Paul. It was only by the effective power of God that he could carry on his ministry; likewise, it is only by the power of God that the readers can continue their service. The author extols the accessibility of this power to the readers in the doxology of 3:20: κατὰ τὴν δύναμιν τὴν ἐνεργουμένην ἐν ἡμῖν. This divine enablement is prerequisite to the continuing mission of the church and effective engagement in spiritual warfare. It is also foundational for enabling (ἐνέργεια) each of the members of the body to contribute to the building up of the body in love (4:16).

Paul's example would serve both as an instructive pattern and as an inspirational model to the readers. God's power is entirely sufficient for them, as it was for Paul.

Early catholicism?

The question of early catholicism is highly relevant for our study since it directly affects how one understands the presence and operation of the divine power within the church. Some have described Ephesians as totally devoid of teaching the dynamic presence of the Spirit within the church. W. Carr, in fact, criticizes E. Käsemann for not giving this fact more recognition. Concerning Ephesians, Carr asserts, "a dynamic understanding of the Spirit is largely lacking; it is difficult to understand the Spirit in terms of Christian experience ... on the whole it is institutionalised as an accepted part of the life of the Church and scarcely shows signs of being a dynamic force."[131]

Ernst Käsemann was probably the first to describe Ephesians in terms of a tendency toward institutionalization, or "early catholicism."[132] He argues that the effectiveness of the world-wide mission necessitated a total ecclesiastical consciousness. The need was further enhanced by the historical situation of Gentile Christians gaining ascendancy, with the resultant threat of "enthusiasm" in the church. The unity of the church needed to be stressed and shielded by a thorough redefinition of the church. This new definition gave the "head" a more prominent role in giving the body cohesion versus Paul, who stressed the Spirit as ruling the body.[133] Even so, Christology lost its decisive significance and ecclesiology assumed paramount importance. In fact, Käsemann contends that *Christology has become a function of ecclesiology* in Ephesians.[134]

H. Merklein has recently attempted to modify Käsemann's view. He argues that Christology is not a function of ecclesiology, but rather Christology and ecclesiology have been incorporated into each other.[135] In this perspective the church is understood as the property of heaven and as the sphere of salvation. It is not to be regarded as an independent entity or seen in its institutional or sociological form of appearance. The church exists as an entity in Christ. Such a view of the church juxtaposing ecclesiology and Christology could lead the historical church to a flamboyant theology of glory or ecclesiastical triumphalism. Merklein argues that the Ephesian author (and Colossians) recognized this danger and tempered the "ecclesiological Christology" by altering the Pauline eschatological reservation. The Pauline temporal schema of "now—not yet" (*schon—noch nicht*) has become a spatially oriented "now—but yet" (*schon—erst noch*). He coins the formula: "*it still remains for the church to become what it already is*" (italics in original).[136] This means that the church must still first historically realize what it already is in essence in Christ through developing in knowledge, filling, growing, and building.[137] Like Käsemann, Merklein contends that soteriology has become a function of ecclesiology in Ephesians.[138]

An additional variation of the early catholic view has recently been put forward by Horacio Lona, who observes that the Christology of Ephesians has been carefully qualified by the eschatology. The eschatology in turn can be described as an *ecclesiological eschatology* (my italics).[139] The presence and future of salvation are spoken of in connection with the reality of the church. Specifically, the church represents the presence of salvation.[140] It appears that Lona would regard soteriology as a function of ecclesiology except for the fact that he sees a future aspect to the salvation presented in Ephesians. He would distinguish himself from Käsemann not only by leaving a future expectation intact in Ephesians (and Colossians), but primarily also by tying the ecclesiological developments in the epistles to a fairly specific situation (see above, section 5).

My analysis of the evidence leads to a conclusion which substantially varies from the nuanced views of these advocates of an early catholicism. I would argue that Ephesians still maintains the Pauline primacy of Christology. Specifically, *ecclesiology is a function of Christology* in Ephesians. Further, salvation is presented as a function of Christology. Christ is the one who has created the church. By his work on the cross he took away the enmity between wayward humanity and God (2:16, 18). Upon his resurrection and ascension he created a body of those identified with him. As head of the church and as the ascended and victorious Lord with power and authority, he is the one who endows his people with gifts and enabling power. Likewise, he is the one who instructs the church and gives it direction. Ultimately, the church will be presented to Christ at the consummation holy and unblemished, without spot or wrinkle (5:27). The church thus has its beginning, continuation, and consummation in Christ according to Ephesians.

There has been little attempt by interpreters to classify Colossians as a product of "early catholicism" in spite of its striking similarity to Ephesians. This derives mainly from the fact that there are occurrences of the term "church" in a local sense in Colossians, there appears to be a concrete heresy in the background, there is not a delineation of offices, and there is a strong emphasis on Christology – the main theme of the epistle appears to be the lordship of Christ.[141] Hence some interpreters have argued that ecclesiology therefore marks the decisive disjuncture between Ephesians and Colossians. I have attempted to demonstrate, however (see above, section 2), that Christology receives a very strong emphasis in Ephesians. With regard to the apparent lack of a situation in Ephesians, I have been attempting to show that there indeed is at least a general situation to which the epistle is addressed in Asia Minor. Although Ephesians refers to some "offices," they are not presented and developed as part of an organized institution. No qualifications are listed and no job description is subsequently provided; they are plainly mentioned in the context of the church building itself up in love and unity.

Kümmel finds the apparently exclusive use of ἐκκλησία in a non-local sense (1:22; 3:10, 21; 5:23–25, 27, 29, 32) an indication of the early catholic nature of the epistle.[142] This is not as large a problem as it may appear since we can safely observe that Paul was capable of using "church" to refer to more than one local church (e.g. 1 Cor 1:2; 10:32; Gal 1:13; Phil 3:6).[143] One would also expect the author to use the term "church" in a broader sense if the letter was written as a circular to a number of churches in western Asia Minor. The emphasis on unity (viz. "one body") may also have influenced his choice of the singular ("church") over the plural ("churches"). Furthermore, one cannot be certain that there was only one local church in Ephesus itself. Given the fact that Paul labored and evangelized in Ephesus for two and a half years combined with the fact that the population of Ephesus at that time could have ranged between 200,000 and 400,000, there may have been a number of "house-churches" to which the epistle circulated.

Finally, Ephesians has not lost sight of the future consummation of salvation (see above). Temporal coordinates have not given way to spatial coordinates. The church still awaits the consummation of all things by Christ (Eph 1:10; cf. Col 1:20). Christology has therefore not been subordinated to ecclesiology.

Ephesians is therefore not devoid of affirmations about the dynamic presence of the Spirit in favor of a bland institutionalization. On the contrary, the writer can pray to the Father that, "He might grant to you according to the riches of his glory to be strengthened with power *through his Spirit* in the inner man" (3:16). The epistle is filled with statements and allusions to the dynamic presence of the power of God in people (believers), not institutions. These people do not come to possess this dynamic power through merely fulfilling a rite, viz. baptism, but by the exercise of faith through prayer (1:19: 2:8; 3:17; Col 2:12).

7. Summary

(1) Ephesians was written to a general but concrete situation facing the church(es) at Ephesus and other churches in western Asia Minor. The believers needed instruction and encouragement on how to cope with the continuing influence and attacks of the sinister cosmic "powers." The theological concepts the author chooses and stresses are particularly appropriate to this situation. The writer endeavors to communicate to the readers their close identification with Christ and their access to his divine power.

(2) The author therefore emphasizes a "cosmic Christology." Christ has been raised to a position of supremacy and authority over these hostile forces. Christ is not rivaled by these "powers," and he alone is sufficient for believers. Through their incorporation into Christ, believers share his "fullness" and power, and, in particular, his authority over the "powers."

(3) The readers would by no means have confused the author's terminology for the "powers" with the abstract notions of sin, flesh, and death. They would have understood the "powers" as actual spirit beings wielding harmful influence over humanity. The author of the epistle speaks of the "flesh" and the devil as

two ontologically distinct forces working in confluence against humanity.

(4) Ephesians strongly highlights the two motifs of the transfer of dominions and the incorporation into Christ of believers. Among other purposes, these two motifs stress the identification of believers with Christ and their sharing in the power of God.

(5) In terms of ethics, the epistle advocates the primacy of conducting oneself according to the pattern of love exemplified by Christ himself. Integral to following this illustrious example is the necessity of "taking off the old self" and "putting on the new self" by the power of God. Underlying this framework for ethics, Ephesians emphasizes resisting the demonic forces which are bent on preventing believers from attaining these objectives. They must be resisted by appropriating the power of God.

(6) Although the writer stresses the realized aspect of eschatology and the spatial categories of existence to a greater extent than the accepted Paulines, the future aspect of salvation has not been abandoned. The partially "realized eschatology" highlights the accessibility to the readers of the power of God, and this is precisely what the writer seeks to impress on his readers. They have been so closely identified with Christ in the mind of the author that he can actually say that they have been "raised with Christ." His intention in affirming this is to bolster the confidence of the readers in Christ so they do not resign themselves to the compelling influence of the "powers" or seek other magical or mystical means of averting their influence. Believers share Christ's position of heavenly authority over the "powers."

(7) Ephesians does not represent a stage of institutionalization where Christology has become a function of ecclesiology. Ecclesiology is still a function of Christology. The term "church" occurs in a non-local sense, but this is consistent with its intended recipients not consisting of one church but a group of churches.

7

CONCLUSION

The overarching problem in research on Ephesians has been in trying to understand the "life setting" or circumstances which occasioned the epistle. Was there a situation that prompted the writing of the epistle and, if so, how would understanding this assist in explaining the letter's distinctive features?

I have set forth an hypothesis — an hypothesis that could potentially contribute to a more precise understanding of the nature and purpose of Ephesians.

Ephesians appears to have been written to a group of churches in western Asia Minor needing help in developing a Christian perspective on the "powers" and encouragement in their ongoing struggles with these pernicious spirit-forces.

Following Paul's two-and-a-half year ministry in Ephesus, his new churches undoubtedly experienced increased growth with many new converts being added. New churches were established in the regions around Ephesus, the Lycus valley, and elsewhere in the province of Asia. Believers in these young Christian communities lived in a milieu characterized by flourishing magical practices, the renowned Artemis cult, and a variety of other Phrygian mysteries and astrological beliefs. Yet a single common feature may be discerned among all the religious diversity in western Asia Minor: people had an extraordinary fear of the hostile spiritual "powers." Through their practices and rituals (some of which the various cults shared), local religion and magic claimed to offer relief from this oppressive fear, and even promised means of control over the dreaded demonic realm. Although many of the new Christians in this area forsook their magical practices and burned their magical papyri, as Luke records, a good number would have been tempted to conflate their magical beliefs with Christianity. "What could be wrong with wearing a magical amulet or invoking magical names for additional protection?" they may have asked. On an even larger scale, there would also have been the danger of sects

167

developing within the churches combining magical and mystery beliefs with Christianity and offering protection from the "powers." Such a segment was probably addressed in the epistle to the Colossians. But what would prevent such aberrant teaching from appearing elsewhere in other churches? A need for apostolic instruction clearly existed.

It may be objected that my description of the setting and therefore the "situation" to which Ephesians was written was not essentially different from that present at Rome, Philippi, Corinth, or Jerusalem — magic, mysteries, and astrology were present throughout the Hellenistic world. Why is the religious climate of western Asia Minor special in this respect? Ephesus stands out as unique among Hellenistic cities because of the widespread and pervasive influence of her patron goddess Artemis — a goddess of the underworld and intimately linked with magical practices. In addition, Ephesus does bear the reputation of being something of a center for magical practices, as reflected by Luke and the proverbial Ephesia Grammata. My thesis does not depend, however, on proving that Ephesus or its environs was different than other Hellenistic cities with regard to these beliefs. I have merely documented that magical practices *flourished* at Ephesus and that the underlying concern in connection with magic — fear of the demonic realm — was *addressed* as a primary theme in Ephesians.

The issue of the "powers" was by no means avoided in the other Pauline letters — the "powers" are referred to in Romans (8:38), 1 Corinthians (2:6–8; 10:19–21; 15:24–26), Galatians (4:3, 9), and Philippians (2:10) — it merely does not receive the prominence it receives in Ephesians.

While my reconstruction of the situation is not sufficient to give a full account of the reasons Ephesians was written, or sufficient to explain all of the theological peculiarities of the epistle, it does provide an explanation for the prominence of the power-motif — the emphasis on the power of God working on behalf of believers juxtaposed to the might of the "powers" of evil working against believers.

The teaching of the epistle on power, while universally relevant and applicable, would prove particularly helpful to converts from a background of strong demonic beliefs and fears. The teaching of the epistle on the power of God and the "powers" of evil can be summarized in the following six points. The epistle teaches:

(1) *The superiority of the power of God and the supremacy of Christ.* The epistle strongly emphasizes the supremacy of God's power, demonstrated especially in the resurrection of Christ from the

dead and his exaltation to a position of preeminence (1:19–23). No "power" is equal to or superior to the power and authority of Christ – all things (τὰ πάντα) ultimately fall into the domain of his sovereign lordship (4:8–10). This encompasses the so-called goddesses of the underworld – Artemis, Hekate, Selene, and Ereschigal – who were ascribed cosmic power and supremacy over the underworld "powers," together with the nature demons, and the astral "powers." It also includes the Ephesia Grammata and the names of any other divinities/demons which were frequently invoked by the pagan and Jewish neighbors of the Christians in Asia Minor. There is truly only one Lord and one God and Father who is over all things. This message would bring great comfort to the Christians. There is no longer any reason to fear the tyrannical evil "powers" in light of the superior power of God the Father, who brings about all things in accordance with his will through Christ.

(2) *The access of the believer to the power of God.* God's superior power is available to believers and is working for their best interest – he desires to mediate it to his people for their protection and growth. Believers are depicted as having been transplanted from one sphere of power (kingdom, or dominion) and placed in another. This transfer forms the basis for their access to the power of God. There is therefore no need for believers to seek any additional protection from the "powers" by any means. This would include the devising of ways to manipulate the demons or the invoking of angelic assistance.

(3) *A new means of access to divine power.* Believers should no longer seek access to power along pagan and magical-mystical Jewish lines. This means that rigorous asceticism, incantations, amulets, the repetition of names, or any other similar means was entirely unnecessary in view of the new state of affairs which obtains for believers. The people of God are brought into the closest possible union with their resurrected and exalted Lord – to the extent that the author could plainly state that believers are already co-resurrected and co-exalted with Christ. Conversely, Christ (and the Holy Spirit) is said to indwell believers, providing them with strengthening and making them sharers of the divine πλήρωμα. This power, however, needs to be appropriated by believers through faith. Therefore, the epistle highlights the role of faith for obtaining God's strengthening (1:19; 3:17; 6:16). One did not really need faith to practice magic; results were guaranteed through carefully following a prescribed formula. Faith is an essential and foundational component, however,

of the Christian life. The primary means of expressing faith in God for his strengthening is in prayer (cf. 6:18–20, and the example set by the author himself in praying for the divine strengthening of the readers in the two prayers). The pieces of armor which God supplies for protection from the "powers" are not magical, material weapons to be worn; the armor consists of spiritual endowments and qualities mediated through faith and prayer.

(4) *A new perspective on the "powers."* Throughout the epistle, the author reaffirms the existence of an evil spiritual order led by one described as "the prince of the authority of the air" (2:2). This one is also known as the διάβολος, who wields an enslaving influence over the pagan world, leading people into disobedience and sin (2:2ff.; 4:27; 6:10–20). He is surrounded by a host of "powers" who are bent on the same aim (6:12). The author intimates that even the "powers" which were once believed to be most helpful and easily manipulated, such as Artemis-Hekate and the Ephesia Grammata, were actually the ones who enslaved! While all of these evil forces still retain a large measure of their power, their authority and sway has been effectively broken by the resurrection and exaltation of Christ. Therefore, all who are "in Christ" need not succumb to the authority of the "powers." At the consummation, these "powers" will be completely subjected by Christ and brought totally under his headship.

(5) *A new posture toward the "powers."* With the "powers" now attempting to reassert their control and authority over the convert, believers are admonished to take up a resistant stance (6:10–20). They are exhorted to appropriate the power of God in order to withstand the vicious attacks of these forces. Furthermore, believers are encouraged to take aggressive action against this kingdom of evil by proclaiming the gospel of Christ.

(6) *A new purpose for divine power.* The epistle sets forth a new purpose for supernatural power which stands in bold relief to the attitude of the non-Christians toward power. Whereas the supernatural power tapped through magical practice has the individual in view, the instruction surrounding God's power imparted to believers has others in view. The power of God strengthens the believer *to love* after the pattern of Christ (3:16–17; 5:2). The rigorous responsibility of this kind of love requires divine enablement in order for it to be fulfilled. With love as the primary ethical imperative of the Christian life, the all-surpassing power of God available to the believer serves as the foundation and basis for ethical living. The strengthening enables the believer to resist the onslaught of the devil, who would

like to see the convert fall into disobedience through lying, stealing, etc. The power of God enables the church to fulfill its mission of proclaiming the gospel in spite of the opposition of the devil and his host of "powers."

The Epistle to the Ephesians is therefore not a response to cosmic speculation. It is a response to the felt needs of the common people within the churches of western Asia Minor, who perceived themselves as oppressed by the demonic realm.

This explanation also provides a more plausible background to Ephesians than the views which appeal to the anachronistic and dubious Gnostic redeemer myth (e.g. Lindemann, Fischer, Schmithals, Käsemann, and Pokorný, among others). The references to the cosmic "powers" are better explained on the basis of the flourishing belief in the demonic realm evidenced in the papyri, inscriptions, and Jewish texts. The setting I postulate also has the advantage of explaining the motivation behind the author's accentuation of "cosmic Christology" and "realized eschatology." The Ephesian author does not betray Gnostic influence on his thought; rather, he has the pastoral intention of admonishing his readers to depend completely upon Christ in their struggle with the forces of evil.

This understanding of the power-motif in light of the epistle's setting naturally has some obvious implications for the question of authorship. The power-motif in its variety of facets is not an alien addition to Pauline theology, but rather appears to be a Pauline emphasis called for by the "situation" addressed. My view of the "situation" also provides helpful perspective on the motive behind the letter's distinctive accents in Christology and eschatology. I have not found a sufficient basis for characterizing these aspects of the theology of Ephesians as discontinuous with the generally accepted Paulines. In light of this, and having been informed by the often overlooked works of E. Percy and A. van Roon as well as the magisterial two-volume work by M. Barth, I believe that the apostle Paul himself surfaces as the most viable candidate for the role of author. There is no difficulty in regarding Paul's personal awareness of their situation, and his demonstrated pastoral and apostolic concern for Christians in western Asia Minor − whom he knew lived in genuine *dread* of the demonic realm − as having prompted him to send them such relevant instruction and encouragement.

I cannot offer a more precise identification of the destination of the epistle. My research into the religious background corroborates the unanimous historical tradition that the epistle was sent to western

Asia Minor. This study does, however, highlight the very significant role played by Ephesus upon the religious climate of western Asia Minor.

The method of research incorporating material from magic, local inscriptional data, and literary testimony to the cult of Artemis and other Phrygian/Lydian religious traditions merely breaks the ground for the use of this material to understand the mind-set of the readers and some of the terms and concepts of the epistle. The inscriptional data have become much more accessible to the NT scholar with the publication of the multi-volume series Inschriften Griechischer Städte aus Kleinasien. Similarly, the use of the magical papyri for English speakers has been greatly assisted by the even more recent publication of *The Greek Magical Papyri in Translation*. Both sources provide a wealth of material, with much still to be tapped for its relevance to interpreting Ephesians and other portions of the NT.

NOTES

1 Introduction

1 M. Barth, *Ephesians* (Anchor Bible, 2 vols., New York, Doubleday), 1.33.

2 See H.-M. Schenke and K.M. Fischer, *Einleitung in die Schriften des Neuen Testaments* (2 vols., Gütersloh, Mohn, 1978), 2.174, 188, and R.P. Martin, "An Epistle in Search of a Life Setting," *ET* 79 (1967–68), 296–302.

2 The religious climate of western Asia Minor in the first century A.D.

1 G.S. Duncan, *St. Paul's Ephesian Ministry* (London, 1929), 8–9, assigns an early date to Ephesians and sees the epistle written at Ephesus by Paul during a postulated Ephesian imprisonment. He suggests that the epistle was written to the Christians of Ephesus as well as to a group of other churches in western Asia Minor.

2 Some see a Pauline school active at Ephesus from where it is believed the epistle was written; this thesis was first advocated by H. Conzelmann, "Paulus und die Weisheit," *NTS* 12 (1965–66), 233. See also J. Gnilka, *Der Epheserbrief* (HTKNT 10/2, Freiburg, 1980), 6; E. Lohse, "Pauline Theology in the Letter to the Colossians," *NTS* 15 (1968–69), 218.

3 E.g. T.K. Abbott, *The Epistles to the Ephesians and to the Colossians* (ICC, Edinburgh, 1897), viii, comments, "there is no difficulty in understanding how the title 'to the Ephesians' would come to be attached to the Epistle, since it was from Ephesus that copies would reach the Christian world generally." N.A. Dahl, "Adresse und Proömium des Epheserbriefes," *TZ* 7 (1951), 241–64, esp. p.248, stresses that the epistle was intended for the new congregations in the neighborhood of Ephesus, but that it was still valued by the old *Kerngemeinde* in Ephesus. Dahl still sees Ephesians as written to churches of Asia Minor, but now by a personal disciple of Paul; see "Gentiles, Christians, and Israelites in the Epistle to the Ephesians," *HTR* 79 (1986), 38.

4 See the recent monograph of K. Usami, *Somatic Comprehension of Unity: The Church in Ephesus* (Analecta biblica 101, Rome,

1983), 12, who *assumes* an Ephesian destination and bases his thesis of the epistle as written to "urban Christians" on this assumption.

5 Most interpreters find it incredible to think that Paul could only speak of "hearing of" their faith and love (1:15; see also 3:2; 4:21) since he had worked among them for two and a half years. On the other hand, if the epistle is authentic, many years had elapsed since Paul had been with them and the congregation(s) had no doubt been inflated by numerous new converts.

6 For an excellent up-to-date discussion of the problem, see E. Best, "Ephesians 1:1 Again," *Paul and Paulinism* (FS. C.K. Barrett, London, 1982), 273–79.

7 See T.R.S. Broughton, "Roman Asia Minor," *An Economic Survey of Ancient Rome*, vol. 4 (Baltimore, 1938), 813 (cited approvingly in R. Oster, "The Ephesian Artemis as an Opponent of Early Christianity," *Jahrbuch für Antike und Christentum* 19 (1976), 24, n. 3). Apollonius of Tyana said that Ephesus was larger than any cities in Ionia or Lydia (Philostr., *Vit. Ap.* 8.7.8).

8 This observation may obviate the often repeated argument that the epistle could not have been written to Ephesus since the content is too general to have been addressed to *one* church.

9 R. Schnackenburg, "Der Epheserbrief im heutigen Horizont," *Maßstab des Glaubens* (Freiburg, 1978), 158–59.

10 See K. Rudolph, *Gnosis* (Edinburgh, 1983), 56–57, 380 n. 17.

11 R. McL. Wilson, "Nag Hammadi and the New Testament," *NTS* 28 (1982), 292.

12 Rudolph, *Gnosis*, 57.

13 Schenke, "Die Gnosis," *Umwelt*, 1.380–82. Refer to his discussion for a more precise understanding of each of the elements.

14 In his 1981 address to the Society of Biblical Literature, J.M. Robinson noted, "pre-Christian Gnosticism as such is hardly attested in a way to settle the debate once and for all"; in "Jesus: From Easter to Valentinus (Or to the Apostles' Creed)," *JBL* 101 (1982), 5. On the whole question of pre-Christian Gnosis, see E. Yamauchi, *Pre-Christian Gnosticism*, 2nd edn (Grand Rapids, 1983) and his article, "Pre-Christian Gnosticism, the New Testament and Nag Hammadi in Recent Debate," *Themelios* 10 (1984), 22–27. Yamauchi is rather skeptical about the existence of a "pre-Christian Gnosticism," but he provides an excellent review of the discussion of this question.

15 C. Colpe, *Die religionsgeschichtliche Schule* (FRLANT 78, 2 vols., Göttingen, 1961); H.-M. Schenke, *Der Gott "Mensch" in der Gnosis* (Göttingen, 1962), maintains that there was no Redeemer-myth in the full sense before Manicheism.

16 See also G. Quispel, *Gnosis als Weltreligion* (Zürich, 1951); R. McL. Wilson, *The Gnostic Problem* (London, 1958).

17 I. Culianu, "The Angels of the Nations and the Origins of Gnostic Dualism," *Studies in Gnosticism and Hellenistic Religions* (EPRO 91, FS. G. Quispel, Leiden, 1981), 78–80.

18 A. F. Segal, *Two Powers in Heaven. Early Rabbinic Reports about Christianity and Gnosticism* (SJLA 25, Leiden, 1977), 265. He further concludes, "gnosticism arose in Judaism out of the polarization of the Jewish community over the issue of the status of God's primary angel ... [therefore], radical gnosticism superseded rather than preceded Christianity as a target for the rabbinic debate."

19 E. Yamauchi, "Jewish Gnosticism? The Prologue of John, Mandaean Parallels, and the Trimorphic Protennoia," *Studies in Gnosticism and Hellenistic Religions* (EPRO 91, FS. G. Quispel, Leiden, 1981), 491.

20 Yamauchi, "Jewish Gnosticism?" 491–92; see also G. Scholem, "Jaldabaoth Reconsidered," *Mélanges d'histoire* (FS. H. C. Puech), 405–21 (cited in Yamauchi).

21 Quispel, *Gnosis*, 9; R. McL. Wilson, "Gnosis and the Mysteries," *Studies in Gnosticism and Hellenistic Religions* (EPRO 91, FS. G. Quispel, Leiden, 1981), 451–57, concurs with Quispel on this point and demonstrates how Gnosis borrowed from the mysteries.

22 See esp. in this regard M. Krause, "The Christianization of Gnostic Texts," *The New Testament and Gnosis: Essays in Honour of Robert McL. Wilson* (Edinburgh, 1983), 187–94.

23 *Sophia of Jesus Christ; Apocryphon of John; Hypostasis of the Archons; The Book of Thomas the Contender; Acts of Peter and the Twelve Apostles.* Tröger finds even more works with Christian elements.

24 For more discussion on this, see R. A. Wild, "The Warrior and the Prisoner: Some Reflections on Ephesians 6:10–20," *CBQ* 46 (1984), 284ff.

25 See C. J. A. Lash, "Where Do the Devils Live? A Problem in the Textual Criticism of Ephesians 6.12," *VC* 30 (1976), 161–74.

26 Wilson, "Gnosis," 457.

27 G. Haufe, "Hellenistische Volksfrömmigkeit," *Umwelt*, 1.82.

28 Wilson, "Gnosis," 456, maintains that some of the ideas and traditions of the mysteries no doubt passed into Gnosticism, but problems arise when the researcher attempts to identify specific points of contact. S. E. Johnson, "Asia Minor and Early Christianity," *Christianity, Judaism and Other Greco-Roman Cults* (SJLA 12, FS. M. Smith, (Leiden, 1975), 2.135, affirms that when Gnosticism actually developed in Asia Minor it borrowed from the local popular religions and magic.

29 A. D. Nock, "Greek Magical Papyri," *Essays on Religion and the Ancient World*, (Oxford, 1972), 1.193.

30 E. R. Goodenough, *Jewish Symbols in the Greco-Roman Period*, (New York, 1953), 2.189, remarks, "Gnosticism seems to me sharply to distinguish itself from this sort of material [magical texts]. For the superhuman beings of the popular cults reflected here are presented as a welter of confused names and conflicting or overlapping functions. The Gnostics accepted this spiritual world but tried to organize and systematize it, and knowledge of this organization was precisely the gnosis by virtue of which the Gnostics felt that they had superior power and hope."

31 Nock, "Greek Magical Papyri," 193.

32 Colpe, *Die religionsgeschichtliche Schule*, 187.

33 H.D. Betz, "Introduction to the Greek Magical Papyri," *The Greek Magical Papyri in Translation* (Chicago, 1986), xlii.

34 J.B. Lightfoot, *St. Paul's Epistles to the Colossians and to Philemon* (London, 1975), 71–113, was one of the first to postulate an Essene Judaism which had been influenced by "Gnosis." See also G. Bornkamm, "The Heresy of Colossians," *Conflict at Colossae* (SBLSBS 4, ed. F.O. Francis and W.A. Meeks (Missoula, 1973), 123–46; et al.

35 F.F. Bruce, *The Epistles to the Colossians, to Philemon, and to the Ephesians* (NICNT, Grand Rapids, 1984), 21–26.

36 G.G. Scholem, *Major Trends in Jewish Mysticism* (New York, 1971), esp. chapter 2, entitled, "Merkabah Mysticism and Jewish Gnosticism," 39–78; see also his work, *Jewish Gnosticism, Merkabah Mysticism, and Talmudic Tradition* (New York, 1965).

37 I. Gruenwald, "Knowledge and Vision," *Israel Oriental Studies* 3 (1973), 90; see also J.M. Robinson, *The Nag Hammadi Codices* (Claremont, 1974), 7, who says that some of Scholem's material may go back to the pupils of Johanan ben Zakkai, who flourished at the end of the first century A.D., but most of his references come from the second century and much later.

38 I. Gruenwald, "The Problem of Anti-Gnostic Polemic in Rabbinic Literature," *Studies in Gnosticism and Hellenistic Religions* (EPRO 91, FS. G. Quispel, Leiden, 1981), 176–77; "Knowledge and Vision," 91; see also Yamauchi, "Jewish Gnosticism?" 489, who cites H. Jonas, D. Flusser, and H.J.W. Drivers as objecting to Scholem's interpretation of Merkabah Mysticism as Gnostic.

39 I. Gruenwald, *Apocalyptic and Merkavah Mysticism* (AGJU 14, Leiden, 1980), 111.

40 Gruenwald, *Apocalyptic*, 110.

41 See the section entitled, "Ephesos als Hauptstadt der Provinz Asia," in D. Knibbe, "Ephesos," *PW* Supp. XII (Stuttgart, 1970), cols. 263–67. Ephesus' boast of primacy (πρωτεῖα) was disputed during the second century A.D. by Pergamum and Smyrna, who both claimed superiority in coins and inscriptions. See A.D. Macro, "The Cities of Asia Minor under the Roman Imperium," *ANRW* II.7.2 (Berlin, 1980), 641ff., 683.

42 Knibbe, "Ephesos," cols. 259–60, 268; V. Chapot, *La Province romaine proconsulaire d'Asie depuis ses origines jusqu'à la fin du Haut-Empire* (Paris, 1904), 138ff. M.P. Nilsson, *Geschichte der griechischen Religion* (2 vols., Münich, 1950), 2.325, states, "In the time of the Caesars, Ephesus, the seat of the proconsul, was the most distinguished and prosperous city of the province of Asia." A few have argued unconvincingly that since Pergamum was the center of the ruler cult, it was also the official capital. For a discussion of this problem, see C. Hemer, *The Letters to the Seven Churches of Asia in their Local Setting* (JSNTSS 11, Sheffield, 1986), 824.

43 Strabo, 12.8.15, regarded Ephesus as the principal trading center of Asia, with Apameia Celaenai (about 90 km north-east of Colossae) as next in importance. See Macro, "Cities of Asia Minor," 670ff. H. Koester, *Introduction of the New Testament* (2 vols., Philadelphia, 1982), 1.328, thus rightly observes, "Ephesus, Antioch, and Alexandria, among others maintained their importance as centers of reshipment because they were situated at the terminals of important trade routes from the inland areas."

44 See D. Magie, *Roman Rule in Asia Minor* (2 vols., Princeton, 1950), 1.74–75, 2.885–86; F. Miltner, *Ephesos* (Wien, 1958), 2, summarizes the significance of Ephesus: "in the middle of the first century A.D., Ephesus was not merely one of the many cities in which the life of the Imperium Romanum was concentrated; it was already much more – in spirit as in substance and not least in the execution of commerce – as the leading harbor city on the coast of Asia Minor."

45 Magie, *Roman Rule*, 1.74–75.

46 Magie, *Roman Rule*, 1.47.

47 W. M. Ramsay, *The Cities and Bishoprics of Phrygia*, vol. 2 (Oxford, 1897), 131.

48 D. H. French, "The Roman Road-System of Asia Minor," *ANRW* II.7.2 (Berlin, 1980), 698–729. French comments, "Ramsay said that in earlier times all roads ran to Ephesus – he was right" (711).

49 French, "Road-System," 707. See also Knibbe, "Ephesos," col. 259; Magie, *Roman Rule*, 2.1048, n. 39.

50 W. M. Ramsay, *The Letters to the Seven Churches of Asia* (London, 1904), 171–96. This hypothesis has received recent support by Hemer, *Seven Churches*, 14–15.

51 J. Lähnemann, "Die Sieben Sendschreiben der Johannes-Apokalypse," *Studien zur Religion und Kultur Kleinasiens* (EPRO 66, 2 vols., Leiden, 1978), 2.525.

52 B. M. Metzger, "St. Paul and the Magicians," *Princeton Seminary Bulletin* 38 (1944), 27; see also W. M. Ramsay, "Ephesus," *HDB* 1.722; E. Kuhnert, "Ephesiae litterae," *PW* 5 (Stuttgart, 1905), col. 2772, speaks of a "flourishing magical practice" in Ephesus.

53 O. Meinardus, *St. Paul in Ephesus and the Cities of Galatia and Cyprus* (Athens, 1979), 91. He also adds, "Ephesus was well known among the cities of the eastern Roman world as a center for the study and practice of magic."

54 E. Haenchen, *The Acts of the Apostles* (Oxford, 1971), 567, seriously questions the historical trustworthiness of the details of the account in Acts 19. However, even if it could be demonstrated that Luke exaggerated the details of the account (e.g. the value of the books), the tradition of prolific magical activity at Ephesus would still persist. Betz, "Introduction," xli, upholds the general reliability of the account, suggesting that the episode is typical of many such instances.

55 K. Preisendanz, "Ephesia Grammata," *RAC* 5 (1965), cols. 515–20; Kuhnert, "Ephesia litterae," cols. 2771–73; Metzger,

"Magicians," 27–30; A. Deissmann, "Ephesia Grammata," *Abhandlung zur Semitischen Religionskunde und Sprachwissenschaft* (BZAW 33, Giessen, 1918), 121–24; C.C. McCown, "The Ephesia Grammata in Popular Belief," *Transactions of the American Philological Association* 54 (1923), 128–40; B. Hemberg, "Die Idaiischen Daktylen," *Eranos* 50 (1952), 41–59, esp. pp. 42–43; T. Hopfner, *Griechisch-Ägyptischer Offenbarungszauber* (2 vols., Amsterdam, 1974 = reprint of the 1921 edition), vol. 1, pars. 763–66; A. Audollent, *Defixionum tabellae* (Paris, 1904), lxvii–lxxii; C. Wessely, "Ephesia Grammata aus Papyrusrollen, Inschriften, Gemmen," *Zwölfter jahresbericht über das k. k. Franz-Josef-Gymnasium in Wien* (Wien, 1886), 1–38 (Wessely's discussion encompasses all the magical names found in eight magical papyri which he generically refers to as "Ephesia Grammata," as opposed to the six specific names of the tradition).

56 See Clem. of Alex., *Strom.* 1.15; 5.8; Hesych., *s.v.*; Plut., *Quaest. conv.* 7.5; Anaxilas, "The Harp-maker," quoted by Athenaeus, *Deipnosophistae* 12.548c; Eustathius, *Comm. ad Hom.* 19.247; Michael Apostolius 4.23; 8.17; 11.29 in *Corpus paroemiographorum Graecorum*, vol. 2 (Göttingen, 1851), 169, 429, 523. Many of the texts are cited in full in *FIE* 1.248, nos. 130–37 and also in Hopfner, *Offenbarungszauber*, vol. 1, pars. 763–66.

57 McCown, "Ephesia Grammata," 132ff.; Preisendanz, "Ephesia Grammata," col. 515.

58 Preisendanz, "Ephesia Grammata," col. 517.

59 Anaxilas, "The Harp-maker," quoted by Athenaeus, *Deipnosophistae* 12.548c;* text cited in Hopfner, *Offenbarungszauber*, vol. 1, par. 765.

60 The Suda, *s.v.*; Eustathius, *Comm. ad Hom.* 19.247.

61 Menander, *Paidion* 371; text cited in Hopfner, *Offenbarungszauber*, vol. 1, par. 765. See also McCown, "Ephesia Grammata," 131 n. 17.

62 McCown, "Ephesia Grammata," 133ff. He cites their use in a fourth-century B.C. Cretan tablet, where they are appealed to as beneficent, protecting spirits.

63 For a discussion of magic in Ephesus, especially as it relates to the Jews, see A. T. Kraabel, "Judaism in Asia Minor under the Roman Empire," unpublished Th.D. Thesis, Harvard University, 1968, 54–59.

64 R. Wünsch, *Antikes Zaubergerät aus Pergamon,* Jahrbuch des Kaiserlich Deutschen Archäologischen Instituts Ergänzungsheft 6 (Berlin, 1905).

65 See J. Keil, "Ein rätselhaftes Amulett," *JhhÖArchInst* Beiblatt 32 (1940), 79–84.

66 Goodenough, *Symbols*, 2.221.

67 See McCown, "Ephesia Grammata," 128.

68 K. Preisendanz, *Papyri graecae magicae: Die griechischen Zauberpapyri* (2 vols., Leipzig & Berlin, 1928, 1931). A third volume, including additional texts and indexes, was ready for the press when the Teubner publishing house in Leipzig was destroyed by an air

raid during the Second World War. Fortunately, the galley proofs survived and a few xeroxed copies were made from these. (I was able to use a poor-quality photocopy housed in the rare manuscripts room of Cambridge University Library. This was made from a tightly bound photocopy belonging to University College London. As far as I am aware, these two are the only copies of the third volume in Britain.) A second edition of the work in two volumes appeared in 1973–74 edited by A. Heinrichs (Stuttgart, 1973, 1974). This two-volume work includes all of the texts of the prior three-volume work, but the indexes have been omitted.

69 See the excellent and concise summary of sources in J. M. Hull, *Hellenistic Magic and the Synoptic Tradition* (SBS 28, London, 1974), 5–15. See also D. E. Aune, "Magic in Early Christianity," *ANRW* II.23.2 (Berlin, 1980), 1516–17.

70 Cf. Aune, "Magic," 1519; Haufe, "Hellenistische Volksfrömmigkeit," 77, refers to the first two centuries of the Christian era as the "heyday" (*Blütezeit*) of magic.

71 Suet., *Aug. Caes.* 31.1. (cited in Betz, "Introduction," xli).

72 Nilsson, *Geschichte*, 2.44ff. T. Hopfner, "Mageia," *PW* 27 (Stuttgart, 1928), 307.

73 *PGM* XVI; XX (1 c. B.C.); LVII; LXXII; LXXXV, CXXII (1 c. B.C.).

74 *PGM* VI; XIc; XVIIb; XXI; XXXII; XXXIV; LIX; LXIII; LXVIII; LXIX; LXXI; LXXVII; CIII; CX.

75 H. D. Betz, "The Formation of Authoritative Tradition in the Greek Magical Papyri," *Jewish and Christian Self Definition* (3 vols., London, 1982), 3.161–70.

76 For Egyptian influence upon Asia Minor, see G. Hölbl, *Zeugnisse ägyptischer Religionsvorstellungen für Ephesus* (EPRO 73, Leiden, 1978); R. Salditt-Trappmann, *Tempel der ägyptischen Götter in Griechenland und an der Westküste Kleinasiens* (EPRO 15, Leiden, 1970).

77 H. Kee, *Medicine, Miracle and Magic in New Testament Times* (SNTSMS 55, Cambridge, 1986), 111–12.

78 F. Cumont, *The Oriental Religions in Roman Paganism* (Chicago, 1911), 185, describes the nature of magical practice: "By means of his charms, talismans, and exorcisms, the magician now communicated with the celestial or infernal 'demons' and compelled them to obey him. But these spirits no longer opposed him with the blind resistance of matter animated by an uncertain kind of life; they were active and subtle beings having intelligence and will power." See also Betz, "Introduction," xlvii; Goodenough, *Symbols*, 2.162.

79 Cited in A. F. Segal, "Hellenistic Magic: Some Questions of Definition," *Studies in Gnosticism and Hellenistic Religions* (EPRO 91, Leiden, 1981), 358.

80 Aune, "Magic," 1515–16. Segal, "Hellenistic Magic," 349–75, has similarly argued that many scholars have been too easily beset by their own cultural assumptions in arriving at a definition of magic. Instead of distinguishing magic too sharply from religion,

Segal would like to see agreement on a broader definition of magic which in some social contexts may even be considered as coterminous with religion. Aune's two-fold definition of "magic" more precisely reaches into the heart of what is distinctively magic.

81 Kee, *Medicine*, 112, elaborates, "What is sought is not to learn the will of the deity, but to shape the deity's will to do the bidding of the one making the demand or to defeat the aims of the evil powers."

82 See E. Yamauchi, "Magic in the Biblical World," *TB* 34 (1983), 174—77.

83 Aune, "Magic," 1521.

84 *Ibid.*

85 Betz, "Introduction," xli.

86 An important and concise article summarizing the interface between the Ephesian Artemis and the Christian gospel has been written by R. Oster, "The Ephesian Artemis as an Opponent of Early Christianity," *Jahrbuch für Antike und Christentum* 19 (1976), 24—44. He clearly demonstrates the prominence of the cult of the Ephesian Artemis during the first century and rightly criticizes the marginal attention given to her in the commentaries on Acts.

87 Paus., *Descr.* 4.31.8: "But all cities worship Artemis of Ephesus and individuals hold her in honor above all the gods. The reason, in my view, is the renown of the Amazons, who traditionally dedicated the image, also the extreme antiquity of this sanctuary. Three other points as well have contributed to her renown, the size of the temple, surpassing all buildings among men, the eminence of the city of the Ephesians and the renown of the goddess who dwells there." See also Xenoph., *Anab.* 5.3.4.

88 For descriptions of the sizeable attendance, see R. MacMullen, *Paganism in the Roman Empire* (New Haven, 1974), 22, who cites *SIG* (3rd), 867, and Xenoph., *Ephes.* 1.2.3.

89 Oster, "Ephesian Artemis," 43. K. Wernicke, "Artemis," *PW* 2 (Stuttgart, 1896), cols. 1385—86, provides a list of the numerous cities where the cult of Artemis had been planted.

90 Oster, "Ephesian Artemis," 34.

91 See L. R. Farnell, *The Cults of the Greek States* (3 vols., Oxford, 1896), 2.480.

92 Oster, "Ephesian Artemis," 40. Most of his evidence comes from the inscriptional and literary evidence about Artemis gathered in volumes 1 and 2 of *Forschungen in Ephesos*.

93 E. Heinzel, "Zum Kult der Artemis von Ephesos," *JhhÖArchInst* 50 (1972—73), 246ff.; Oster, "Ephesian Artemis," 41. See the more detailed discussion in section 5.

94 This attribution of cosmic power to the Ephesian Artemis is further confirmed by an analysis of magical gems found near Paris. Artemis is portrayed in the presence of the sun and the moon, thereby becoming a cosmic divinity: see O. V. Névéron, "Gemmes, bagues et amulettes magiques du sud de l'URSS," *Hommages à Maarten J. Vermaseren* (EPRO 68, 3 vols., Leiden, 1978), 3.842.

95 Cited in R. C. Kukala, "Literary Witnesses of the Artemis Temple," *FiE* 1.253 (my translation).
96 See *FiE* 1.249.
97 O. Jessen, "Ephesia," *PW* 5 (Stuttgart, 1905), col. 2761.
98 *PGM* LXXVIII, in Preisendanz, *Papyri graecae magicae*, 3.207. The same volume contains a facsimile of the image in table IV 2.
99 T. Hopfner, "Hekate-Selene-Artemis and Verwandte in den griechischen Zauberpapyri und auf den Fluchtafeln," *Pisciculi* (FS. F. J. Dölger, Münster, 1939), 125–45. He examines five pieces out of the great Paris magical papyrus and two out of *PGM* VII which Preisendanz regarded as "hymns" to the deities: (1) *PGM* IV. 2243–47; (2) 2441–2621; (3) 2622–2706; (4) 2709–84; (5) 2785–2890; (6) *PGM* VII.756–95; (7) 862–918.
100 Wünsch, *Zaubergerät*, 26–27. The epithet, Λευκοφρυηνή, was commonly used for the worship of Artemis at Magnesia on the Maeander. Wünsch concludes, "it was originally the same barbaric goddess which in Ephesus proved to be Artemis; since antiquity Hekate has been identified with Artemis."
101 C. Bonner, *Studies in Magical Amulets Chiefly Graeco-Egyptian* (Ann Arbor, 1950), 262–63; see in particular D. 56, 63, 64, 65, 66.
102 As quoted by Eustathius, *Comm. ad Hom.* 19.247.
103 McCown, "Ephesia Grammata," 129, Preisendanz, "Ephesia Grammata," col. 517, Hopfner, *Offenbarungszauber*, vol. 1, par. 764, and W. H. Roscher, "Weiteres über die Bedeutung des E zu Delphi und die übrigen γράμματα Δελφικά," *Philologus* 60 (1900), 90, concur, however, in upholding the accuracy of Pausanias' statement.
104 *PGM* IV.2844–48. Hopfner, *Offenbarungszauber*, vol. 1, par. 764, thinks this serves to confirm the observation of Pausanias.
105 McCown, "Ephesia Grammata," 129–30. McCown cites Roscher, "Weiteres," 88ff. and Gruppe, *Griechische Mythologie*, vol. 2 (München, 1906), 884, in support of this conclusion; see also Metzger, "St. Paul and the Magicians," 28. Deissmann, "Ephesia Grammata," 121–24, conjectures that the epithet ἐφέσια is derived from the Babylonian epêšu, "to bewitch." This is not an impossible hypothesis, but it does fail to provide an explanation for the origin of the six Ephesian letters.
106 *PGM* LXX.12. For a full discussion of this entire recipe, see H. D. Betz, "Fragments from a Catabasis Ritual in a Greek Magical Papyrus," *HistRel* 19 (1980), 287–95. These two Ephesian letters occur only one other time in Preisendanz's collection, where they are enigmatically referred to as "the Orphic formula."
107 D. Wortmann, "Neue Magische Texte," *Bonner Jahrbücher* 168 (1968), 56–84. Surprisingly, the text is not included in *The Greek Magical Papyri in Translation*.
108 Wortmann, "Texte," 76, does acknowledge the connection between Artemis and Δαμνομενία.
109 Clem. of Alex., *Strom.* 1.15. *PGM* LXX.13–15 also attributes them to the Dactyls. See Betz, "Catabasis Ritual," 291–93. On the Idaean Dactyls, see Hemberg, "Idaiischen Daktylen," 41–59. With regard

to their relation to the Ephesian Artemis, Hemberg remarks that they "were probably engraved on the statue of the Ephesian Artemis" (50—51).

110 Wünsch, *Zaubergerät*, 41—42. He adds, "They are likewise at home in the anterior of Asia Minor and are known as demons of magic power."

111 See J. Keil, "Kulte im Prytaneion von Ephesos," *Anatolian Studies Presented to William Hepburn Buckler* (Manchester, 1939), 119—28; D. Knibbe, "Ephesos — nicht nur die Stadt der Artemis. Die 'anderen' ephesische Götter," *Studien zur Religion und Kultur Kleinasiens* (EPRO 66, 2 vols., Leiden, 1978), 2.489—505.

112 The names of the Ephesian Artemis, as well as the Ephesia Grammata, although occuring quite frequently in the magical papyri, do not appear more frequently than other divinities. In fact, the Egyptian divinities occur with a great deal more frequency. This can be explained by the fact that (1) one would expect Egyptian deities to be named more frequently than Anatolian deities in Egyptian papyri, and (2) the comprehensive number of deities named in the papyri indicates more of an interest in obtaining power through naming every conceivable divinity than devotion to a particular deity. We would expect the Ephesian Artemis and the Ephesia Grammata to be named with substantially more frequency if magical papyri were to be discovered in Asia Minor.

113 The most comprehensive work in this respect (including numerous illustrations) is by R. Fleischer, *Artemis von Ephesos und verwandte Kultstatuen aus Anatolien und Syrien* (EPRO 35, Leiden, 1973); see also the brief article by Fleischer together with 136 pictures of the Ephesian Artemis in "Artemis Ephesia," *Lexicon iconographicum mythologiae classicae*, vol. 2, parts 1 & 2 (Zürich & München, 1984). See also E. Lichtenecker, "Die Kultbilder der Artemis von Ephesos," Inaugural-Dissertation zur Erlangung des Doktorgrades einer hohen philosophischen Fakultät der Universität zu Tübingen, 1952.

114 See the most recent discussion in W. Helck, "Zur Gestalt der Ephesischen Artemis," *Archäologischen Anzeiger* (1984, Heft 2), 281—82; see also R. Fleischer, "Neues zu kleinasiatischen Kultstatuen," *Archäologischen Anzeiger* (1983), 81—93. Fleischer, who has done by far the most research on this cultic image, has not found any of the interpretations compelling and prefers to leave it as an open question.

115 Lichtenecker, "Kultbilder," 125.

116 *Ibid.*, 124.

117 Hieronymus, *Comm. Ep. Pauli ad Ephes*, as referred to in Fleischer, *Artemis von Ephesos*, 75.

118 M. P. Nilsson, *Greek Popular Religion* (New York, 1940), 16; see also S. Onurkan, "Artemis Pergaia," *Istanbuler Mitteilungen* 19—20 (1969—70), 295.

119 Hopfner, "Hekate-Selene-Artemis," 134.

120 See M. P. Nilsson, "Die Religion in den griechischen Zauberpapyri," *Kung. Humanistiska Vetenskapssamfundet I Lund. Årsberattelse 1947—48* (Lund, 1948), 73.

121 Hopfner, "Hekate-Selene-Artemis," 144.
122 See Farnell, *Cults*, 1.480–82; A.D. Nock, *Early Gentile Christianity and its Hellenistic Background* (New York, 1964), 3–4. There is also some evidence for Persian influence in her development (Plutarch, *Lysander* 3).
123 A. Bammer, *Das Heiligtum der Artemis von Ephesos* (Graz, 1984), 259.
124 Oster, "Ephesian Artemis," 27. He cites C. Picard, *Ephèse et Claros* (Paris, 1922), 452–74, in support of this conjecture.
125 Oster, "Ephesian Artemis," 28, finds evidence supporting the notion that in the period contemporary with early Christianity there was an increased tendency to identify her with the Greek Artemis, daughter of Leto and sister of Apollo.
126 *IvE* 989.10; see also 26.3; 213.3; 667a.10; 702.13; 987.11; 988.14; et al.
127 Oster, "Ephesian Artemis," 38–39.
128 *PGM* IV.2523, 2819, 2747. In Inv. T. 1.66 (= Wortmann, "Texte," 79), Hekate, Selene, Artemis, and Persephone are called a τετραδαίμων.
129 Cumont, *Oriental Religions*, 67. See also G. Haufe, "Die Mysterien," *Umwelt*, 1.115–16.
130 J.G. Griffiths, "Xenophon of Ephesus on Isis and Alexandria," *Hommages à Maarten J. Vermaseren* (EPRO 68, Leiden, 1978), 419; Farnell, *Cults*, 1.481; Wernicke, "Artemis," cols. 1372–73.
131 The "Laudatio" text of the *Acts of Andrew*; see *NTApoc*, 2.399.
132 *IvE* 1351 (see also *FiE*, 1.103).
133 *Acts of John*, 43; translation by K. Schäferdiek, in *NTApoc*, 2.237.
134 However, Markus Barth, "Traditions in Ephesians," *NTS* 30 (1984), 16, has offered some interesting suggestions. He proposes that the extended discussion on marriage in Eph 5:21–33 "may contain a factual, though critical dialogue with the Kybele-Artemis tradition." He also suggests that the Artemis temple (in addition to the Jerusalem temple) may be in the mind of the author as he pens Eph 2:20–22.
135 Oster, "Ephesian Artemis," 27, never considers the evidence of Ephesians since on the basis of 1:1 he concludes that the epistle "was in fact not addressed to Ephesus."
136 See chapter 3, esp. the discussion of κοσμοκράτωρ in section 2.
137 See A.D. Nock, "Astrology and Cultural History," *Essays on Religion and the Ancient World* (2 vols., Oxford, 1972), 1.359–68; F. Cumont, *Astrology and Religion among the Greeks and Romans* (New York, 1912); Nilsson, *Geschichte*, 2.465ff.; M. Hengel, *Judaism and Hellenism* (2 vols., London, 1974), 1.236. Even W. Carr, *Angels and Principalities* (SNTSMS 42, Cambridge, 1981), 15, concedes the presence of astrological beliefs in this time frame.
138 For a full treatment of the relationship of magic and astrology in the magical papyri, see H.G. Gundel, *Weltbild und Astrologie in den griechischen Zauberpapyri* (Münchener Beiträge zur Papyrusforschung und Antiken Rechtsgeschichte 53, München, 1968).

139 Gundel, *Weltbild*, 13, 33.
140 *Ibid.*, 49.
141 Heinzel, "Artemis von Ephesos," 246ff.; Oster, "Ephesian Artemis," 40–41. That these zodiacal signs were present on the first-century Ephesian Artemis is established by Fleischer, *Artemis von Ephesos*, 72. Lichtenecker, "Kultbilder," 97–106, considers the zodiacal signs an essential part of the primary type (*Haupttypus*) of the Ephesian Artemis. Most of the statues contain five or more signs displayed in a half circle on her chest; a few other statues have only three signs or even just one (the crab). Lichtenecker thinks these may have been inscribed on Artemis as early as the third century B.C. (102, 106).
142 Heinzel, "Artemis von Ephesos," 241–51, suggests that although the chest decoration was originally meant to depict a fertility motif, it was later given religious-astral significance. The "egg-forms" are interpreted by Heinzel as representing planets and are related to the zodiacal signs engraved around her neck. Heinzel observes that the classification of the planets within a month (her explanation of the rows of egg forms) is attested as early as the beginning of the second century A.D.
143 Cumont, *Oriental Religions*, 163.
144 *Ibid.*, 182.
145 H. Bietenhard, *Die himmlische Welt* (WUNT 2, Tübingen, 1951), 106ff. See, for example, *Jub* 11:8: "And he [Nahor] grew up and lived in Ur of the Chaldees, and his father instructed him in the learning of the Chaldees, how to divine and foretell the future from the signs of heaven."
146 J. Daniélou, *Primitive Christian Symbols* (Baltimore, 1964), 132–34.
147 J.M. Allegro, "An Astrological Cryptic Document from Qumran," *JSS* 9 (1964), 291–94. For a brief discussion and bibliography on this text, see J.J. Gunther, *St. Paul's Opponents and their Background. A Study of Apocalyptic and Jewish Sectarian Teachings* (NovTSup 35, Leiden, 1973), 206ff.; see also Hengel, *Judaism and Hellenism*, 1.236–38.
148 For further discussion on the pervasive influence of astrology in Judaism, see J.H. Charlesworth, "Jewish Astrology in the Talmud, Pseudepigrapha, the Dead Sea Scrolls, and Early Palestinian Synagogues," *HTR* 70 (1977), 183–200.
149 For a detailed study on this aspect of Judaism, see Kraabel, "Judaism of Asia Minor under the Roman Empire," unpublished Th.D. Thesis, Harvard University, 1968. See also the more general volume by E.M. Smallwood, *The Jews Under Roman Rule* (SJLA 20, Leiden, 1976), esp. 121–43.
150 For further literary references to the Jewish presence in Ephesus and its environs, see Kraabel, "Judaism," 51–52.
151 Goodenough, *Symbols*, 2.102, 108, reports that a number of lamps with menorahs and a glass painted with Jewish symbols have been discovered at Ephesus. See A.T. Kraabel, "The Diaspora

Synagogue," *ANRW* II.19.1 (Berlin, 1979), 477–510, for a discussion of the synagogues which have been discovered in Asia Minor (Sardis, Miletus, Priene).

152 Koester, *Introduction*, 2.114, regards the account as "legendary": "The unmasking of the Jewish exorcists and the burning of the magical books go back to an older Christian or pagan tale."

153 *Str-B*, 4.533ff., e.g. *Shab.* 67a; see also Picard, *Ephèse et Claros*, 132 n.2.

154 Betz, "Introduction," xlv. For additional discussion of Jewish magic, see Goodenough, *Symbols*, 2. 153–295; M. Simon, *Verus Israel* (Paris, 1964), 394–431 (= chapter 12, "Superstition et magie"); J. G. Gager, *Moses in Greco-Roman Paganism* (SBLMS 16, Nashville, 1972), 134–61 (= chapter 4, "Moses and Magic"). For a bibliography on Jewish magic, see Aune, "Magic," 1520 n.52.

155 J. H. Charlesworth, "Prayer of Jacob," *OTP*, 2.714–23.

156 Charlesworth, "Prayer of Jacob," 715.

157 Simon, *Verus Israel*, 399–404; Goodenough, *Symbols*, 2.161; Charlesworth, "Prayer of Jacob," 716.

158 M. Margalioth, *Sepher Ha-Razim* (Jerusalem, 1966). The text has recently been translated by M. Morgan, *Sepher Ha-Razim. The Book of the Mysteries* (SBL Texts and Translations 25, Pseudepigrapha Series 11, Chico, 1983); see also the discussion in Gruenwald, *Apocalyptic*, 225–34.

159 Morgan, *Sepher Ha-Razim*, 9, states, "It is crucial to recognize that what fascinates us most about this text, the magic, is part of a folk tradition which dates from an earlier time."

160 Gruenwald, *Apocalyptic*, 228, 230.

161 Kraabel, "Judaism," 51–59.

162 Keil, "Amulett," 79–84; see also Kraabel, "Judaism," 56–57.

163 Goodenough, *Symbols*, 2.221. He cites H. J. van Lennep, *Travels in Little Known Parts of Asia Minor* (1870), 1.20.

164 Wünsch, *Zaubergerät*, 33.

165 For the Greek text and an introduction, see C. C. McCown, *The Testament of Solomon* (Leipzig, 1922); see also the introduction and English translation by D. C. Duling, *OTP*, 1.935–88.

166 McCown, *Testament*, 110; M. R. James, "The Testament of Solomon," *JTS* 24 (1922), 468. The view has not attracted a consensus, however. Babylon, Egypt, and Palestine have also been put forward as possible areas of origin.

167 The name "Salama" occurs in a list of other names thought to be laden with power in *PGM* XII.80; demons are conjured by his seal in *PGM* IV.3040; charms, spells, rites, and magical books are attributed to Solomon in the magical papyri (*PGM* IV.850ff.; et al.). Josephus, *Antiq.* 8.2.5, gives an account of a Jewish magician named Eleazar who performed an exorcism in the presence of Vespasian with the help of a Solomonic magical formula. A number of Solomon amulets have been discovered in Jewish graves in Palestine: see Goodenough, *Symbols*, 2.235.

168 Goodenough, *Symbols*, 2.236–37.

169 *PGM* XXVIIIa.2; XXVIIIb.6; P3.2.
170 McCown, *Testament*, 136.
171 See esp. K. G. Kuhn, "The Epistle to the Ephesians in Light of the Qumran Texts," *Paul and Qumran* (London, 1968) 115–31; see also the other essays in that volume.
172 Kraabel, "Judaism," 146, is less optimistic about the possibility of this influence. With regard to understanding the Colossian heresy, he states, "[it is] premature at the very least to make direct connections between the Colossian heresy and the Dead Sea Scrolls."
173 P. Benoit, "Qumran and the New Testament," *Paul and Qumran* (London, 1968), 15.
174 M-M, 172. See also the study of K. Prümm, "Dynamis in griechisch-hellenistischer Religion und Philosophie als Vergleichsbild zu göttlicher Dynamis im Offenbarungsraum," *ZKT* 83 (1961), 393–430.
175 A. D. Nock, "Studies in the Graeco-Roman Beliefs of the Empire," *JHS* 45 (1925), 84–101.
176 *Ibid.*, 87.
177 *Ibid.*, 88–93.
178 *Ibid.*, 94.
179 Knibbe, "Ephesos – Nicht nur die Stadt der Artemis," 489–503; Keil, "Kulte im Prytaneion von Ephesos," 119–28.
180 W. M. Ramsay, "Artemis-Leto and Apollo-Lairbenos," *JHS* 10 (1889), 228.
181 Nilsson, *Geschichte*, 1.69.
182 O. Schmitz, "Der Begriff δύναμις bei Paulus," *Festgabe für Adolf Deissmann* (Tübingen, 1927), 139–67; see also F. Preisigke, *Die Gotteskraft der frühchristlichen Zeit* (Papyrusinstitut Heidelberg 6, Berlin & Leipzig, 1922); W. Grundmann, *Der Begriff der Kraft in der neutestamentlichen Gedankenwelt* (BWANT 8, Stuttgart, 1932), esp. 3–39.
183 Schmitz, "Begriff," 157–58.
184 *Ibid.*, 164ff.
185 For a history of the establishment of the ruler cult throughout the Greek world, see R. Mellor, ΘΕΑ ΡΩΜΗ. *The Worship of the Goddess Roma in the Greek World*, Hypomnemata 42, Göttingen, 1975). On Pergamum, see pp. 141ff., 200ff. On the ruler cult generally, see Nilsson, *Geschichte*, 2.132–85, 384–95; L. R. Taylor, *The Divinity of the Roman Emperor* (Middletown, 1931); G. Hansen, "Herrscherkult und Friedenidee," *Umwelt*, 1.127–42. For Asia Minor, see also Macro, "Cities of Asia Minor," 681–82.
186 Ancient Greek Inscriptions of the British Museum, 522. See Mellor, ΘΕΑ ΡΩΜΗ, 138.
187 Mellor, ΘΕΑ ΡΩΜΗ, 138. Mellor indicates that an Ephesian temple, however, is depicted on an imperial cistophorus issued at Ephesus during the reign of Claudius with the legend ROM. ET. AUG. COM. ASI. Smyrna became the second νεωκόρος in A.D. 26.
188 G. W. Bowersock, "The Imperial Cult: Perceptions and Persistence," *Jewish and Christian Self-Definition* (3 vols., London,

1982), 3.172. Bowersock claims that A. D. Nock pointed this out many times.

189 Bowersock, "Imperial Cult," 173.

190 Mellor, ΘΕΑ ΡΩΜΗ, 16. So also Hansen, "Herrscherkult," 141–42, who observes that the ruler cult was widespread, "but in general, there was seldom a participation in genuine religious feeling."

191 F. W. Norris, "Asia Minor Before Ignatius: Walter Bauer Reconsidered," *SE* VII (= *TU* 126, Berlin, 1982), 370.

192 See the revised edition by A. Heinrichs. Unfortunately, these have not been included in Betz's English translation.

193 Origen, *Contra Celsum* 6.40. See also 6.41; et al. See further in Hippolytus, *Refutation* 6.15; 7.20; 9.9; et al.

3 The presentation of the "powers" in Ephesians

1 For a brief history of the interpretation of the Pauline "powers" prior to the twentieth century, see K. L. Schmidt, "Die Natur- und Geistkräfte bei Paulus," *ErJb* 14 (1946), 87–143.

2 O. Everling, *Die paulinische Angelologie und Dämonologie* (Göttingen, 1888).

3 M. Dibelius, *Die Geisterwelt im Glauben des Paulus* (Göttingen, 1909).

4 Of course, for us, this question will be even more complicated by the growing realization that Judaism in the first century was already "Hellenized" to a large extent.

5 Dibelius, *Geisterwelt*, 169. His skepticism about Pauline authorship comes when he compares Ephesians with Colossians and finds irreconcilable differences between the two epistles (169–75). He concludes that Paul could not possibly have written both epistles and Colossians more accurately reflects Paul; therefore Ephesians must not be authentic (174). This is confirmed for Dibelius in noticing the "institutionalization" (*Verkirchlichung*) tendency in Ephesians in a measure not seen before in Paul.

6 Grundmann, *Begriff der Kraft*, esp. chapter 3: "Gewalten, Mächte, Kräfte," 39–55.

7 For a more complete summary of the views of these interpreters than can be afforded here, see the recent study by P. T. O'Brien, "Principalities and Powers: Opponents of the Church," in *Biblical Interpretation and the Church: Text and Context* (Exeter, 1984), 110–50, esp. pp. 111–28.

8 H. Schlier, *Principalities and Powers in the New Testament* (London, 1961). This represents a translation of a much earlier German work of Schlier's: "Mächte und Gewalten im Neuen Testament," *Theologische Blätter* IX/11 (1930), 289ff.

9 Schlier, *Principalities*, 30–32. Markus Barth takes a similar view; see Barth, *Ephesians*, 1.215; Comment V.A. on 1:15–23, "Origin and Definition of Powers" (170–76), and Comment II on 2:1–10, "The Realm of the Evil One."

10 O. Cullmann, *Christ and Time* (London, 1951); *The State in the New Testament* (London, 1957), esp. pp. 95−114.
11 C. Morrison, *The Powers That Be* (SBT 29, London, 1960).
12 Morrison, *Powers*, 130.
13 Cf. O'Brien, "Principalities and Powers," 118−19; F.F. Bruce, "Paul and 'The Powers That Be,'" *BJRL* 66.2 (1983−84), 78−96; C.E.B. Cranfield, *The Epistle to the Romans* (2 vols., Edinburgh, 1979), 2.657−68; et al.
14 H. Berkhof, *Christ and the Powers* (Scottdale, 1962).
15 For example, Ronald Sider, *Christ and Violence* (Scottdale, 1979), 51, who follows Berkhof's view of the "powers," and advocates a very aggressive role for the Christian today: "Announcing Christ's lordship to the powers [Eph. 3:10] is to tell governments that they are not sovereign ... to witness in a biblical way to the principalities and powers is to engage in dangerous, subversive political activity."
16 G.B. Caird, *Principalities and Powers: A Study in Pauline Theology* (Oxford, 1956).
17 O'Brien, "Principalities and Powers," 149, n. 47.
18 G.B. Caird, *Paul's Letters from Prison* (Oxford, 1976), 91.
19 O'Brien, "Principalities and Powers," 143, "The principalities and powers continue to exist, inimical to man and his interests, hell-bent on carrying out their tyrant's destructive plans, ..."
20 G.H.C. MacGregor, "Principalities and Powers: The Cosmic Background of Paul's Thought," *NTS* 1 (1954−55), 17−28. A very similar view was held by W.L. Knox, *St. Paul and the Church of the Gentiles* (Cambridge, 1939), esp. pp. 104−7, 151, 220.
21 J.Y. Lee, "Interpreting the Demonic Powers in Pauline Thought," *NovT* 12 (1970), 54−69.
22 P. Benoit, "Pauline Angelology and Demonology: Reflexions on the Designations of the Heavenly Powers and on the Origin of Angelic Evil," *Religious Studies Bulletin* 3 (1983), 1−18.
23 Benoit, "Angelology," 11.
24 For example, Benoit quickly dismisses *1 Enoch* 61:10 on the basis that the Similitudes are suspected of "being entirely Christian, [or] at least of containing Christian interpolations" (7). Modern research is more positive with regard to the date. J.H. Charlesworth, *The Pseudepigrapha and Modern Research* (SBL Septuagint and Cognate Studies 7, Missoula, 1976), 98 contends that, "If, as most specialists concur, the early portions of 1 Enoch date from the first half of the second century B.C., chapters 37−71 could have been added in the first century B.C., or the first century A.D."
25 J.H. Charlesworth, *The Old Testament Pseudepigrapha and the New Testament* (SNTSMS 54, Cambridge, 1985), 68, remarks, "The understanding of the cosmos and humanity − the *Zeitgeist* of Early Judaism − is perhaps the single most important contribution the documents in the Pseudepigrapha can make to our research as New Testament scholars."
26 Charlesworth, *Old Testament Pseudepigrapha*, 66.
27 Carr, *Angels and Principalities*.

28 See Clinton E. Arnold, "The 'Exorcism' of Ephesians 6.12 in Recent Research," *JSNT* 30 (1987), 71–87.

29 W. Wink, *Naming the Powers* (Philadelphia, 1984). The second volume, *Unmasking the Powers* (1986), and the prospective third volume, *Engaging the Powers*, focus on interpreting the significance of the biblical presentation of the "powers," aiming at making the discussion relevant to contemporary existence.

30 See the index to *IvE*, s.v., which compiles numerous instances of both terms used for political rulers. See also Macro, "Cities of Asia Minor," 677–78. He observes that ἀρχαί was a commonly used term in Asia Minor to refer to the elective offices of the state, whereas ἄρχοντες was the generic term for the governing board of magistrates, whether *strategoi* or *prytaneis*.

31 Wink, *Naming*, 66. Wink does waver slightly after this analysis when he says, "That all these terms were in fact used of social structures in the New Testament is beyond question, as our earlier survey shows. Whether the author intended such an analysis of social structures here is an open question."

32 Wink, *Naming*, 84, n. 96.

33 See the survey of the early Christian use of Ps 110 in D. M. Hay, *Glory at the Right Hand* (SBLMS 18, Nashville, 1973).

34 G. Delling, "ἀρχή," *TDNT* 1 (1964), 483.

35 Unfortunately, the Greek original of this text is not extant, but the conjectures are probably accurate. These particular conjectures are from Bietenhard, *Die himmlische Welt*, 105. There are also some significant Christian texts using the terms for evil spirits, although these may very well have come under the influence of Ephesians: *Acts of John* 79, 98, 104, 114; *PGM* P13.15, 17; P21:2–3. For further texts and discussion regarding the sources, see Dibelius, *Geisterwelt*, 99–101, and Bietenhard, *Himmlische Welt*, 104–108.

36 As with *2 Enoch*, we can only conjecture the Greek equivalents of the terminology for the angelic "powers" since this portion of *1 Enoch* is only extant in Ethiopic. We may also add *1 Enoch* 41:9: "Surely no authority (ἐξουσία) or power (δύναμις) has the ability to hinder" (a different MS reads, "Surely, neither an angel nor Satan has the power to hinder").

37 For further texts and discussion regarding the background of this term, see Grundmann, *Begriff der Kraft*, 41–47, and his article, "δύναμαι," *TDNT* 2 (1964), 292–99.

38 M-M, 172; see also *PGM* IV.1275.

39 See *BAG*, 461; W. Foerster, "κυριότης," *TDNT* 3 (1965), 1096–97, gives additional texts supporting the angelic interpretation.

40 Contra Wink, *Naming*, 62, and others who see a demythologizing trend in Ephesians.

41 See the discussion of the function of names in the magical papyri in H. Bietenhard, "ὄνομα," *TDNT* 5 (1967), 250–52. See also Aune, "Magic in Early Christianity," 1546–47.

42 Kee, *Medicine*, 107, observes that the efficacy of magic depends on "the recitation of an adequate number of names of divinities as a means of forcing their cooperation."

43 See also the numerous occurrences of ὄνομα in the cursing tablets;
    see the indexes to Audollent, *Defixionum tabellae*, s.v.
44 F. C. Conybeare, "The Demonology of the New Testament," *JQR*
    8 (1895—96), 585.
45 For further discussion, see G. B. Caird, "The Descent of Christ in
    Eph 4, 7—11," *SE* II (= *TU* 87, part 1, Berlin, 1964), 535—45, and
    the more recent discussion in A. T. Lincoln, "The Use of the OT
    in Ephesians," *JSNT* 14 (1982), 18—25.
46 Dibelius, *Geisterwelt*, 163.
47 F. Mußner, *Christus, das All und die Kirche* (TTS 5, Trier, 1955),
    44. Mußner and Barth, 2.477, argue convincingly against Gnostic
    interpretations which see the souls as captive in the realm of matter
    and finiteness.
48 Incarnation: Mußner, *Christus*, 27—28; H. Schlier, *Der Brief an
    die Epheser* (Dusseldorf, 1957), 192; et al.; descent of Holy Spirit:
    Lincoln, "Use of the OT," 21—25; Caird, "Descent," 537, would
    rather speak of Christ's return at Pentecost to bestow his spiritual
    gifts on the church.
49 Betz, "Catabasis Ritual," 287—95.
50 *Ibid.*, 292.
51 See chapter 2, sections 4 and 5 for an explanation of the connection
    of these names with Ephesus and western Asia Minor.
52 P. Köln Inv. T.1.58 (= Wortmann, "Texte," 62, 78). See also *PGM*
    IV.2333ff., 2293ff., VII.780ff.; see Wortmann, "Texte," 78, and
    Hopfner, "Hekate-Selene-Artemis," 131ff., for further texts.
53 G. H. R. Horsley, *New Documents Illustrating Early Christianity*
    (1976) (Australia, 1981), 35. His observations are made in the
    context of commenting on a recently discovered magical papyrus
    which also uses the imagery of the "keys of Hades."
54 *IvS* 550.1—2, speaks of the "dreadful shores of Hades." Another
    gravestone epitaph pleads, "O grave and demon, let my child Paula
    go free for a short time into the light (from Hades)" (*IvS* 549.7—9).
    See also *IvE* 2104.3, 5; 2105.4; *IvS* 517.3; 523.5; 528.2; 529.4; et al.
    Most of these date between the second century B.C. and the second
    century A.D.
55 This term may refer to a nation, family, clan, or even a relation-
    ship: see *BAG*, 636. The use of it here was probably motivated by
    the prior use of πατήρ. It is not necessary to think of the angelic
    world as a "family," but rather that they have their source in the
    one creator, the "Father."
56 This view of the term in Eph 2:2 commands a wide array of support:
    Barth, 1.214; Bruce, 281; J. Gnilka, *Der Epheserbrief* (HTKNT 10/2,
    Freiburg, 1971), 114; R. Schnackenburg, *Der Brief an die Epheser*
    (EKKNT 10, Zurich, Einsiedeln & Köln, 1982), 91; Schlier, 102; H.
    Saase, "αἰών," *TDNT* 1 (1964), 207; Mußner, *Christus*, 26; et al.
57 See Dibelius, *Geisterwelt*, 156; Everling, *Angelologie*, 105; Abbott,
    40; Wink, *Naming*, 82—83; A. van Roon, *The Authenticity of
    Ephesians* (NovTSup 39, Leiden, 1974), 225; E. Percy, *Die
    Probleme der Kolosser- und Epheserbriefe* (Lund, 1964), 259.

58 See G. Delling, "ἄρχων," *TDNT* 1 (1964), 488–89. Surprisingly, this word never occurs in Preisendanz's collection of magical papyri, which makes the Jewish provenance all the more significant in terms of linking it with spiritual "powers."

59 Dibelius, *Geisterwelt*, 156; Gnilka, 115; et al.

60 E.g. Everling, *Angelologie*, 108–109; Mußner, *Christus*, 19.

61 M. Smith, *Clement of Alexandria and a Secret Gospel of Mark* (Cambridge, Mass., 1973), 216, cites this magical text as a commentary on Eph 2:2.

62 For additional texts, see *PGM* I.49; IV.1134, 2699, 3042; VII.314; XIII.278; et al.

63 See also Philo, *De Gig.* 1.263; *1 Enoch* 15:10–11 has the demons dwelling in the clouds; *Asc. Is.* 7:9–12; 10:20 (these two texts may be post first century A.D.?). For further texts, see Everling, *Angelologie*, 106–109, and *BAG*, 20; see also Dibelius, *Geisterwelt*, 56–57; Abbott, 42; Schnackenburg, 91; *Str-B* 4.516.

64 Wink, *Naming*, 83, claims that there are no sources which give evidence for the idea of *evil* spirits in the air in the time of Paul. The magical papyri and Jewish tradition demonstrate the contrary. The logic of his argument is in error, however. He earnestly contends throughout his work (contra Carr) that there was a widespread belief in evil spirits in the first century. Where then are these evil spirits thought to reside? Wink deprives them of a home. He is right in affirming that there are a number of pre-Christian references to good spirits dwelling in the air, but it does not follow that their evil counterparts could not also abide in the air, especially when there are no texts pointing to the contrary coupled with a strong post-first-century tradition which puts them in the air. See also Schlier, *Principalities*, 30–32.

65 The expression τοῦ πνεύματος should be understood as in apposition to ἄρχων. The genitive case is retained because of the anacoluthon; see Gnilka, 115.

66 This is a prominent idea in the first section of *Asc. Is.*: see 1:9; 3:11; 4:2; see also *Jub* 10:1–2 ("And in the third week of this jubilee the unclean demons began to lead the children of Noah's sons astray and to mislead them and destroy them"); 10:6–11; 11:4–5 ("And malevolent spirits egged them on and seduced them, so that they indulged in every kind of sin and uncleanness. And the prince Mastema exerted himself to do all this, and he sent out as agents the spirits that were under his control to do all kinds of wrong and sin ..."); 12:20; 19:28; the devil (Mastema) is seen even to inspire a "mob spirit" in 48:12; *Test. Dan* 1:6 ("And one of the spirits of Beliar was at work within me, saying, 'take this sword, and with it kill Joseph'"); 5:6.

67 Wink, *Naming*, 83–84, as we noted earlier, has attempted to explain this by contending that the author has "taken a radical step away from mythicization of evil in personified demonic spirits." The unparalleled emphasis on the role of the "powers" in Ephesians

proves just the contrary. Our author has sought to highlight the place of the "powers," otherwise we could have expected him to eliminate totally such references and emphasize "the flesh."

68 For additional discussion of the "mystery," see chapter 6.

69 Dibelius, *Geisterwelt*, 161, n. 1, concurs by noting that it is "not through words and deeds, but through its complete existence."

70 Wink, *Naming*, 89; see also Barth, 1.363–66.

71 Wink, *Naming*, 93, 95–96.

72 *Ibid.*, 96, n. 127.

73 See *1 Enoch* 12:4; *Jub* 4:15, 21, 22; 5:1–6; *Test. Reub.* 5:6; *Test. Naph.* 3:5; et al.

74 See Everling, *Angelologie*, 11–14, and G. Delling, "ἄρχων," *TDNT* 1 (1964), 489, for evidence affirming the demonic interpretation of ἄρχοντες in 1 Cor 2:6, 8.

75 E. F. Scott, *The Epistles of Paul to the Colossians, to Philemon, and to the Ephesians* (MNTC, London, 1930), 189.

76 See C. L. Mitton, *The Epistle to the Ephesians. Its Authorship, Origin and Purpose* (Oxford, 1951), 8, 209.

77 Van Roon, *Authenticity*, 174.

78 E.g. H. Kee, "Testaments of the 12 Patriarchs," *OTP* 1.782, n. 2a, comments, "The devil (διάβολος) is somewhat more common than Satan in T12P." See *Test. Reub.* 2:1; *Test. Naph.* 8:4, 6.

79 See Carr, *Angels and Principalities*, 106.

80 In *Test. Sol.* 8:2 the στοιχεῖα are called κοσμοκράτορες and in 18:2 the spirits come to Solomon and call themselves the "κοσμοκράτορες of the darkness of this age." This usage may have been influenced by Eph 6:12, however. F. C. Conybeare, "The Testament of Solomon," *JQR* 11 (1898), 6, on the other hand, argues that the phrase κοσμοκράτορες τοῦ σκότους cannot be regarded as imported from Ephesians into the Testament. He sees the phrase as reflecting Jewish demonology.

81 Carr, *Angels and Principalities*, 107; Wink, *Naming*, 85, regards this as the first occurrence.

82 F. Cumont and L. Canet, "Mithra ou Sarapis ΚΟΣΜΟΚΡΑΤΩΡ?" *CRAI* (1919), 313–28.

83 Cumont and Canet, "ΚΟΣΜΟΚΡΑΤΩΡ," 318, n. 3. Cumont and Canet cite numerous other occurrences of the term, primarily in the magical papyri and astrological writings, especially Proclus, Simplicius, Iamblichus, Hephestion, Damascius, et al.

84 The cosmic and astrological significance of Mithras is illustrated by two images of the deity described by G. Ristow, "Zum Kosmokrator im Zodiacus, ein Bildvergleich," *Hommages à Maarten J. Vermaseren* (EPRO 68, 3 vols., Leiden, 1978), 3.985–87. The similarity to the images of the Ephesian Artemis are quite striking with regard to the astrological motifs. Both deities have a wreath with the signs of the stars as well as an animal-circle (*Tierkreis*), the most significant cosmic trait. For an explanation of the importance and meaning of the *Tierkreiszeichen* for the Ephesian Artemis, see Heinzel, "Artemis von Ephesos," 241–51. See also chapter 2.

85 Cumont and Canet, "ΚΟΣΜΟΚΡΑΤΩΡ," 320–21.
86 Cumont and Canet, "ΚΟΣΜΟΚΡΑΤΩΡ," 322–23; W. Michaelis, "κοσμοκράτωρ," *TDNT* 3 (1965), 913; Nilsson, *Geschichte*, 2.374.
87 We have no extant evidence of this term being applied to Artemis, but Artemis possesses all of the traits of a cosmic deity who holds the power over fate.
88 There is substantial evidence to support the presence of the worship of these and other Egyptian deities in first-century Asia Minor; see G. Hölbl, *Zeugnisse ägyptischer Religionsvorstellungen für Ephesus* (EPRO 73, Leiden, 1978).
89 Everling, *Angelologie*, 27–32, esp. p. 28. Conybeare, "Demonology," 584, remarks, "Paul, the apostle of the Gentiles, believed in another and fresh mode of demoniac activity, never referred to in the Gospels. The gods of the heathen were devils, i.e. really supernatural beings exercising their powers and knowledge for sinister aims." For further discussion of the Pauline concept of "demons" animating the heathen gods, see M. Dibelius and H. Greeven, *An die Kolosser, Epheser, an Philemon* (HNT 12, Tübingen, 1953), 67–71.
90 See Billerbeck's summary of the attitude of the ancient synagogue to heathen gods in *Str-B*, 3.48–60. See also C. K. Barrett, "Things Sacrificed to Idols," *NTS* 11 (1964–65), 148–49.
91 Abbott, 182; *BAG*, 679.
92 See chapter 6; see also H. Schlier, "ἀνακεφαλαιόομαι," *TDNT* 3 (1965), 682; Barth, 1.88–91; Dibelius–Greeven, 61. Col. 1:20 closely parallels this passage in meaning but uses the term ἀποκαταλάσσω.
93 A. Lindemann, *Die Aufhebung der Zeit* (SNT 12, Gütersloh, 1975), 98ff.
94 For further arguments against the position of Lindemann, see the excursus, "The Cosmic Anakephalaiosis," in C. Caragounis, *The Ephesian Mysterion* (ConB 8, Lund, 1977), 143–46.
95 This was also the conclusion of Dibelius in his monograph on the "powers": "Far be it from him to contradict the existence of the spirits; they *exist*, but we Christians are prepared for them; they can no longer rule us" (Dibelius, *Geisterwelt*, 207).

4 The power of God for believers

1 R. Schnackenburg, "Die große Eulogie Eph 1,3–14," *BZ NF* 21/1 (1977), 85–86.
2 N. A. Dahl, 'Adresse und Proömium," 241–64, esp. p. 262, C. Maurer, "Der Hymnus von Epheser 1 als Schlüssel zum ganzen Brief," *EvT* 11 (1951–52), 151–72, esp. p. 168, and J. T. Sanders, "Hymnic Elements in Ephesians 1–3," *ZNW* 56 (1965), 230, all contend that the eulogy serves as an introduction to the whole epistle by prefiguring the main themes of the letter. Barth, 1.98, has also given assent to this conclusion by commenting that the eulogy is "a digest of the whole epistle and replete with key terms and topics that anticipate what follows."

3   P. T. O'Brien, "Ephesians 1: An Unusual Introduction to a New
    Testament Letter," *NTS* 25 (1978), 510.
4   O'Brien, "Introduction," 512.
5   *Ibid.*, 511–12.
6   Some see Eph 1:20–23 as part of a hymnic piece which the author
    has inserted as a Christological excursus motivated by his final
    request: Dibelius–Greeven, 64, refer to it as "a kind of hymn'';
    G. Schille, *Frühchristliche Hymnen* (Berlin, 1965), 55, also speaks
    of it as a kind of hymn, but he does not examine the passage in detail;
    Käsemann, "Epheserbrief," *RGG*, 2.519, sees a hymnic fragment
    lying at the base of the passage; R. Deichgräber, *Gotteshymnus und
    Christushymnus in frühen Christenheit* (SUNT 5, Göttingen, 1967),
    161–65, K. M. Fischer, *Tendenz und Absicht des Epheserbriefes*
    (FRLANT 111, Göttingen, 1973), 118–20, and J. Ernst, *Pleroma
    und Pleroma Christi* (BU 5, Regensburg, 1970), 106–107 (Ernst
    follows Deichgräber) attempt detailed reconstructions of the sup-
    posed hymn. Some see it as part of the free composition of the
    author elaborating on his final request: Schnackenburg, 70–71;
    Barth, 1.154. My thesis is not affected either way if the passage could
    be conclusively demonstrated as hymnic or non-hymnic.
7   P. T. O'Brien, *Introductory Thanksgivings in the Letters of Paul*
    (NovTSup 46, Leiden, 1977), 13–15.
8   O'Brien, "Introduction," 514.
9   Fischer, *Tendenz*, 118, has correctly observed this emphasis: "from
    verse 15 on, [the author of] Ephesians prays for the reader that he
    might be filled with the power of God, the power by which God
    raised Jesus from the dead." F. W. Beare, *The Epistle to the
    Ephesians* (IB, New York, 1955), 630, corroborates this conclusion:
    "The whole prayer moves forward to the exposition of the third
    [v. 19] of these elements."
10 The term μέγεθος is a hapax legomenon in the NT and seldom
    occurs in the LXX (but see Ezek 31). Likewise, ὑπερβάλλω is rare
    in the LXX and only occurs twice in Paul, viz. in reference to the
    New Covenant (2 Cor 3:10) and the grace of God (2 Cor 9:14). The
    Ephesian author uses it twice to describe the vast grace (2:7) and
    love (3:19) of God.
11 For μέγεθος, see *IvE* 211.2; 212.2; 449.12; 666a.10; *PGM* III.601.
12 See also *PGM* IV.649; *IvE* 11a.15–19. The significance of this local
    and magical usage is heightened by the fact that the participle occurs
    only once in the LXX (Job 15:11).
13 See G. Bertram, "ἐνεργέω," *TDNT* 2 (1964), 652. See also Wis
    7:17.
14 See Wis 7:26; 2 Macc 3:29; 3 Macc 4:21; 5:12; 5:28.
15 Grundmann, *Begriff der Kraft*, 58. This same conclusion is upheld
    by K. W. Clark, "The Meaning of 'Ενεργέω and Καταργέω in the
    New Testament," *JBL* 54 (1935), 93–101, esp. 96–97; see also G.
    Bertram, "ἐνεργέω," *TDNT* 2 (1964), 652; *BAG*, 265.
16 See also *PGM* I.274; III.284, 290, 412, 596; IV.160, 1718, 2570.
17 Eph 3:7; 4:16; Col 1:29; 2:12; Phil 3:21; 2 Thess 2:9, 11.

18 For κράτος, see *PGM* IV.518; VII.1020; XII.134; XIII.629, 803, 881. For ἰσχύς, see *PGM* II.182; IV.1025, 1653, 1665, 1820; VII.924; XXXVI.224; LXIX.1,2.

19 E.g. Abbott, 31, and B.F. Westcott, *St. Paul's Epistle to the Ephesians* (London, 1906), 25–26, regard ἰσχύς as denoting inherent power or strength absolutely, whereas κράτος refers to power expressing itself in overcoming resistance, i.e. strength regarded as abundantly effective in relation to an end to be gained or a dominion to be exercised. W. Michaelis, "κράτος," *TDNT* 3 (1965), 908, on the other hand, would stress that κράτος denotes the outer aspect of strength, perhaps its supremacy. This actually comes closer to Abbott and Westcott's definition of ἰσχύς.

20 See also 1QH 7:9ff.; 18:8ff.; 15:4; 1QS 11:19ff.; similarly, but with other synonyms for "might," 1QH 2:8; 1QM 11:5; 1QH 14:23; 1QH 11:29. For further discussion, see Grundmann, *Begriff der Kraft*, 109–10; "ἰσχύω," *TDNT* 3 (1965), 402; Gnilka, 92; R. E. Murphy, "GBR and GBWRH in the Qumran Writings," *Lex tua veritas* (FS. H. Junker, Trier, 1961), 137–43; Kuhn, "Qumran," 117.

21 In her study of δύναμις in Paul, Helge Nielsen, "'Paulus' Verwendung des Begriffes Δύναμις. Eine Replik zur Kreuzestheologie," *Die Paulinische Literatur und Theologie* (Århus, 1980), 140–41, concludes, "If one explores Paul's use of the word δύναμις more closely, it will soon be evident that it is fundamentally related to the Pauline use of the concept of δόξα." Although Nielsen omits Ephesians from her study, Schlier, 77, delineates the same conclusion in his comments on the phrase in Ephesians when he remarks that δόξα and δύναμις are interchangeable terms in Paul; see also H. Schlier, "Doxa bei Paulus als heilsgeschichtlicher Begriff," *Besinnung auf das Neue Testament* (Freiburg, 1964); H. Kittel, *Die Herrlichkeit Gottes* (BZNW 16, Giessen, 1934), 232.

22 Schnackenburg, 73; et al.

23 Schlier, 77–78. He produces a significant number of references to an expected Messianic Spirit of inspiration in the apocalyptic tradition of Judaism and in the wisdom literature. See also J. L. Houlden, *Paul's Letters from Prison* (Baltimore, 1970), 274.

24 E. Käsemann, *Leib und Leib Christi* (BHT 9, Tübingen, 1933), 125. In his comments on 1:17, Houlden, 274, notes, "Spirit is again a word which carries the idea of God's power."

25 Schnackenburg, 73; Beare, 629.

26 Scott, 154. For references, see *BAG*, 873. See also R. Reitzenstein, *Hellenistic Mystery Religions* (Pittsburgh, 1978), 335–36.

27 Scott, 154.

28 J. A. Fitzmyer, "'To Know Him and the Power of His Resurrection' (Phil 3:10)," *Mélanges bibliques en hommage au R. P. Béda Rigaux* (Gembloux, 1970), 420.

29 B. Metzger, "The Meaning of Christ's Ascension," *Search the Scriptures* (Leiden, 1969), 166, notes, "In claiming that Christ is at the right hand of God the author is affirming the absolute and complete authority of Christ over the whole universe so that to say

'Christ has ascended and now sits at the right hand of God,' means simply that he lives and rules with the power and authority of God himself.'' See also P. D. Overfield, "The Ascension, Pleroma and Ecclesia Concepts in Ephesians," unpublished Ph.D. Thesis, St. Andrews, 1976, 79.

30 The adverb ὑπεράνω does occur in *Test. Levi* 3:4 to denote the abode of God: "And above them [the spirits of error and of Beliar] are the Holy Ones. In the uppermost heaven of all dwells the Great Glory in the Holy of Holies superior to all holiness."

31 E.g. Judg 10:18; 11:8–9, 11; 1 Sam 15:17; 2 Sam 22:44; 1 Kings 21:12; Isa 7:8–9; Ps 17:44; Hos 1:11. See also *Jub* 1:16; Philo, *Praem. poen.*, 20.

32 For example, in Judg 11:8–9, A reads κεφαλή twice while B has ἄρχων both times, although it has κεφαλή in 11:11. In 1 Kings 20:12, the text reads ἀρχή while A prefers κεφαλή. See further, H. Schlier, "κεφαλή," *TDNT* 3 (1965), 675, Gnilka, 103–105, and van Roon, *Authenticity*, 289–90.

33 E.g. Schnackenburg, 79.

34 H. Schlier, *Christus und die Kirche im Epheserbrief* (BHT 6, Tübingen, 1930), 37–48; Käsemann, *Leib*, 137–59.

35 See chapter 2, section 2. See also Colpe's rejection of this derivation in his study, "Zur Leib-Christi-Vorstellung im Epheserbrief," *Judentum, Urchristentum, Kirche* (BZNW 26, Berlin, 1960), 172–87.

36 Colpe, "Leib-Christi," 179–82; see also E. Schweizer, "σῶμα," *TDNT* 7 (1971), 1054–55; Schenke, *Der Gott "Mensch,"* 153–56, and his article, "Der Widerstreit gnostischer und kirchlicher Christologie im Spiegel des Kolosserbriefes," *ZTK* 61 (1964), 400; Fischer, *Tendenz*, 76–79. E. Schweizer, "Die Kirche als Leib Christi in den paulinischen Antilegomena," *Neotestamentica* (Zürich, 1963), 293–316, on the basis of his summary of the usage of σῶμα in Greek writings presented in his *TDNT* article also argues for a widespread non-Gnostic macroanthropos view of σῶμα in the Hellenistic world which influenced the Christology of the Christ-hymn in Colossians and thereby the Christology of Colossians and Ephesians. He depends most heavily on passages in Philo plus references to Plato and the Stoics which speak of the animating "body" of all things, or the cosmos.

37 The actual papyrus *PGM* XXI may be dated as early as the second century, with the strong likelihood that its readings date much earlier.

38 H. Wheeler Robinson, "The Hebrew Conception of Corporate Personality," *Werden und Wesen des Alten Testaments* (BZAW 66, Berlin, 1936), 49–62. For the application of this concept to Paul and Ephesians, see: T. G. Allen, "Exaltation and Solidarity with Christ: Ephesians 1.20 and 2.6," *JSNT* 28 (1986), 110, 119; E. Percy, *Der Leib Christi* (Lund & Leipzig, 1942); E. Best, *One Body in Christ* (London, 1955), 115–59; W. D. Davies, *Paul and Rabbinic Judaism* (London, 1955), 36–57; et al.

39 Lightfoot, *Colossians*, 366—67; J. A. Robinson, *St. Paul's Epistle to the Ephesians* (London, 1907), 104.
40 Lightfoot, *Colossians*, 227.
41 Barth, 1.183—92. So also, Usami, *Somatic Comprehension*, 140—42.
42 Barth, 1.190.
43 Contra E. Käsemann, "The Theological Problem Presented by the Motif of the Body of Christ," *Perspectives on Paul* (London, 1971), 113.
44 Lightfoot, *Colossians*, 267; Robinson, 104; P. Benoit, "Corps, tête et plérôme dans les épîtres de la captivité," *RB* 63 (1956), 27. Barth 1.186, n. 204, cites this conclusion of these interpreters approvingly.
45 Beare, 637; Robinson, 43, 152, 259; Best, *One Body*, 141—43; P. D. Overfield, "Pleroma: A Study in Content and Context," *NTS* 25 (1978—79), 393; P. Benoit, "The 'plérôma' in the Epistles to the Colossians and the Ephesians," *Svensk Exegetisk Årsbok* 49 (1984), 156; R. Yates, "A Re-examination of Ephesians 1:23," *ET* 83 (1971—72), 146—51; I. de la Potterie, "Le Christ, Plérôme de l'Eglise (Ep. 1, 22—23)," *Bib* 58 (1977), 500—24.
46 Gnilka, 98—99; Barth, I.209; C. Masson, *L'Epître de Saint Paul aux Ephésiens* (Neuchatel & Paris, 1953), 156; Schnackenburg, 80—81; Schlier, 97—99; Dibelius—Greeven, 65; H. Hegermann, *Die Vorstellung vom Schöpfungsmittler im hellenistischen Judentum und Urchristentum* (*TU* 82, Berlin, 1961), 152; Lightfoot, *Colossians*, 329. Ernst, *Pleroma*, 118—20, attempts to set forth a third view by conflating the evidence set forth by both views. He therefore takes πλήρωμα as both active and passive ("Fülle und Vollendung") and likewise the participle as having both active and passive significance ("erfüllen" und "erfüllt sein").
47 This is not consistently the case in the gospels, where on one occasion πλήρωμα is used in an active sense, viz. in Mark 2:21, where the term may be regarded as synonymous with "patch" and therefore denotes that which completes or restores.
48 *BDF*, par. 316 (1).
49 Schnackenburg, 80; Hegermann, *Schöpfungsmittler*, 152.
50 See the study of Overfield, "Pleroma," 384—96, who delineates the decisive differences.
51 Benoit, "The plérôma," 136—58. He finds the use of the term in Stoicism and in this context opposed to later Valentinian usage by the expansiveness of its meaning, "far from being the fulness of a divine world opposed to the material one, he [Christ] encompasses all, the divine, the human, and the whole created framework of the universe" (142). This explanation too closely approximates the pantheistic identification of the one and the all of which Ephesians and Colossians know nothing.
52 G. Münderlein, "Die Erwählung durch das Pleroma," *NTS* 8 (1962), 264—76; see also Barth, 1. Comment VI.C., "Fullness," 200—10. Hellenistic Judaism, as represented by Philo, used the verb in a similar way to express the divine fullness of being, e.g. "The Father and Creator of all things ... who truly with his being fills

all things with his powers for the salvation of all" (Philo, *Qu. gen.* 4.130; see also *Leg. all.*, 3.4; *Som.*, 2.221). See Hegermann, *Schöpfungsmittler*, 106ff. See also H. Merklein, *Das Kirchliche Amt nach dem Epheserbrief* (SANT 33, Munich, 1973), 70; G. Delling, "πληρόω," *TDNT* 6 (1968), 288–90.

53 Münderlein, "Erwählung," 272: "*as a striking paraphrase of the Holy Spirit*" (italics in original). See also N. Kehl, *Der Christushymnus im Kolosserbrief* (SBM 1, Stuttgart, 1967), 120–25; J. G. Gibbs, *Creation and Redemption* (NovTSup 26, Leiden, 1971), 99ff., 108; R. P. Meyer, *Kirche und Mission im Epheserbrief* (SBS 86, Stuttgart, 1977), 44; A. J. Bandstra, "Plērōma as Pneuma in Colossians," *Ad Interim* (FS. R. Schippers, Kampen, 1975), 96–102. Bandstra seeks to overcome one of the objections to Münderlein's interpretation, viz. that no instances of πλήρωμα can be found where it is used as an equivalent for the Spirit. He is not able to find such an equation with the Greek term, but he does find two examples using a Semitic equivalent (1QH 16:2–3; *2 Baruch* 21:4).

54 Lightfoot, *Colossians*, 329.

55 So Schlier, 97–99, and others who see a Gnostic background to the use of πλήρωμα here.

56 Schnackenburg, 81, 83. Meyer, *Kirche und Mission*, 43–46, prefers seeing τὰ πάντα in 1:23 as a reference to the lost world to whom the gospel should be preached by the church, which has been empowered by the πλήρωμα. Christ's filling of "all things" therefore refers to the extensive growth of the church through the addition of individuals (ἐν πᾶσιν = masculine). It is likely that the preaching of the gospel may be one of the ideas in the mind of the author in referring to Christ's filling of all things, but there is no basis for restricting "all things" to unevangelized humanity.

57 As for example, Barth, 1.156.

58 Schnackenburg, 83; Gnilka, 99; Dibelius–Greeven, 65. It is unlikely that it is a masculine noun denoting the individual members of the church (thus Schlier, 99) because of the cosmic emphasis.

59 Schlier, 146.

60 This is also the view of Mußner, *Christus*, 73, who explains that the final clause functions as a résumé of the whole prayer. He retains this view in his commentary; see *Der Brief an die Epheser* (ÖTK 10, Gutersloh, 1982), 109.

61 The closest parallel to this expression is found in 2 Kings 22:33: ὁ ἰσχυρὸς ὁ κραταιῶν με δυνάμει; see W. Michaelis, "κραταιόω," *TDNT* 3 (1965), 913. Kuhn, "Qumran," 117–18, and Gnilka, 183, point to close parallels in the Qumran texts (1QH 7:17, 19; 12:35; 13:35). The verb κραταιόω never occurs in Preisendanz's collection of magical papyri.

62 Hopfner, "Hekate-Selene-Artemis," 142.

63 *Ibid.*, 142.

64 This is the view of most of the commentaries: see Schlier, 169; Gnilka, 184; Abbott, 96; Barth, 1.369–70; Westcott, 51. Beare, 678, however, views v. 17a as a second means of strengthening.

65 For further discussion of v. 17a in relation to Pauline theology, see S. Mattam, "Eph. 3:17: A Study of the Indwelling of Christ in St. Paul," *Biblehashyam* 6 (1980), 125–50; G. Söhngen, "Christi Gegenwart in und durch den Glauben (Eph 3, 17)," *Die Messe in der Glaubensverkündigung* (Freiburg, 1950), 14–28.

66 Barth, 1.370–71.

67 J. Behm, "καρδία," *TDNT* 3 (1965), 612.

68 Cf. Gnilka, 184; Schlier, 169.

69 Schnackenburg, 151.

70 Dibelius–Greeven, 77.

71 *BAG*, 276.

72 Barth, 1.372. See, for example, Judg 9:45; 2 Kings 12:26; 1 Macc 1:19; 5:28.

73 Job 11:7–9 speaks of four dimensions to the wisdom of God, although the terminology is not precisely the same as in Ephesians: "Can you find out the deep things of God? Can you find out the limit of the Almighty (παντοκράτωρ)? It is higher (ὑψηλός) than heaven … deeper (βαθύτερα) than Sheol, its measure is longer (μακρότερα) than the earth, and broader (εὔρους) than the sea." See also Job 28:12–14, 21–22; Amos 9:2–3; Ps 139:8–9; Wis 1:3. Those who see the infinite scope of the divine wisdom as the object of the dimensional language in Ephesians are: A. Feuillet, "L'Eglise plérôme du Christ d'après Ephés., I, 23," *NRT* 78 (1956), 593–602; Barth, 1.395–97; Bruce, 327–28. Schnackenburg, 154, finds the Wisdom literature the source for the dimensional terminology, but refers to the salvation "mystery" as the object. It is important for our purposes to note that an integral part of understanding the personified divine "Wisdom" is apprehending the nature of God as "all-powerful" (παντοκράτωρ).

74 N. A. Dahl, "Cosmic Dimensions and Religious Knowledge," *Jesus and Paul* (Göttingen, 1978), 57–75, traces a development in which he believes that Jewish wisdom literature and Greek philosophy converge into a notion of revealed knowledge of cosmological secrets and mystical visions of the universe. He suggests that the actual terminology is of Greek origin (60). J. Dupont, *Gnosis* (Louvain, 1949), 476–89, cites a number of texts from Philo.

75 *Corp. Herm.* 10:25; 11:19ff.; *Pistis sophia* 133; see Dibelius–Greeven, 77. Mußner, *Christus*, 74, rightly observes that Eph 3:18 has nothing in common with the spatial speculation of Gnosis. Furthermore, the Hermetic texts do not use the same terminology as Ephesians. Schlier, 173–74, and in his article, "βάθος," *TDNT* 1 (1964), 518, binds the conception of the Gnostic primal man and his cosmic body which encompasses the earth with the idea of the cross of Christ encompassing the earth with its redemptive significance. He sees this concept taken up in some of the apocryphal acts (*Acts of Andrew* 14; *Acts of Peter* 38) and in Irenaeus, *Adv. Haer.* 5.17.4. Against this view, it should be mentioned that "cross" only appears once in Ephesians (2:16) in an instrumental sense without this kind of symbolic significance. In addition, these

later passages may be partly influenced by the Ephesian passage: see Schnackenburg, 154.

76 See Herm., *Vis.* 3.2.5, and the rabbinic texts cited in *Str-B*, 3.849–50, and Schlier, 173. This background has the additional NT support of Rev 21:16, which uses all of the same terms as Ephesians, except βάθος, to describe the dimensions of the heavenly Jerusalem.

77 Dupont, *Gnosis*, 476ff., supposes that the author has taken over a Stoic formula indicating the idea of totality.

78 *BAG*, s.v. βάθος, 130.

79 Dahl, "Cosmic Dimensions," 66, n. 18.

80 R. Reitzenstein, *Poimandres* (Darmstadt, 1966), 25–26.

81 So also Dahl, "Cosmic Dimensions," 66–67. Reitzenstein, *Poimandres*, 25–26, therefore finds von Soden's interpretation of the dimensions in Ephesians as the spiritual temple of the heart which God fills the most compelling.

82 Reitzenstein, *Poimandres*, 25, regards the magical formula in *PGM* IV as the source of this passage. Knox, *Paul*, 192, n. 1, argues for the opposite conclusion. He contends, "there is no reason for a fourth dimension in magic." This statement is true if one regards the four dimensions as a spatial expression, but the argument falls if the four dimensions are seen as a rhetorical expression of supernatural power.

83 Gnilka, 189; Abbott, 99–100; van Roon, *Authenticity*, 265.

84 Schnackenburg, 154; Percy, *Probleme*, 310; Robinson, 86, 176; Mußner, *Christus*, 74; Usami, *Unity*, 176.

85 Feuillet, "L'Eglise," 593–602; Barth, 1.396–97; Bruce, 327–28.

86 Dibelius–Greeven, 77; H. Conzelmann, *Der Brief an die Epheser* (NTD 8, Göttingen, 1965), 106; N. Dahl, *Das Volk Gottes* (Darmstadt, 1963), 58ff.; G. Bertram, "ὕψος," *TDNT* 8 (1972), 604.

87 Schlier, 173–74.

88 Ambrosiaster, cited in Schlier, 172.

89 Dahl, "Cosmic Dimensions," 73–74.

90 *Ibid.*, 60–64.

91 It is significant to note 1 Cor 2:10, where Paul states that the depths (βάθη) of God are revealed διὰ τοῦ πνεύματος.

92 Gnilka, 189.

93 The term βάθος is used twice with a defined object. It is used to describe the "depth" of the wisdom and knowledge of God (Rom 11:33) and the "depths" of God himself (1 Cor 2:10). On both occasions Paul seems to utilize the term in a metaphorical sense as a way of expressing extent.

94 H. Schlier, "βάθος," *TDNT* 1 (1964), 517, states, "in Rom 8:39 βάθος is a κτίσις like δύναμις etc."; H. Lietzmann, *Die Briefe des Apostels Paulus* (HNT, Tübingen, 1919), 89, sees ὕψωμα as an astrological expression usually linked with ταπείνωμα used to indicate the approaching or withdrawing of a star from its zenith (Plutarch, *Sept. sap. conv.* 3.149a); βάθος is also an astrological expression for the *Himmelsraum* existing under the horizon out of which the stars ascend. Lietzmann concludes that in v. 39 the two

terms refer to "sidereal powers ... that rule in the heights and depths." Similarly, O. Michel, *Der Brief an die Römer*, MeyerK (14th edn, Göttingen, 1977), 285, thinks the terms refer to "spirit beings in the heavenly and underworld spheres." See also E. Käsemann, *Commentary on Romans* (Grand Rapids, 1980), 250–251; U. Wilckens, *Der Brief and die Römer* (EKKNT, 3 vols., Neukirchener, 1980), 3.177.

95 See Cranfield, *Romans*, 2.443.
96 Dahl, "Cosmic Dimensions," 57–75.
97 Schlier, 171.
98 See Barth, 1.383, who refers to the Synoptic examples of the appointing of the Twelve and Peter (Luke 6:13–14; Matt 10:1, 13; Mark 3:14; see also Matt 16:18–19).
99 Contra the thesis of Lindemann, *Aufhebung*, who sees this tension as completely lost in the fully realized eschatology of Ephesians. See Mußner, 113.
100 A few interpreters connect ἐν ἀγάπῃ with the preceding clause: see Robinson, 85–86, 175; Goodspeed, cited in Beare, 678–79; WH; NEB. This construal seems highly unlikely, especially in view of the fact that a ground for "rooting" and "founding" is expressed in both of the Colossian parallels (1:23; 2:7).
101 Schnackenburg, 152; Dibelius–Greeven, 77. Barth, 1.371–72, however, regards this clause as an "exhortatory digression." In addition, both *BDF*, par. 468(2)b, and J. H. Moulton and N. Turner, *A Grammar of New Testament Greek* (Edinburgh, 1963), 3.343e, cite this phrase as an example of the imperatival participle. It is difficult and inconsistent to see this phrase as an exhortation, however, since the context is not paraenesis but prayer.
102 G. Scholem, *Major Trends in Jewish Mysticism* (London, 1955), 56.
103 L. G. Champion, *Benedictions and Doxologies in the Epistles of Paul* (Oxford, 1934), 24, regards 3:20–21 as a "clear example" of a doxology complete in itself; see also G. Delling, *Der Gottesdienst im Neuen Testament* (Göttingen, 1952), 67; and the commentaries.
104 Deichgräber, *Gotteshymnus*, 25.
105 *Ibid.*, 24.
106 *Ibid.*, 39. See also Gnilka, 192; Barth, 1.374; Champion, *Doxologies*, 45.
107 This is not a unique phrase. It occurs also in the doxologies of Rom 16:25, Jude 24, and *Mart. Pol.* 20:2.
108 Clark, "Meaning of Ἐνεργέω," 93–101, convincingly argues for a passive understanding of ἐνεργέομαι here and in its other occurrences in the NT with the divine subject implicit.
109 Deichgräber, *Gotteshymnus*, 28.

5 The conflict with the "powers"

1 A. Lindemann, "Bemerkungen zu den Adressaten und zum Anlaß des Epheserbriefes," *ZNW* 67 (1976), 242–43, 250. See also P. Pokorný, "Epheserbrief und gnostische Mysterien," *ZNW* 53 (1962), 190, for a similar view.
2 Martin, "Life Setting," 299–301.
3 Schnackenburg, "Horizont," 155–75; Fischer, *Tendenz*, 201–203.
4 H. Lona, *Die Eschatologie im Kolosser- und Epheserbrief* (FzB 48, Würzburg, 1984), 425–26, 428–48.
5 Not only is this passage neglected in summarizing the theology of the epistle, especially the eschatology, but some writers fail even to mention the passage: e.g. F. J. Steinmetz, *Protologische Heilszuversicht* (Frankfurt, 1969), makes only one reference, in a footnote, to the passage.
6 Gnilka, 304, n. 1; Schnackenburg, 277.
7 The author may have wanted to enhance the parallelism of ἐνδυναμοῦσθε ... ἐνδύσασθε by adding the ἐν prefix to the verb δυναμόω in order to render them stylistically parallel. The verbs δυναμόω and ἐνδυναμόω are synonymous in meaning: see W. Grundmann, "δύναμις," *TDNT* 2 (1965), 287. Manuscripts P 46, B, and 33 actually read δυναμοῦσθε.
8 Wild, "Warrior," 286. Conversely, Wild is correct in noticing that 6:12 is extremely important in terms of the argument of Ephesians. The "powers" do indeed hold a prominent place in the epistle, but the structure of this passage clearly suggests that "standing" is the ultimate goal the author seeks to impress upon his readers as he writes this section. The disproportionate attention given this verse by second-century commentators does not accurately reflect the importance of the verse for the total context as Wild suggests, but rather reflects the interest in the novel delineation of the "powers" as well as reflecting the importance of these terms in second-century Gnosticism.
9 Gnilka, 309; Schnackenburg, 274.
10 Wild, "Warrior," 286.
11 Abbott, 187; Masson, 222; Schnackenburg, 275.
12 Gnilka, 313.
13 P. Carrington, *The Primitive Christian Catechism* (Cambridge, 1940). See also Davies, *Paul*, 120–30; E. Selwyn, *The First Epistle of Peter* (London, 1947), 393–406.
14 Carrington, *Catechism*, 31–57; see his table comparing the four epistles (42–43).
15 Carrington, *Catechism*, 3–10, 13–21. See also Davies, *Paul*, 129.
16 Schlier, 223. See also Fischer, *Tendenz*, 172, who refers to 6:10–20 as typical teaching for new believers (*Neophytenparänese*).
17 Schlier, 289; Barth, 2.760; Abbott, 180–81.
18 Bruce, 403, however, understands it as a middle voice with the sense of "strengthen yourselves in the Lord." He finds this to be more consistent with its integral place within the paraenesis of the epistle

(4:1–6:20) and with the active significance, "put on the armor of God" (v. 11). The requisite dependence on the power of God is not lessened by this interpretation, but the necessary ethical implications are stressed (esp. faith, prayer).

19 Barth, 2.762, observes that the verb δύναμαι normally bears the significance of the presence and exercise of sufficient power "in a pragmatic, almost mechanical sense." He finds this sense of the verb confirmed by the LXX translators' preference for δύναμαι in the translation of the Hebrew *yakhol*, "to be able, to hold, to endure, to stand, to have it in one's power, to prevail."

20 Grundmann, *Begriff der Kraft*, 108.

21 Wild, "Warrior," 287.

22 This is a tendency held in common with Paul, who cites Isaiah 26 per cent of the time in his OT quotations. See C. J. A. Hickling, "Paul's Reading of Isaiah," *Studia biblica 1978: III* (JSNTSS 3, Sheffield, 1980), 215–23.

23 Lincoln, "Use of the OT," 43; Wild, "Warrior," 293; Barth, 2.788, n. 175; Caird, 93; Schlier, 294–97; Schnackenburg, 284–87; E. Ellis, *Paul's Use of the Old Testament* (London, 1957), 154.

24 Lindemann, *Aufhebung*, 64, n. 81, argues that the author was drawing from Wisdom alone and therefore not from Isaiah or from Paul (1 Thess 5:18). Carr, *Angels and Principalities*, 111, sees the armor as reminiscent of Isaiah and Wisdom. A number of other commentators point out the similarity of the description of the armor in Wisdom with the Ephesian passage, but maintain that Isaiah is the primary source for the author of Ephesians; see e.g. Wild, "Warrior," 293.

25 Contra Kuhn, "Qumran," 131; see also his article, "πανοπλία," *TDNT* 5 (1967), 297ff.

26 H. Braun, *Qumran und das Neue Testament* (Tübingen, 1956), 223; Fischer, *Tendenz*, 168–69.

27 Gnilka, 28, 310; Fischer, *Tendenz*, 166, contends that the author depends on a primitive baptismal understanding by which baptism was an equipping for the final apocalyptic battle. For Fischer (pp. 166–67), the metaphorical weapons of God are ultimately derived from Persian influence; in this regard, Fischer depends heavily on E. Kamlah, *Die Form der katalogischen Paränese im Neuen Testament* (WUNT 7, Tübingen, 1964). See also Reitzenstein, *Mystery Religions*, 259. For a critique of Kamlah's view, see Barth, 2.789–80. Among the points Barth raises are (1) in Iranian anthropology, the soul is the weapon of the Primal Man, but there is no reference to the soul in Eph 6; God himself is the armor in Ephesians; (2) the monotheism of Ephesians (4:4ff., "one Lord ... one God") leaves no room for the thorough-going dualism of the Iranian anthropology; (3) although Ephesians extols the blessings of an intimate union of the church with Christ, it falls short of espousing a mystical identity between the pious and the Messenger of light (or the *Urmensch Erlöser*) as in the Iranian religion.

28 E. Levine, "The Wrestling Belt Legacy in the New Testament," *NTS* 28 (1982), 563. See also Barth, 2.767.
29 W. Foerster, "διάβολος," *TDNT* 2 (1964), 71–72.
30 E. Käsemann, "'The Righteousness of God' in Paul," *New Testament Questions of Today* (London, 1969), 173.
31 See below, where it will be shown that the offensive proclamation of the gospel is presented by the author as a key part of the resistance strategy which deals a heavy blow to the devil and his "powers."
32 Schlier, 298, however, describes prayer as the "seventh weapon."
33 Cf. *Apoc. Abr.* 29:2, 8ff., 13; 30:4; *2 Baruch* 48:31; *Jub* 23:16–21; *T. Dan* 5:4ff. This was also a common concept and expression at Qumran (cf. "the time/day of distress" in 1QM 15:1–2; 16:3; 18:10, 12; "the time of the rule of Belial" in 1QS 2:19; "the last days of distress (evil)" in 1Qp Hab 5:7; 7:1ff.). For further references, see Schlier, 292–93, J. Ernst, *Der Brief an die Philipper, an Philemon, an die Kolosser, an die Epheser* (RNT, Regensburg, 1974), 399, and P. Volz, *Die Eschatologie der jüdischen Gemeinde im neutestamentlichen Zeitalter* (Tübingen, 1934), 147–65 (cited in Lona, *Eschatologie*, 425).
34 Bruce, 406; G. Harder, "πονηρός," *TDNT* 6 (1968), 554, 566.
35 See the many references to the character of "those days" in Mark 13 (and parallels).
36 A. L. Moore, *The Parousia in the New Testament* (NovTSup 13, Leiden, 1966), 161.
37 G. Harder, "πονηρός," *TDNT* 6 (1968), 554.
38 Contra Lindemann, *Aufhebung*, 64–65, who argues against an eschatological understanding of the phrase in favor of an ethical interpretation, viz. this passage admonishes believers to participate in an ethical repetition (*Wiederholung*) of God's already attained victory over the "powers" of evil. Fischer, *Tendenz*, 166, argues that the phrase has lost its strong apocalyptic sense and now signifies the normal situation of the Christian.
39 See B. B. Hall, "Battle Imagery in Paul's Letters: An Exegetical Study," Unpublished Th.D. Thesis, Union Theological Seminary, New York, 1973.
40 Hall, "Battle Imagery," 117–18.
41 Evald Lövestam, *Spiritual Wakefulness in the New Testament* (Lund, 1962), 45.
42 Carr, *Angels and Principalities*, 105. Knox, *Paul*, 202, interprets this section as an exhortation to the Christians not to resign themselves to the decrees of fate.
43 This general sense is well attested in Greek literature: see *LSJ*, s.v.; H. Greeven, "πάλη," *TDNT* 5 (1967), 721. Philo can speak of the "wrestling" of the ascetic, but his use of the term never goes beyond the metaphor of actual wrestling (*Leg. all.*, 3.190; *Mut. nom.*, 14; *Abr.* 243).
44 V. C. Pfitzner, *Paul and the Agon Motif* (NovTSup 16, Leiden, 1967), 159.
45 I. R. Arnold, "Festivals of Ephesus," *AJA* 76 (1972), 20.

46 These annual pan-Ionian games were held in Ephesus since the fourth century B.C. See H. Engelmann and D. Knibbe, "Aus ephesischen Skizzenbüchern," *JhhÖArchInst* 52 (1980), 35, nr. 40. According to local tradition the foundation of the Epheseia reached back as far as 2000 or 1900 B.C., which was the legendary date of the birth of Artemis and the founding of Ephesus.

47 Arnold, "Festivals," 18–19; Engelmann and Knibbe, "Skizzenbüchern," 35, nr. 39.

48 See *IvE* 1109.2; 1111.10; 1123.4, 9, 11, 14, 16; 1118.3; 1119.4; 3809.9. See also *Die Inschriften von Magnesia am Sipylos* 6.4, 9, 11, which uses πάλη in these three occurrences in referring to wrestling as a part of the Olympiads in Ephesus and Pergamum.

49 *IvE* 1123 = Engelmann and Knibbe, "Skizzenbüchern," 35, nr. 39 (my translation).

50 Pausanias as cited in Eustathius, *Comm. ad Hom.* 19.247. The account is also cited in The Suda, s.v., and Photius, *Lexicon*, s.v. The text from Eustathius is cited in full in Hopfner, *Offenbarungszauber*, vol. 1, par. 765.

51 A. Oepke, "ὅπλον," *TDNT* 5 (1967), 294.

52 Here the order is transposed from the usual Pauline order of expression, "flesh and blood" (1 Cor 15:50; Gal 1:16). Percy, *Probleme*, 184, suggests that the order is reversed to prevent the readers from thinking that they are no longer urged to struggle against the flesh as a designation of the principle of the "old self" (and hence a power against which they should struggle – cf. Rom 8:13; Gal 5:7).

53 W. Michaelis, "μεθοδεία," *TDNT* 5 (1967), 103.

54 Schlier, 297; see also Schnackenburg, 285.

55 Contra Lindemann, *Aufhebung*, 65, who asserts that defeat is not possible for the Christian engaged in conflict with the "powers" since the believer is seated with Christ in the heavens (cf. 2:5–8) and cannot stumble from that position.

56 Schnackenburg, 277.

57 Bruce, 408, sees the "preparation" as part of the gospel – "appropriated and proclaimed."

58 C. L. Mitton, *Ephesians* (NCB, London, 1976), 227.

59 Schnackenburg, 286.

60 Pfitzner, *Agon Motif*, 195.

6 Features of the theology of Ephesians in light of its background

1 See the two Ph.D. theses written specifically on this theme: Overfield, "Ascension," and more recently, E. Penner, "The Enthronement Motif in Ephesians," Unpublished Ph.D. Thesis, Fuller Theological Seminary, 1983.

2 Van Roon, *Authenticity*, 259.

3 W. Bousset, *Kyrios Christos* (Nashville, 1970), 142. See his footnote 77 for the references in the primary literature. See also Ramsay, "Artemis-Leto," 228.

4 See Overfield, "Ascension," 10–27, for a detailed form-critical approach to this subject. He sees Eph 1:20–23 as "having a direct relationship with the kerygma and confessions of the early church." Among the other NT passages Overfield finds reflecting this tradition of interpreting the ascension–exaltation in terms of Christ's total authority in both the earthly and heavenly spheres are Matt 28:18; Acts 2:32; Rom 1:3f.; 14:9; Col 1:18; 3:1; 1 Thess 1:10; 1 Pet 1:21.

5 See Caragounis, *Mysterion*, 143–46; R.E. Brown, *The Semitic Background of the Term "Mystery" in the NT* (Philadelphia, 1968), 60.

6 Inscriptional data testify to the performance of "mysteries" in the cult of the Ephesian Artemis; see above in chapter 2, section 5 and Oster, "Ephesian Artemis," 38.

7 The term μυστήριον does occur frequently in the magical papyri, however; see G. Bornkamm, "μυστήριον," *TDNT* 4 (1967), 810, for a summary of this usage. Betz, "Tradition," 164, observes, "The whole of magic as well as its parts can be called μυστήριον or μυστήρια ... Furthermore, handing over the magical tradition to a student becomes the purpose of a mystery-cult initiation."

8 For a discussion of this text, see Smith, *Clement of Alexandria*, 180.

9 See Brown, *Mystery*, 1–30, 56–66, and G. Bornkamm, "μυστήριον," *TDNT* 4 (1967), 824.

10 Caragounis, *Mysterion*, 121–35. Others see more similarity with the use of *raz* in the Qumran Hodayoth: e.g. Kuhn, "Qumran," 117ff.; Merklein, *Das Kirchliche Amt*, 210–14; et al.

11 E.g. Dibelius-Greeven, 24, 83–85; Dibelius, *Geisterwelt*, 171–72; Mitton, *Epistle*, 86–88; Sanders, "Hymnic Elements," 231–32.

12 Schlier, 149; Barth 1.331; S. Kim, *The Origin of Paul's Gospel* (WUNT 2/4, Tübingen, 1981), 22.

13 This is essentially the conclusion of Caragounis, *Mysterion*, 136–37, 143, who remarks, "The Ephesian mysterion is a comprehensive concept ... they are not different mysteria, but wider or narrower aspects of one and the same mysterion – God's mysterion in Christ."

14 Cf. Rom 1:10; 2:18; 12:2; 15:32; 1 Cor 1:1; Gal 1:4; 1 Thess 4:3; 5:18; see also 2 Tim 1:1.

15 For the similar use of προορίζω in Paul, see Rom 8:29, 30; 1 Cor 2:7. For πρόθεσις, see Rom 8:28; 9:11, and also 2 Tim 1:9; 3:10.

16 This term also only appears elsewhere in Paul: see Rom 9:23.

17 This verb is used elsewhere in the NT only in Paul, cf. Rom 1:23; 3:25.

18 J.C. Beker, *Paul the Apostle* (Edinburgh, 1980), 189–92.

19 Beker, *Paul*, 189.

20 Wink, *Naming*, 61–63; for a critique of Wink's book, see chapter 3.

21 Beker, *Paul*, 189.

22 *Ibid.*, 188.

23 *Ibid.*, 188.

24 Wink, *Naming*, 61.

25 See the critique of Wink's book in chapter 3, section 1.
26 E. Schweizer, "σάρξ," *TDNT* 7 (1971), 133.
27 The author has therefore not "taken a radical step away from the mythicization of evil in personified demonic spirits" (Wink, *Naming*, 83). Wink does not give an adequate basis for interpreting ἐξουσία in this context as abstract versus personified.
28 See Barth 1.290–91: "Christ has abrogated the divisive function of the law − and therefore not God's holy law itself" (291).
29 This observation obviously assumes an interpretation of στοιχεῖα as personal spirits in this context. This view will be given fresh support in a separate publication on the Colossian heresy.
30 R. C. Tannehill, *Dying and Rising with Christ* (BZNW 32, Berlin, 1967), 14–15, 17.
31 *Ibid.*, 71.
32 Dahl, "Adresse und Proömium," 261, and "Epistle to the Ephesians," 38; van Roon, *Authenticity*, 55, n. 1; Percy, *Probleme*, 447; Carrington, *Catechism*, 23ff., 31ff., 59ff., 77; R. A. Wilson, " 'We' and 'You' in the Epistle to the Ephesians," *SE* II (*TU* 87, Berlin, 1964), 676–80, suggests that "we" in the epistle always refers to all Christians and "you" refers to a much smaller group within the church, the newly baptized.
33 A. T. Lincoln, *Paradise Now and Not Yet* (SNTSMS 43, Cambridge, 1981), 135–36, describes Ephesians as a "liturgical homily" intended to be read at worship services on the occasion of the baptism of new converts and functioning simultaneously to remind other believers of the meaning of their baptism. Gnilka, 33, describes Ephesians as a "liturgical homily," but does not see it as written to "neophytes." Rather, he views it as directed to baptized believers who were instructed on the theme of the church and their relationship to it by a sermon designed to remind them of the significance of their baptism.
34 Schlier, 16–22, esp. 21. Schlier sees the epistle as a meditation on the "wisdom" of the mystery of Christ (cf. 1 Cor 2:6–8).
35 Caragounis, *Mysterion*, 46, n. 83.
36 E.g. Gnilka, 85.
37 G. Fitzer, "σφραγίς," *TDNT* 7 (1971), 949, concurs, arguing that there is no reference to baptism in the occurrences of the term in Eph 1:13, 4:30, and 2 Cor 1:21. See also J. D. G. Dunn, *Baptism in the Holy Spirit* (London, 1970), 160; Barth 1.135–43. The substantive "seal" (σφραγίς) is used in later writings for baptism (e.g. *2 Clem.* 7:6; 8:6), but as Schnackenburg, 64, concedes, it is not used in this sense in the NT.
38 D. Lull, *The Spirit in Galatia* (SBLDS 49, Chico, 1980), 66, contends that for Paul, "The Spirit is a power which makes baptism effective; but it is bestowed on the believer *before* [italics in original] baptism. Its Sitz im Leben is in Paul's missionary preaching."
39 J. A. Allan, "The 'In Christ' Formula in Ephesians," *NTS* 5 (1958–59), 54.
40 Beker, *Paul*, 272–73.

41 See Allen, "Exaltation and Solidarity," 116.
42 Beker, *Paul*, 274–75.
43 Usami, *Somatic Comprehension*, 186. For Usami, this "somatized dynamism" aims at creating greater unity within itself and also grows and expands by integrating all kinds of people into the one body of Christ through mission.
44 L. Cerfaux, *Christ in the Theology of St. Paul* (New York, 1959), 426.
45 See J. Adai, *Der Heilige Geist als Gegenwart Gottes* (Regensburger Studien zur Theologie, Frankfurt am Main, Bern & New York, 1985), whose thorough study of the Holy Spirit in Ephesians rightly elevates the importance of this theme in the epistle.
46 See D. Black, *Paul, Apostle of Weakness* (New York, 1984).
47 See especially, J. Moltmann, *The Crucified God* (New York, 1974).
48 See P. Stuhlmacher, "Achtzehn Thesen zur paulinischen Kreuzestheologie," *Rechtfertigung* (FS. E. Käsemann, Tübingen, 1976), 509–25. This article summarizes the conclusions of a 1975 seminar held at Tübingen on the Pauline "theology of the cross." Stuhlmacher also includes a good bibliography of works published on this theme through 1975.
49 *Ibid.*, 514–15.
50 *Ibid.*, 518.
51 *Ibid.*, 519.
52 H. Nielsen, "Paulus' Verwendung des Begriffes Δύναμις. Eine Replik zur Kreuzestheologie," *Die Paulinische Literatur und Theologie* (Århus, 1980), 137–58.
53 *Ibid.*, 138–39.
54 *Ibid.*, 139, 156–58.
55 *Ibid.*, 154–55.
56 *Ibid.*, 156–58.
57 Beker, *Paul*, 291–94, esp. p. 294.
58 W. Schrage, *Ethik des Neuen Testaments* (GNT 4, Göttingen, 1982), 237, writes, "in both epistles love functions as the decisive criterion and summary of all that is essential for the new man to do."
59 Schrage, *ibid.*, 233, finds significant correspondence in the use of the indicative-imperative in Ephesians (and Colossians) with its use in Paul.
60 See Tannehill, *Dying and Rising*, 81–83.
61 As, for example, Beker, *Paul*, 278, claims is true of Ephesians (and Colossians).
62 Barth, "Traditions," 16.
63 F. Hahn, *Mission in the New Testament* (SBT 47, London, 1965), 143–52; Meyer, *Kirche und Mission*, 15–16, 59.
64 Schrage, *Ethik*, 238.
65 See esp. Lindemann, *Aufhebung*. See also Conzelmann, 86–88; Schlier, *Christus*; Käsemann, *Leib*, 145–47; Beker, *Paul*, 356; P. J. Achtemeier, "An Apocalyptic Shift in Early Christian Tradition: Reflections on Some Canonical Evidence," *CBQ* 45 (1983), 231–48, esp. p. 237.

66 For a good bibliography on Gnostic eschatology, see G. Sellin, " 'Die Auferstehung ist schon Geschehenen.' Zur Spiritualisierung apokalyptischer Terminologie im neuen Testament," *NovT* 25 (1983), 223, n. 5.

67 Sellin, "Die Auferstehung," 223.

68 See, for example, Percy, *Probleme*, 114–16, 299–300; Moore, *Parousia*, 161; Schlier, 111, 227, 292; Bruce, 233–35; van Roon, *Authenticity*, 262.

69 Lona, *Eschatologie*, 427–28.

70 He finds some differences and new accents which suggest to him an alteration of the Pauline tradition in its appropriation to the concrete situation to which he believes Ephesians was addressed (449).

71 Lona, *Eschatologie*, esp. the section, "Eschatologie und Situation," 428–48.

72 H. Chadwick, "Die Absicht des Epheserbriefes," *ZNW* 51 (1960), 152, and Gnilka, 45–49, also see this crisis as influential in the Ephesian author's presentation.

73 Lona, *Eschatologie*, 439.

74 *Ibid.*, 437–40.

75 More important to Lona is how the Ephesian author allegedly confronts this scenario through an ecclesiology especially adapted to this situation: see Lona, *Eschatologie*, 442–44.

76 Sanders, "Hymnic Elements," 218.

77 Schille, *Hymnen*, 53–60, 104, finds the author dependent upon a hymnic tradition which speaks of an experienced salvation. He sees Colossians as dependent upon the same tradition, which for him explains the similarities.

78 E.g. A. T. Lincoln, "Ephesians 2:8–10: A Summary of Paul's Gospel?" *CBQ* 45 (1983), 619.

79 See Dibelius-Greeven, 67, who also argues that this means that the Ephesian author thus did not take over and edit Col 2:10–13.

80 Lincoln, "Summary," 621–22.

81 The term αἰών in 2:7 cannot be interpreted in a personal sense (viz. as the god Aion) for two reasons: (1) such an interpretation destroys the balance and parallelism with the undisputed temporal use of αἰών in 1:21; (2) it also renders meaningless the participle ἐπερχομένος, "the coming, or future ages."

82 Lincoln, "Summary," 620.

83 *Ibid.*, 623.

84 Conzelmann, 88.

85 H. Merklein, "Paulinische Theologie in der Rezeption des Kolosser- und Epheserbriefes," *Paulus in den Neutestamentlichen Spät-schriften zur Paulusrezeption im Neuen Testament* (QD 89, Freiburg, 1981), 44.

86 P. Tachau, *"Einst" und "Jetzt" im Neuen Testament* (FRLANT 105, Göttingen, 1972). He contends that it was part of the rhetorical vocabulary of early Christian preaching. He suggests that the schema was used particularly in connection with the preaching associated

with baptism or even on the event of conversion (133). His research also led him to conclude that the schema did not have its roots in the OT or Judaism (including Qumran), although he does not deny its occurrence there (e.g. 2 Sam 15:34). He contends that the book *Joseph and Aseneth* reflects a formal use of ποτέ–νῦν similar to what is found in the NT (68–70). Specifically, he draws attention to a literary form in the book which he terms a "judicial doxology" (*Gerichtsdoxologie*) where "once" is used to describe the past as a time of sin and the "now" as a time of forgiveness and hope in the Lord (52–58).

87 Tachau, *Einst*, 143.
88 Lindemann, *Aufhebung*, 191–92.
89 This is not a personal reference to the god Aion or a synonym of ἀρχή or ἐξουσία, as I have demonstrated above. Such a reinterpretation is required by those who would see an elimination of all temporal references in Ephesians.
90 Tachau, *Einst*, 142.
91 Lincoln, *Paradise*, 140; Schnackenburg, 48–49; Schlier, 45–48; Gnilka, 62–63; Dibelius-Greeven, 58.
92 E. Käsemann, "Epheserbrief," *RGG*, 2.518; Conzelmann, 87–88; Lindemann, *Aufhebung*, 54–56; Schlier, *Christus*, 13, cf. 1–18.
93 Schlier, 47–48.
94 Abbott, 32; Beare, 634; R.M. Pope, "Studies in Pauline Vocabulary: Of the Heavenly Places," *ET* 23 (1912), 365–68, sees a Platonic influence on all the references except 3:10 and 6:12, which he describes as local and Jewish (as cited in Lincoln, *Paradise*, 140).
95 Ps 67:14; Dan 4:26 A (Theodotian); 2 Macc 3:39; 3 Macc 6:28; 7:6; 4 Macc 4:11; 11:13.
96 A.T. Lincoln, "A Re-Examination of 'the Heavenlies' in Ephesians," *NTS* 19 (1972), 468–83; *Paradise*, 135–68.
97 Lincoln, "The Heavenlies," 478–79. See also H. Traub, "ἐπουράνιος," *TDNT* 5 (1967), 539.
98 See van Roon, *Authenticity*, 213; A. Deissmann, *Light from the Ancient East* (London, 1927), 257.
99 Deissmann, *Light*, 250, suggested that the entire passage (lines 3007–86) was originally a Jewish recipe taken over and used by pagans, W.L. Knox, "Jewish Liturgical Exorcism," *HTR* 31 (1938), 191–203, agrees with Deissmann's general conclusion, but suggests that the text may be a rare example of an orthodox Jewish exorcism recipe.
100 H. Traub, "ἐπουράνιος," *TDNT* 5 (1967), 540; Percy, *Probleme*, 182, thinks the author used it because it has more of a liturgical-ceremonial ring to it in contrast to οὐράνιοι, which for Percy is more consistent with the overall style of the epistle. Schille, *Hymnen*, 68, regards it as a traditional formula taken from the worship of the early church.
101 *Die Inschriften von Magnesia am Sipylos* (IGSK 8, Bonn, 1978), no. 28, lines 10–11.
102 Lincoln, "The Heavenlies," 479.

He who began a good work in you will perfect it until the day of Christ Jesus.
Philippians 1:6 NASB

If children grow up with an abundance of love (expressed both verbally and physically), positive attention, and discipline from both a father and a mother, they will develop a basic sense of trust, self-worth, and a healthy comfort with their sexual identity.

Southern Cafe

261-1404

2000 MacArthur

2 bloks post fruitvale

103 *Ibid.*, 481; see also Percy, *Probleme*, 181; Caragounis, *Mysterion*, 150; Schille, *Hymnen*, 106, remarks that the formula characterizes "the life of the baptized as life in the new age."
104 Lincoln, "The Heavenlies," 483.
105 Lincoln, *Paradise*, 138.
106 *Ibid.*, 138—39; "The Heavenlies," 483. Lincoln here follows Martin, "Life Setting," 296—302.
107 This is also part of the conclusion of Lona, *Eschatologie*, 448.
108 Hall, "Battle Imagery," 123. She finds such a connection with eschatology in Paul's use of military terminology in 1 Thess 5:8; 1 Cor 15:23—26, 52—55; Rom 8:35, 37; 13:12. It is less clear in 2 Cor 6:7; 7:5; 10:3—6, but she feels that Paul could reasonably assume that 1 Cor 15 would be remembered by his Corinthian readers. In each case, Paul has in mind two opposing spheres of power in the present time.
109 Hall, "Battle Imagery," 174—76.
110 She points particularly to many concepts shared with Qumran (esp. 1QS 3:13—25), for example: (1) the conviction that affliction is due to the enemy and his group, (2) an understanding that men live according to the "way of walking" to which God has destined them, and (3) the use of light—darkness imagery in relation to battle in an eschatological context: see Hall, "Battle Imagery," 17—20.
111 Hall, "Battle Imagery," 22—23, 55.
112 A. Grabner-Haider, *Paraklese und Eschatologie bei Paulus* (NTAbh 4, Münster, 1968), 139—40.
113 Lindemann, *Aufhebung*, 64—65, does attempt to make sense of 6:10—20 in light of a fully realized eschatology. He contends that Eph 6:10ff. has been completely ethicized − believers practice an ethical repetition of God's already attained victory over the "powers" of evil.
114 Rudolph, *Gnosis*, 252.
115 Grabner-Haider, *Paraklese*, 104—105.
116 The verb ἀνακεφαλαιόομαι can be acceptably translated, "to bring under one head." It should be noted that the word itself is derived from κεφάλαιον and not κεφαλή. It is possible, however, that the writer himself may have connected it with κεφαλή, which is a prominent word in Ephesians, Colossians, and Paul; see Dupont, *Gnosis*, 425; Brown, *Mystery*, 59.
117 Caragounis, *Mysterion*, 145, similarly concludes, "The final *anakephalaiosis* of the powers envisages a subjugation of the most humiliating kind."
118 This verse is frequently neglected in the descriptions of the eschatology of Ephesians. The text describes the promised future perfection of the church, not a present status or possession. See Bruce, 389; Barth, 2.628.
119 E.g. Chadwick, "Absicht," 146, writes, "the main theme of the epistle is the church."
120 Barth, 1.274.
121 Gnilka, 160.

122 Bruce, 353.
123 Gnilka, 220, observes, "in him [the body] obtains the divine ἐνέργεια and on him all the members are dependent."
124 Barth, 2.450.
125 Schnackenburg, 136; Schlier, 151; Gnilka, 169.
126 On this verse and on the theme of the power of God manifested in the weakness of man, see Black, *Weakness*, 146–67. With P. Hughes, Black regards this verse as the "summit of the epistle" and the crowning point of Paul's view of weakness (151). Unfortunately, Black provides us with no discussion of Ephesians (or Colossians), since his study is limited to ἀσθένεια and its cognates.
127 See Percy, *Probleme*, 412.
128 There are Semitic stylistic parallels for this (*1 Enoch* 60:16; 1QH 4:32; 1QM 11:5; 1QS 11:19); see further Gnilka, 92, n. 3.
129 See Schlier, 151; see also G. Bertram, "ἐνεργέω," *TDNT* 2 (1964), 653.
130 Paul frequently represents himself as a model (or *Vorbild*) to believers as in 1 Cor 4:16, "I urge you therefore, be imitators (μιμηταί) of me." He could say this only insofar as he was a follower of Christ (1 Cor 11:16) and the risen Christ empowered him for service. J. H. Schütz, *Paul and the Anatomy of Apostolic Authority* (SNTSMS 26, Cambridge, 1975), 231, aptly remarks, "It is no accident that Paul counsels the imitation of himself. His whole apostolic self-consciousness is shot through with this awareness of his personal service in weakness which is at the same time God's power in him ... What Paul reflects as an apostle is only a facet of the possibility, the demand of the new life in Christ."
131 Carr, *Angels and Principalities*, 95.
132 E. Käsemann, "Paul and Early Catholicism," *New Testament Questions of Today* (London, 1969), 237–50; "Theological Problem," 102–21; "Epheserbrief," *RGG*, 2.517–20. His view has attracted a number of adherents: see J. L. Houlden, "Christ and Church in Ephesians," *SE* 6 (*TU* 112, Berlin, 1973), 267–73, esp. 272; Chadwick, "Absicht," esp. 146–47; Beker, *Paul*, 342–43; et al.
133 Käsemann, "Theological Problem," 120.
134 *Ibid.*, 120; "Epheserbrief," *RGG*, 2.518.
135 Merklein, "Rezeption," 25–69. He claims, "Ephesians does not write ecclesiology next to Christology, but rather an ecclesiological Christology" (62).
136 *Ibid.*, 51.
137 *Ibid.*, 51.
138 *Ibid.*, 48, 62.
139 Lona, *Eschatologie*, 442.
140 *Ibid.*, 445.
141 See, for example, Chadwick, "Absicht," 146–48; E. Lohse, "Christusherrschaft und Kirche im Kolosserbrief," *NTS* 11 (1964–65), 203–16. Lohse also sees a decisive difference in the objects of the revelation of the "mystery." In Col 1:26 it is

revealed to the apostles and prophets. For Lohse, this betrays the early catholic tendencies of Ephesians as opposed to Colossians since the apostolic office is there regarded as the guardian of the truth (214–15).

142 W. G. Kümmel, *Introduction to the New Testament* (London, 1975), 360.

143 For further argumentation on this same line, see Bruce, 237–40.

SELECT BIBLIOGRAPHY

ACHTEMEIER, Paul J. "An Apocalyptic Shift in Early Christian Tradition: Reflections on Some Canonical Evidence," *CBQ* 45 (1983), 231–48

ALLAN, John A. "The 'In Christ' Formula in Ephesians," *NTS* 5 (1958–59), 54–62

ALLEGRO, J.M. "An Astrological Cryptic Document from Qumran," *JSS* 9 (1964), 291–94

ALLEN, Thomas G. "Exaltation and Solidarity with Christ: Ephesians 1.20 and 2.6," *JSNT* 28 (1986), 103–20

ARNOLD, Clinton E. "The 'Exorcism' of Ephesians 6.12 in Recent Research," *JSNT* 30 (1987), 71–87

ARNOLD, Irene R. "Festivals of Ephesus," *AJA* 76 (1972), 17–22

AUDOLLENT, Augustus. *Defixionum tabellae*, Paris, Alberti Fontemoing, 1894

AUNE, David E. "Magic in Early Christianity," *ANRW* II.23.2, Berlin, Walter de Gruyter, 1980, 1507–57

BAMMER, Anton. *Das Heiligtum der Artemis von Ephesos*, Graz/Austria, Akademische Druck- u. Verlagsanstalt, 1984

BARTH, Markus. "Traditions in Ephesians," *NTS* 30 (1984), 3–25

BEKER, J. Christiaan. *Paul the Apostle*, Edinburgh, T. & T. Clark, 1980

BENOIT, Pierre. "Qumran and the New Testament," *Paul and Qumran*, ed. J. Murphy-O'Connor, London, Geoffrey Chapman, 1968

"Pauline Angelology and Demonology. Reflexions on the Designations of the Heavenly Powers and on the Origin of Angelic Evil According to Paul," *Religious Studies Bulletin* 3 (1983), 1–18

"The 'plèrōma' in the Epistles to the Colossians and the Ephesians," *Svensk Exegetisk Årsbok* 49 (1984), 136–58

BERKHOF, Hendrik. *Christ and the Powers*, tr. J.H. Yoder, Scottdale, Herald, 1977

BEST, Ernest. *One Body in Christ. A Study in the Relationship of the Church to Christ in the Epistles of the Apostle Paul*, London, SPCK, 1955

"The Power and Wisdom of God." *Paolo a una Chiesa divisa (1 Cor. 1–4)*, Serie Monografica di "Benedictina" 5, Rome, Abbazia, 1980, 9–39

"Dead in Trespasses and Sins (Eph. 2:1)," *JSNT* 13 (1981), 9–25

"Ephesians 1:1 Again." *Paul and Paulinism*, FS. C.K. Barrett, ed. M.D. Hooker and S.G. Wilson, London, SPCK, 1982, 273–79

BETZ, Hans Dieter. "Fragments from a Catabasis Ritual in a Greek Magical Papyrus," *HistRel* 19 (1980), 287–95
"The Delphic Maxim 'Know Yourself' in the Greek Magical Papyri," *HistRel* 21 (1981), 156–71
"The Formation of Authoritative Tradition in the Greek Magical Papyri," *Jewish and Christian Self-Definition*, vol. 3, ed. B. F. Meyer and E. P. Sanders, London, SCM, 1982, 161–70
BETZ, Hans Dieter, ed. *The Greek Magical Papyri in Translation*, vol. 1: Text, Chicago, Univ. of Chicago Press, 1986
BETZ, Otto. "Das Volk seiner Kraft: zur Auslegung der Qumran-hodajah iii, 1–18," *NTS* 5 (1958–59), 67–75
BIELER, Ludwig. "Δύναμις und ἐξουσία," *Wiener Studien* 55 (1937), 182–190
BIETENHARD, Hans. *Die Himmlische Welt im Urchristentum und Spätjudentum*, WUNT 2, Tübingen, Mohr, 1951
BLACK, David A. *Paul, Apostle of Weakness. Astheneia and its Cognates in the Pauline Literature*, American University Studies, Series 7, Theology and Religion 3, New York, Bern, Frankfurt/M., & Nancy, P. Lang, 1984
BÖCHER, O. *Dämonenfurcht und Dämonenabwehr. Ein Beitrag zur Vorgeschichte der christlichen Taufe*, BWANT 10, Stuttgart, Kohlhammer, 1970
Christus Exorcista. Dämonismus und Taufe im Neuen Testament, BWANT 16, Stuttgart, Kohlhammer, 1972
Das Neue Testament und die dämonischen Mächte, SBS 58, Stuttgart, Katholisches Bibelwerk, 1972
BONNER, Campbell. *Studies in Magical Amulets Chiefly Graeco-Egyptian*, Ann Arbor, Univ. of Michigan Press, 1950
BOWERSOCK, G. W. "The Imperial Cult: Perceptions and Persistence," *Jewish and Christian Self-Definition*, vol. 3, ed. B. F. Meyer and E. P. Sanders, London, SCM, 1982, 171–82
BRASHEAR, William. "Ein Berliner Zauberpapyrus," *ZPE* 33 (1979), 261–78
BROWN, Raymond E. *The Semitic Background of the Term "Mystery" in the NT*, Facet Books, Biblical Series, Philadelphia, Fortress Press, 1968
BRUCE, F. F. "Paul and 'The Powers That Be,'" *BJRL* 66 (1983–84), 78–96
BURGER, Christoph. *Schöpfung und Versöhnung. Studien zum liturgischen Gut im Kolosser- und Epheserbrief*, WMANT 46, Neukirchen, Neukirchener, 1975
BURKERT, Walter. *Greek Religion. Archaic and Classical*, tr. J. Raffan, Oxford, Basil Blackwell, 1985
CADBURY, H. J. "The Dilemma of Ephesians," *NTS* 5 (1958/59), 91–102
CAIRD, G. B. *Principalities and Powers*, Oxford, Clarendon, 1956
"The Descent of Christ in Eph 4, 7–11," *SE* II (= TU 87), part 1, Berlin, Akademie, 1964, 535–45
CARAGOUNIS, Chrys C. *The Ephesian Mysterion. Meaning and Content*, ConB 8, Lund, Gleerup, 1977
CARR, Wesley. *Angels and Principalities. The Background, Meaning and Development of the Pauline Phrase hai archai kai hai exousiai*, SNTSMS 42, Cambridge University Press, 1981

CARRINGTON, Philip. *The Primitive Christian Catechism*, Cambridge University Press, 1940
CHADWICK, H. "Die Absicht des Epheserbriefes," *ZNW* 51 (1960), 145–53
CHAMPION, L. G. *Benedictions and Doxologies in the Epistles of Paul*, Oxford, Kemp Hall, 1934
CHAPOT, V. *La Province romaine proconsulaire d'Asia*, Paris, 1904
CHARLESWORTH, James H. *The Pseudepigrapha and Modern Research*, Society of Biblical Literature Septuagint and Cognate Studies 7, Missoula, Scholar's Press, 1976
  "Jewish Astrology in the Talmud, Pseudepigrapha, the Dead Sea Scrolls, and Early Palestinian Synagogues," *HTR* 70 (1977), 183–200
CHARLESWORTH, James H. ed. *The Old Testament Pseudepigrapha*, 2 vols., New York, Doubleday & co., vol. 1, 1983; vol. 2, 1985
  The Old Testament Pseudepigrapha and the New Testament. Prolegomena for the Study of Christian Origins, SNTSMS 54, Cambridge University Press, 1985
CLARK, Kenneth W. "The Meaning of 'Ενεργέω and Καταργέω in the New Testament," *JBL* 54 (1935), 93–101
COLPE, C. *Die religionsgeschichtliche Schule. Darstellung der Kritik ihres Bildes vom gnostischen Erlösermythus*, FRLANT 78, Göttingen, Vandenhoeck & Ruprecht, 1961
  "Zur Leib-Christi-Vorstellung im Epheserbrief," *Judentum, Urchristentum, Kirche*, FS. J. Jeremias, ed. W. Eltester, BZNW 26, Berlin, Tölpelmann, 1964, 172–87
CONYBEARE, F. C. "The Demonology of the New Testament," *JQR* 8 (1895–96), 576–608
  "The Testament of Solomon," *JQR* 11 (1898), 1–45
Corpus inscriptionum graecarum, vol. 2, ed. A. Boeckhius, Berlin, G. Reimer, 1843
Corpus paroemiographorum graecorum, Göttingen, Sumptus Fecit Libraria Dieterichiana, 1851
CRAMER, F. H. *Astrology in Roman Law and Politics*, Memoirs of the American Philosophical Society 37, Philadelphia, American Phil. Soc., 1954
CULIANU, I. P. "The Angels of the Nations and the Origins of Gnostic Dualism," *Studies in Gnosticism and Hellenistic Religions*, FS. G. Quispel, ed. R. van den Broek and M. J. Vermaseren, EPRO 91, Leiden, Brill, 1981, 78–91
CULLMANN, Oscar. *The State in the New Testament*, London, SCM, 1957
CUMONT, F., and CANET, L. "Mithra ou Sarapis ΚΟΣΜΟΚΡΑΤΩΡ?" *Comptes rendues à l'Académie des inscriptions et belles-lettres*, 1919, 313–28
CUMONT, Franz. *Astrology and Religion among the Greeks and Romans*, New York & London, Putnams, 1912
  The Oriental Religions in Roman Paganism, New York & London, Dover, 1956
DAHL, Nils A. "Adresse und Proömium des Epheserbriefes," *TZ* 7 (1951), 241–64

Das Volk Gottes: Eine Untersuchung zum Kirchenbewusstsein des Urchristentums, Darmstadt, Wissenschaftliche Buchgesellschaft, 1963
"Interpreting Ephesians, Then and Now," *TD* 25 (1977), 305–15
"Cosmic Dimensions and Religious Knowledge," *Jesus and Paulus*, FS. Werner Kümmel, Göttingen, Vandenhoeck & Ruprecht, 1978, 57–75
"Gentiles, Christians, and Israelites in the Epistle to the Ephesians," *HTR* 79 (1986), 31–39
DEICHGRÄBER, R. *Gotteshymnus und Christushymnus in der frühen Christenheit. Untersuchungen zur Form, Sprache und Stil der frühchristlichen Hymnen*, SUNT 5, Göttingen, Vandenhoeck & Ruprecht, 1967
DEISSMANN, Adolf. "Ephesia Grammata," *Abhandlung zur Semitischen Religionskunde und Sprachwissenschaft*, ed. W. Frankenberg & F. Kuchler, BZAW 33, Gießen, Töpelmann, 1918, 121–24
Light from the Ancient East, tr. R.M. Strachan, New York, Doran, 1927
DIBELIUS, Martin. "The Isis Initiation in Apuleius and Related Initiatory Rites," *Conflict at Colossae*, ed. F.O. Francis and W.A. Meeks, SBLSBS 4, Missoula, Scholar's Press, 1973, 61–121
Die Geisterwelt im Glauben des Paulus, Göttingen, Vandenhoeck & Ruprecht, 1909
DUNCAN, G.S. *St. Paul's Ephesian Ministry*, London, Hodder & Stoughton, 1929
DUPONT, Dom J. *Gnosis. La Connaissance religieuse dans les épîtres de Saint Paul*, Universitas Catholica Lovaniensia Series II, Tomus 40, Louvain, Nouvelaerts, 1949
EITREM, S.E. *Some Notes on the Demonology of the New Testament*, Symbolae Osloenes Fasc. Supplement 12, Oslo, A.W. Brogger, 1950
ENGELMANN, Helmut and KNIBBE, Dieter "Aus ephesischen Skizzenbüchern," *JhhÖArchInst* 52 (1980), 19–61
ENGELMANN, Helmut, KNIBBE, Dieter and MERKELBACH, Reinhold (ed.). *Die Inschriften von Ephesos*, IGSK 13, parts 1–8, Bonn, Rudolf Habelt, 1980–84
ERNST, Josef. *Pleroma und Pleroma Christi. Geschichte und Deutung eines Begriffs der paulinischen Antilegomena*, Biblische Untersuchungen 5, Regensburg, Pustet, 1970
EVERLING, Otto. *Die paulinische Angelologie und Dämonologie*, Göttingen, Vandenhoeck & Ruprecht, 1888
FARNELL, Lewis R. *The Cults of the Greek States*, vol.2, Oxford, Clarendon Press, 1896
FILSON, Floyd F. "Ephesus and the New Testament," *BA* 8 (1945), 73–80
FISCHER, Karl M. *Tendenz und Absicht des Epheserbriefes*, FRLANT 111, Göttingen, Vandenhoeck & Ruprecht, 1973
FITZMYER, Joseph A. "To Know Him and the Power of His Resurrection (Phil. 3:10)," *Mélanges bibliques en hommage au R.P. Béda Rigaux*, ed. A. Descamps and A. de Halleux, Gembloux, Duculot, 1970, 411–25
FLEISCHER, Robert. *Artemis von Ephesos und verwandte Kultstatuen aus Anatolien und Syrien*, EPRO 35, Leiden, Brill, 1973
"Artemis von Ephesos und verwandte Kultstatuen aus Anatolien und Syrien. Supplement," *Studien zur Religion und Kultur Kleinasiens*, vol.1,

Select bibliography

218

FS. F. K. Dörner, ed. S. Sahin, E. Schwertheim and J. Wagner, EPRO 66, Leiden, Brill, 1978, 324–58
"Artemis Ephesia und Aphrodite von Aphrodisias," *Die orientalische Religionen im Römerreich*, ed. M. J. Vermaseren, EPRO 93, Leiden, Brill, 1981
"Neues zu kleinasiatischen Kultstatuen," *AA* (1983), 81–93
"Artemis Ephesia," *Lexicon iconographicum mythologiae classicae*, vol. 2, parts 1 & 2, Zürich & München, Artemis, 1984
Forschungen in Ephesos veröffentlicht vom Österreichischen Archäologischen Institute, 7 vols., Wien, Alfred Hölder, 1906–
FORSTER, A. Haire. "The Meaning of Power for St. Paul," *ATR* 32 (1950), 177–85
FRENCH, D. H. "The Roman Road-System of Asia Minor," *ANRW* II.7.2, Berlin, Walter de Gruyter, 1983, 698–729
GAGER, John G. *Moses in Greco-Roman Paganism*, SBLMS 16, Nashville, Abingdon, 1972
GIBBS, John G. *Creation and Redemption. A Study in Pauline Theology.* SupNovT 26, Leiden, Brill, 1971
GOODENOUGH, Erwin R. *Jewish Symbols in the Greco-Roman Period*, vol. 2, *The Archaeological Evidence from the Diaspora*, New York, Pantheon, 1953
GRABNER-HAIDER, A. *Paraklese und Eschatologie bei Paulus. Mensch und Welt im Anspruch der Zukunft Gottes*, NTAbh NS 4, Münster, Aschendorff, 1968
GRIFFITHS, J. Gwyn. "Xenophon of Ephesus on Isis and Alexandria," *Hommages à Maarten J. Vermaseren*, vol. 1, ed. M. B. De Boer and T. A. Edridge, EPRO 68, Leiden, Brill, 1978, 409–37
GRUENWALD, Ithamar. *Apocalyptic and Merkavah Mysticism*, AGJU 14, Leiden, Brill, 1980
"Knowledge and Vision," *Israel Oriental Studies* 3 (1973), 63–107
"The Problem of Anti-Gnostic Polemic in Rabbinic Literature," *Studies in Gnosticism and Hellenistic Religions*, FS. G. Quispel, ed. R. van den Broek and M. J. Vermaseren, EPRO 91, Leiden, Brill, 1981
GRUNDMANN, Walter. *Der Begriff der Kraft in der Neutestamentlichen Gedankenwelt*, BWANT 8, Stuttgart, Kohlhammer, 1932
GUNDEL, Hans Georg. *Weltbild und Astrologie in den griechischen Zauberpapyri*, Münchener Beiträge zur Papyrusforschung und Antiken Rechtsgeschichte 53, München, Beck, 1968
"Imagines Zodiaci. Zu neueren Funden und Forschungen," *Hommages à Maarten J. Vermaseren*, vol. 1, ed. M. B. De Boer and T. A. Edridge, EPRO 68, Leiden, Brill, 1978, 438–54
GUNTHER, John J. *St. Paul's Opponents and their Background. A Study of Apocalyptic and Jewish Sectarian Teachings*, NovTSup 35, Leiden, Brill, 1973
GUTHRIE, W. K. C. "The Religion and Mythology of the Greeks," *The Cambridge Ancient History*, rev. edn. of vols. 1 & 2, Cambridge University Press, 1964
HALL, Barbara Blanche. "Battle Imagery in Paul's Letters: An Exegetical Study," unpublished Th.D. Thesis, Union Theological Seminary in the City of New York, 1973

HANSEN, Günther. "Herrscherkult und Friedensidee," *Umwelt des Ur-Christentums*, vol. 1: *Darstellung des neutestamentlichen Zeitalters*, ed. J. Leipoldt and W. Grundmann, Berlin, Evangelische Verlagsanstalt, 1971, 127–42

HARNACK, Adolf. "Die Adresse des Epheserbriefes des Paulus," *Kleine Schriften zur Alten Kirche*, Leipzig, Zentralantiquariat der Deutschen Demokratischen Republik, 1980, 120–33

Militia Christi, tr. D. Gracie, Philadelphia, Fortress, 1981

HAUFE, Günter. "Hellenistische Volksfrömmigkeit," *Umwelt des Urchristentums*, vol. 1: *Darstellung des neutestamentlichen Zeitalters*, ed. J. Leipoldt and W. Grundmann, Berlin, Evangelische Verlagsanstalt, 1971, 68–100

"Die Mysterien," *Umwelt des Urchristentums*, vol. 1: *Darstellung des neutestamentlichen Zeitalters*, ed. J. Leipoldt and W. Grundmann, Berlin, Evangelische Verlagsanstalt, 1971, 101–26

HAY, David M. *Glory at the Right Hand. Psalm 110 in Early Christianity*, SBLMS 18, Nashville, Abingdon, 1973

HEINZEL, Elma. "Zum Kult der Artemis von Ephesos," *JhhÖArchInst* 50 (1972–73), 243–51

HELCK, W. "Zur Gestalt der ephesischen Artemis," *AA* (1984), 281–82

HEMBERG, Bengt. "Die Idaiischen Daktylen," *Eranos. Acta philologica suecana a Vilelmo Lundström condita* 50 (1952), 41–59

HEMER, Colin. "Unto the Angels of the Churches: 1. Introduction and Ephesus," *Buried History* 11 (1975), 4–25

The Letters to the Seven Churches of Asia in their Local Setting, JSNTSS 11, Sheffield, JSOT Press, 1986

HENGEL, Martin. *Judaism and Hellenism. Studies in their Encounter in Palestine during the Early Hellenistic Period*, 2 vols., tr. J. Bowden, London, SCM, 1974

Christ and Power, tr. E.R. Kalin, Philadelphia, Fortress, 1977

HÖLBL, G. *Zeugnisse ägyptischer Religionsvorstellungen für Ephesus*, EPRO 73, Leiden, Brill, 1978

HOLMBERG, Bengt. *Paul and Power. The Structure of Authority in the Primitive Church as Reflected in the Pauline Epistles*, ConB 11, Lund, C.W.K. Gleerup, 1978

HOPFNER, Theodor. "Hekate-Selene-Artemis und Verwandte in den griechischen Zauberpapyri und auf den Fluchtafeln," *Pisciculi. F.J. Dölger zum 60. Geburtstage*, Münster, Aschendorff, 1939, 125–45

Griechisch-Ägyptischer Offenbarungszauber, Studien zur Palaeographie und Papyruskunde 21, Amsterdam, Adolf M. Hakkert, vol. 1, 1974, vol. 2, 1983 (originally published in Leipzig, Haessel, vol. 1, 1921, vol. 2, 1924).

HORSLEY, G.H.R. *New Documents Illustrating Early Christianity. A Review of the Greek Inscriptions and Papyri Published in 1976*, North Ryde, NSW, Australia, Macquarie University, 1981

HOULDEN, J.L. "Christ and Church in Ephesians," *SE* 6 (= *TU* 112), Berlin, Akademie, 1973, 267–73

HULL, John M. *Hellenistic Magic and the Synoptic Tradition*, SBS 28, London, SCM, 1974

IHNKEN, Thomas, ed. *Die Inschriften von Magnesia am Sipylos*, IGSK 8, Bonn, Rudolf Habelt, 1978

JAMES, M. R. "The Testament of Solomon," *JTS* 24 (1922), 468

JOHNSON, Sherman E. "Laodicea and Its Neighbors," *BA* 13 (1950), 1–18

"Unsolved Questions About Early Christianity in Anatolia," *Studies in New Testament and Early Christian Literature*, FS. A. P. Wikgren, ed. D. E. Aune, NovTSup 33, Leiden, Brill, 1972, 181–93

"Asia Minor and Early Christianity," *Christianity, Judaism and Other Greco-Roman Cults*, vol. 2, FS. M. Smith, SJLA 12, Leiden, Brill, 1975, 77–145

KAMLAH, Ehrhard. *Die Form der katalogischen Paränese im Neuen Testament*, WUNT 7, Tübingen, Mohr, 1964

KÄSEMANN, Ernst. *Leib und Leib Christi. Eine Untersuchung zur paulinischen Begrifflichkeit*, BHT 9, Tübingen, Mohr, 1933

"Epheserbrief," *RGG*, vol. 2, Tübingen, Mohr, 1958, 517–20

"Das Interpretationsprobleme des Epheserbriefes," *Exegetische Versuche und Besinnungen*, vol. 2, Göttingen, Vandenhoeck & Ruprecht, 1964, 253–61

"Ephesians and Acts," *Studies in Luke–Acts*. Nashville, Abingdon, 1966, 288–97

"Paul and Early Catholicism," *New Testament Question of Today*, tr. W. J. Montague, London, SCM, 1969, 237–50

" 'The Righteousness of God' in Paul," *New Testament Questions of Today*, tr. W. J. Montague, London, SCM, 1969, 168–82

"The Theological Problem Presented by the Motif of the Body of Christ," *Perspectives on Paul*, tr. M. Kohl, London, SCM, 1971, 102–21

KEE, Howard C. *Medicine, Miracle and Magic in New Testament Times*, SNTSMS 55, Cambridge University Press, 1986

KEIL, Josef. "Die Kulte Lydiens," *Anatolian Studies Presented to Sir William Mitchell Ramsay*, ed. W. M. Calder and W. H. Buckler, Manchester University Press, 1923, 239–66

"Ein rätselhaftes Amulett," *JhhÖArchInst* 32 (1940), 79–84

Führer durch Ephesos, Wien, Österreichisches Archäologisches Institut, 1964

"Kulte im Prytaneion von Ephesos," *Anatolian Studies Presented to William Hepburn Buckler*, ed. W. M. Calder and J. Keil, Manchester University Press, 1939, 119–28

KIM, Seyoon. *The Origin of Paul's Gospel*, WUNT 2/4, Tübingen, Mohr, 1981

KIRBY, J. C. *Ephesians, Baptism and Pentecost. An Inquiry into the Structure and Purpose of the Epistle to the Ephesians*, London, SPCK, 1968

KNIBBE, Dieter. "Ephesos – nicht nur die Stadt der Artemis. Die 'anderen' ephesische Götter," *Studien zur Religion und Kultur Kleinasiens* II, FS. F. K. Dörner, ed. S. Sahin, E. Schwertheim, and J. Wagner, EPRO 66, Leiden, Brill, 1978, 489–505

KNIBBE, Dieter and ALZINGER, Wilhelm. "Ephesos vom Beginn der römischen Herrschaft in Kleinasien bis zum Ende der Principatszeit," *ANRW* II.7.2, Berlin, Walter de Gruyter, 1983, 748–830

KNIBBE, Dieter, ALZINGER, Wilhelm, and KARWIESE, Stefan. "Ephesos," *PW* Supp. XII, Stuttgart, Alfred Druckenmüller, 1970, 248–364, 1588–1704

KNOX, Wilfred L. *St. Paul and the Church of the Gentiles*, Cambridge University Press, 1961

"Jewish Liturgical Exorcism," *HTR* 31 (1938), 191–203

KOESTER, Helmut. *Introduction to the New Testament*, 2 vols. (vol. 1, *History, Culture, and Religion of the Hellenistic Age*; vol. 2, *History and Literature of Early Christianity*), Philadelphia, Fortress, 1982

KRAABEL, A. T. "Judaism in Asia Minor under the Roman Empire with a Preliminary Study of the Jewish Community at Sardis, Lydia," Unpublished Doctoral Dissertation, Harvard, March 1968

"The Diaspora Synagogue," *ANRW* II.19.1, Berlin, Walter de Gruyter, 1979, 477–510

"The Roman Diaspora: Six Questionable Assumptions," *JJS* 33 (1982), 445–64

KRAFT, Robert. "The Multiform Jewish Heritage of Early Christianity," *Christianity, Judaism and Other Greco-Roman Cults*, vol. 3, FS. M. Smith, SJLA 12, Leiden, Brill, 1975, 174–205

KRAUSE, Martin. "The Christianization of Gnostic Texts," *The New Testament and Gnosis: Essays in Honour of Robert McL. Wilson*, ed. A. H. B. Logan and A. J. M. Wedderburn, Edinburgh, T. & T. Clark, 1983, 187–94

KUHN, Karl G. "The Epistle to the Ephesians in Light of the Qumran Texts," *Paul and Qumran*, ed. J. Murphy-O'Connor, London, Geoffrey Chapman, 1968, 115–31

KUHNERT, E. "Ephesiae Litterae," *PW* 5, Stuttgart, J. B. Metzlerscher, 1905, 2771–73

LÄHNEMANN, Johannes. "Die sieben Sendschreiben der Johannes-Apokalypse. Dokumente für die Konfrontation des frühen Christentums mit hellenistisch-römischer Kultur und Religion in Kleinasien," *Studien zur Religion und Kultur Kleinasiens*, vol. 2, FS. F. K. Dörner, ed. S. Sahin, E. Schwertheim and J. Wagner, EPRO 66, Leiden, Brill, 1978, 516–39

LASH, C. J. A. "Where Do Devils Live? A Problem in the Textual Criticism of Ephesians 6,12," *VigChr* 30 (1976), 160–74

LEE, J. Y. "Interpreting the Demonic Powers in Pauline Thought," *NovT* 12 (1970), 54–69

LEIVESTAD, Ragnar. *Christ the Conqueror. Ideas of Conflict and Victory in the New Testament*, London, SPCK, 1954

LEVINE, E. "The Wrestling Belt Legacy in the New Testament," *NTS* 28 (1982), 560–64

LICHTENECKER, Elisabeth. "Die Kultbilder der Artemis von Ephesos," Inaugural-Dissertation zur Erlangung des Doktorgrades einer hohen philosophischen Fakultät der Universität zu Tübingen, 1952

LINCOLN, Andrew T. "A Re-Examination of 'The Heavenlies' in Ephesians," *NTS* 19 (1972–73), 468–83

"The Use of the OT in Ephesians," *JSNT* 14 (1982), 16–57

"Ephesians 2:8–10: A Summary of Paul's Gospel?" *CBQ* 45 (1983), 617–30

Paradise Now and Not Yet. Studies in the Role of the Heavenly Dimension in Paul's Thought with Special Reference to his Eschatology, SNTSMS 43, Cambridge University Press, 1981

LINDEMANN, Andreas. *Die Aufhebung der Zeit. Geschichtsverständnis und Eschatologie im Epheserbrief*, SNT 12, Gütersloh, Mohn, 1975
"Bemerkungen zu den Adressaten und zum Anlaß des Epheserbriefes," *ZNW* 67 (1976), 235–51

LONA, Horacio E. *Die Eschatologie im Kolosser- und Epheserbrief*. FzB 48, Würzburg, Echter, 1984

LULL, David J. *The Spirit in Galatia. Paul's Interpretation of Pneuma as Divine Power*, SBLDS 49, Chico, Scholar's Press, 1980

McCOWN, Chester C. *The Testament of Solomon*. Untersuchungen zum Neuen Testament 9, Leipzig, J.C. Heinrichs, 1922
"The Ephesia Grammata in Popular Belief," *Transactions of the American Philological Association* 54 (1923), 128–40

MacGREGOR, G.H.C. "Principalities and Powers: the Cosmic Background of Paul's Thought," *NTS* 1 (1954–55), 17–28

McKENZIE, John L. "Authority and Power in the New Testament," *CBQ* 26 (1964), 413–22

MacMULLEN, Ramsay. *Paganism in the Roman Empire*, New Haven, Yale University Press, 1974

MACRO, Anthony D. "The Cities of Asia Minor under the Roman Imperium," *ANRW* II.7.2, Berlin, Walter de Gruyter, 1983, 658–97

MAGIE, D. *Roman Rule in Asia Minor*, 2 vols., Princeton University Press, 1950

MARGALIOTH, M. *Sepher Ha-Razim*, Jerusalem, Yediot Achronot, 1966

MARSHALL, I. Howard. "Palestinian and Hellenistic Christianity: Some Critical Comments," *NTS* 19 (1972–73), 271–87

MARTIN, Ralph P. "An Epistle in Search of a Life Setting," *ET* 79 (1967–68), 296–302

MAURER, C. "Der Hymnus von Eph 1 als Schlüssel zum ganzen Brief," *EvT* 11 (1951–52), 151–72

MEINARDUS, Otto. *St. Paul in Ephesus and the Cities of Galatia and Cyprus*, Athens, Lycabettus, 1979

MELLINK, Machteld J. Review of R. Fleischer, *Artemis von Ephesos. AJA* 79 (1975), 107–108

MELLOR, Ronald. ΘΕΑ ΡΩΜΗ. *The Worship of the Goddess Roma in the Greek World*, Hypomnemata 42, Göttingen, Vandenhoeck & Ruprecht, 1975

MERKLEIN, Helmut. *Das kirchliche Amt nach dem Epheserbrief*, SANT 33, Munich, Kösel, 1973
"Paulinische Theologie in der Rezeption des Kolosser- und Epheserbriefes," *Paulus in den Neutestamentlichen Spätschriften zur Paulusrezeption im Neuen Testament*, QD 89, Freiburg, Basel, & Wien, Herder, 1981, 25–69

METZGER, Bruce M. "St. Paul and the Magicians," *Princeton Seminary Bulletin* 38 (1944), 27–30.

MEYER, Regina P. *Kirche und Mission im Epheserbrief*, SBS 86, Stuttgart, Katholisches Bibelwerk, 1977

MILTNER, Franz. *Ephesos. Stadt der Artemis und des Johannes*, Wien, Franz Deuticke, 1958

MITTON, C. L. *The Epistle to the Ephesians. Its Authorship, Origin and Purpose*, Oxford, Clarendon, 1951

MORGAN, Michael. *Sepher Ha-Razim. The Book of the Mysteries*, SBL Texts and Translations 25, Pseudepigrapha Series 11, Chico, Scholar's Press, 1983

MORRISON, Clinton. *The Powers That Be: Earthly Rulers and Demonic Powers in Romans 13:1–7*, SBT 29, London, SCM, 1960

MOULE, C. F. D. "A Note on Ephesians 1:22–23," *ET* 60 (1948–49), 53

MOULTON, J. H. and MILLIGAN, G. ed. *The Vocabulary of the Greek Testament*, London, Hodder and Stoughton, 1930

MÜNDERLEIN, G. "Die Erwählung durch das Pleroma," *NTS* 8 (1962), 264–76

MURPHY, Roland E. "GBR and GBWRH in the Qumran Writings," *Lex tua veritas*, FS. H. Junker, Trier, Paulinus, 1961, 137–43

MUSSNER, Franz. *Christus, das All und die Kirche. Studien zur Theologie des Epheserbriefes*, TTS 5, Trier, Paulinus, 1955
"Contributions Made by Qumran to the Understanding of the Epistle to the Ephesians," *Paul and Qumran*, ed. J. Murphy-O'Connor, London, Geoffrey Chapman, 1968

NEVERON, O. V. "Gemmes, bagues et amulettes magiques du sud de l'URSS," *Hommages à Maarten J. Vermaseren*, vol. 2, ed. M. B. De Boer and T. A. Edridge, EPRO 68, Leiden, Brill, 1978, 833–48

NIELSEN, Helge K. "Paulus' Verwendung des Begriffes Δύναμις. Eine Replik zur Kreuzestheologie," *Die Paulinische Literatur und Theologie*, ed. S. Pederson, Århus, Aros, 1980, 137–58

NILSSON, Martin P. *Greek Popular Religion*, New York, Columbia University Press, 1940
Geschichte der griechischen Religion, 2 vols., München, D. H. Beck, vol. 1, 1941; vol. 2, 1950
"Die Religion in den griechischen Zauberpapyri," *Kungl. Humanistika Vetenskapssamfundet I Lund. Årsberattelse 1947–48*, Lund, Gleerup, 59–93

NOACK, Bent. *Satanás und Soteria. Untersuchungen zur neutestamentlichen Dämonologie*, København, G. E. C. Gads, 1948

NOCK, A. D. "Studies in the Graeco-Roman Beliefs of the Empire," *JHS* 48 (1928), 84–101 (reprinted in *Arthur Darby Nock: Essays on Religion and the Ancient World*, vol. 1, ed. Z. Stewart, Oxford, Clarendon Press, 1972, 32–48)
"Greek Magical Papyri," *Journal of Egyptian Archaeology* 15 (1929), 219–35 (reprinted in *Arthur Darby Nock: Essays on Religion and the Ancient World*, vol. 1, ed. Z. Stewart, Oxford, Clarendon Press, 1972, 176–94)

"Vocabulary of the New Testament," *JBL* 52 (1933), 131–39
Early Gentile Christianity and its Hellenistic Background, New York, Harper & Row, 1964
"Astrology and Cultural History," *Arthur Darby Nock: Essays on Religion and the Ancient World*, vol. 1, ed. Z. Stewart, Oxford, Clarendon Press, 1972, 359–68
O'BRIEN, Peter T. *Introductory Thanksgivings in the Letters of Paul*, NovTSup 49, Leiden, Brill, 1977
"Ephesians 1: An Unusual Introduction to a New Testament Letter," *NTS* 25 (1978), 504–16
"Principalities and Powers and Their Relationship to Structures," *ERT* 6 (1982), 50–61
"Principalities and Powers: Opponents of the Church," *Biblical Interpretation and the Church: Text and Context*, ed. D. A. Carson, Exeter, Paternoster, 1984, 110–50
O'COLLINS, Gerald G. "Power Made Perfect in Weakness: 2 Cor. 12: 9–10," *CBQ* 33 (1971), 528–37
ODEBERG, H. *The View of the Universe in the Epistle to the Ephesians*, Lunds Universitets Årsskrift, N.F. 29, no. 6, Lund, Gleerup, 1934
ONURKAN, Somay, "Artemis Pergaia," *Ist Mitt* 19–20 (1969–70), 289–98
von der OSTEN-SACKEN, Peter. *Gott und Belial. Traditionsgeschichtliche Untersuchungen zum Dualismus in den Texten aus Qumran*, SUNT 6, Göttingen, Vandenhoeck & Ruprecht, 1969
OSTER, R. "The Ephesian Artemis as an Opponent of Early Christianity," *Jahrbuch für Antike und Christentum* 19 (1976), 24–44
"Christianity and Emperor Veneration in Ephesus: Iconography of a Conflict," *Restoration Quarterly* 25 (1982), 143–49
OVERFIELD, P. D. *The Ascension, Pleroma and Ecclesia Concepts in Ephesians*, unpublished Ph.D. Thesis, St. Andrews University, 1976
"Pleroma: A Study in Content and Context," *NTS* 25 (1978–79), 384–96
PARVIS, Merrill M. "Archaeology and St. Paul's Journeys in Greek Lands. Part IV – Ephesus," *BA* 8 (1945), 62–73
PERCY, Ernst. *Die Probleme der Kolosser- und Epheserbriefe*. Skrifter Utgivna av Kungl. Humanistiska Vetenskapssamfundet i Lund XXXIX, Lund, Gleerup, 1964 (reprint of 1946 edition)
PETZL, G., ed. *Die Inschriften von Smyrna*, IGSK 23, Bonn, Rudolf Habelt, 1978
PFITZNER, V. C. *Paul and the Agon Motif*, NovTSup 16, Leiden, Brill, 1967
PICARD, Charles. *Ephèse et Claros*, Paris, 1922
POKORNY, Petr. "Epheserbrief und gnostische Mysterien," *ZNW* 53 (1962), 160–94
Der Epheserbrief und die Gnosis. Die Bedeutung des Haupt-Glieder-Gedankens in der entstehenden Kirche, Berlin, Evangelische Verlagsanstalt, 1965
POWELL, Cyril H. *The Biblical Concept of Power*, London, Epworth, 1963
POWELL, J. Enoch, ed. *The Rendel Harris Papyri of Woodbroke College, Birmingham*, Cambridge University Press, 1936

PREISENDANZ, Karl. "Die griechischen Zauberpapyri," *APF* 8 (1927), 104–67
Papyri graecae magicae. Die griechischen Zauberpapyri, Leipzig & Berlin, Verlag und Druck von B.G. Teubner, vol.1, 1928; vol.2, 1931; vol.3, 1942 (2nd rev. edn. by A. Heinrichs, Stuttgart, 1973–74)
"Die griechischen und lateinischen Zaubertafeln," *APF* 11 (1935), 153–64
"Ephesia Grammata," *RAC*, vol.5 (1965), 515–20
PREISIGKE, Friedrich. *Der Gotteskraft der frühchristlichen Zeit*, Papyrusinstitut Heidelberg 6, Berlin & Leipzig, Walter de Gruyter, 1922
PRÜMM, Karl. "Dynamis in griechisch-hellenistischer Religion und Philosophie als Vergleichsbild zu göttlicher Dynamis im Offenbarungsraum. Streiflichter auf ein Sondergebiet antik-frühchristlicher Begegnung," *ZKT* 83 (1961), 393–430
"Das Dynamische als Grund-Aspekt der Heilsordnung in der Sicht des Apostels Paulus," *Gregorianum* 42 (1961), 643–700
QUISPEL, Gilles. *Gnosis als Weltreligion*, Zürich, Origo, 1951
RAMSAY, W.M. "Antiquities of Southern Phrygia and the Border Lands," *American Journal of Archaeology and of the History of Fine Arts* 3 (1887), 344–68
"Artemis-Leto and Apollo-Lairbenos," *JHS* 10 (1889), 216–30
"St. Paul at Ephesus," *Expositor* Series 4/2 (1890), 1–22
The Cities and Bishoprics of Phrygia, 2 vols., Oxford University Press, vol.1, 1895, vol.2, 1897
The Letters to the Seven Churches of Asia, London, Hodder & Stoughton, 1904
"Sketches in the Religious Antiquities of Asia Minor," *The Annual of the British School at Athens* 18 (1911), 37–79
"The Mysteries in their Relation to St. Paul," *Contemporary Review* 104 (1913), 198–209
The Teaching of Paul in Terms of the Present Day, London, Hodder & Stoughton, 1914
St. Paul the Traveller and Roman Citizen, London, Hodder & Stoughton, 1920
REITZENSTEIN, R. *Poimandres. Studien zur griechisch-ägyptischen und frühchristlichen Literatur*, Leipzig, Teubner, 1904 (reprinted Darmstadt, 1966)
Das iranische Erlösungsmysterium, Bonn a. Rh., A. Marcus & E. Weber, 1921
Hellenistic Mystery Religions, tr. J.E. Steely, Pittsburgh, Pickwick, 1978
RISTOW, Günter. "Zum Kosmokrator im Zodiacus, ein Bildvergleich," *Hommages à Maarten J. Vermaseren*, vol.3, ed. M.B. De Boer & T.A. Edridge, EPRO 68, Leiden, Brill, 1978, 985–87
ROBINSON, James M. "The Nag Hammadi Library and the Study of the New Testament," *The New Testament and Gnosis: Essays in Honour of Robert McL. Wilson*, ed. A.H.B. Logan and A.J.M. Wedderburn, Edinburgh, T. & T. Clark, 1983, 1–18
ROGERS, Cleon L. "The Dionysian Background of Ephesians 5:18," *BibSac* 136 (1979), 249–57

ROOD, L.A. "Le Christ, Puissance de Dieu," *Littérature et théologie Pauliniennes*, ed. A. Descamps, Recherches bibliques 5, Louvanii, Desclée, 1960, 93–108

VAN ROON, A. *The Authenticity of Ephesians*, NovTSup 39, tr. S. Prescod-Jokel, Leiden, Brill, 1974

ROSCHER, W. H. "Weiteres über die Bedeutung des E zu Delphi und die übrigen γράμματα Δελφικά," *Philologus* 60 (1900), 81–101

RUDOLPH, Kurt. *Gnosis. The Nature and History of an Ancient Religion*, tr. R. McL. Wilson, Edinburgh, T. & T. Clark, 1983

SALDITT-TRAPPMANN, Regina. *Tempel der ägyptischen Götter in Griechenland und an der Westküste Kleinasiens*, EPRO 15, Leiden, Brill, 1970

SANDERS, Jack T. "Hymnic Elements in Ephesians 1–3," *ZNW* 56 (1965), 214–32

SCHENKE, Hans-Martin. *Der Gott "Mensch" in der Gnosis. Ein religionsgeschichtlicher Beitrag zur Diskussion über die paulinische Anschauung von der Kirche als Leib Christi*, Göttingen, Vandenhoeck & Ruprecht, 1962

"Die Gnosis," *Umwelt des Urchristentums*, vol. 1: *Darstellung des neutestamentlichen Zeitalters*, ed. J. Leipoldt and W. Grundmann, Berlin, Evangelische Verlagsanstalt, 1971, 371–415

"Das Weiterwirken des Paulus und die Pflege seines Erbes durch die Paulus-Schule," *NTS* 21 (1974–75), 505–18

SCHENKE, Hans-Martin and FISCHER, Karl Martin. *Einleitung in die Schriften des Neuen Testaments I, Die Briefe des Paulus und Schriften des Paulinismus*, Gütersloh, Mohn, 1978

SCHILLE, Gottfried. *Frühchristliche Hymnen*, Berlin, Evangelische Verlagsanstalt, 1965

SCHLIER, Heinrich. *Christus und die Kirche im Epheserbrief*, BHT 6, Tübingen, Mohr, 1930

Principalities and Powers in the New Testament, QD 3, Freiburg, Herder, 1961

SCHMIDT, Karl L. "Die Natur- und Geistkräfte bei Paulus," *Eranos Jahrbuch* 14 (1946), 87–143

SCHMITHALS, Walter. "The Corpus Paulinum and Gnosis," *The New Testament and Gnosis: Essays in Honour of Robert McL. Wilson*, ed. A. H. B. Logan and A. J. M. Wedderburn, Edinburgh, T. & T. Clark, 1983, 107–24

SCHMITZ, Otto, "Der Begriff Δύναμις bei Paulus," *Festgabe für Adolf Deissmann*, Tübingen, Mohr, 1927, 139–67

SCHNACKENBURG, Rudolf. " 'Er hat uns Mitauferweckt.' Zur Tauflehre des Epheserbriefes," *Liturgisches Jahrbuch* 2 (1952), 159–83

"Christus, Geist und Gemeinde (Eph. 4:1–16)," *Christ und Spirit in the New Testament*, FS. C. F. D. Moule, ed. B. Lindars and S. S. Smalley, Cambridge University Press, 1973, 279–96

"Die große Eulogie Eph. 1, 3–14," *BZ* 21 (1977), 67–87

"Der Epheserbrief im heutigen Horizont," *Maßstab des Glaubens*, Freiburg, Herder, 1978, 155–75

SCHOLEM, Gershom. *Major Trends in Jewish Mysticism*, London, Thames & Hudson, 1955
Jewish Gnosticism, Merkabah Mysticism, and Talmudic Tradition, New York, 1960
SCHRAGE, Wolfgang, *Ethik des Neuen Testaments*, GNT 4, Göttingen, Vandenhoeck & Ruprecht, 1982
SCHÜTZ, John H. *Paul and the Anatomy of Apostolic Authority*, SNTSMS 26, Cambridge University Press, 1975
SCHWEIZER, Eduard. "The Church as the Missionary Body of Christ," *NTS* 8 (1961–62), 1–11
"Die Kirche als Leib Christi in den paulinischen Antilegomena," *Neotestamentica. Deutsche und englische Aufsätze, 1951–1963*, ed. E. Schweizer, Zürich & Stuttgart, Zwingli, 1963, 293–316
SEGAL, Alan F. *Two Powers in Heaven. Early Rabbinic Reports about Christianity and Gnosticism*, SJLA 25, Leiden, Brill, 1977
"Hellenistic Magic: Some Questions of Definition," *Studies in Gnosticism and Hellenistic Religions*, FS. G. Quispel, ed. R. van den Broek and M. J. Vermaseren, EPRO 91, Leiden, Brill, 1981, 349–75
SEITERLE, Gerard. "Artemis – Die Große Göttin von Ephesos. Eine neue Deutung der 'Vielbrüstigkeit' eröffnet einen Zugang zum bisher ungekannten Kult der Göttin," *Antike Welt* 10 (1979), 3–16
SELLIN, Gerhard. " 'Die Auferstehung ist schon Geschehen.' Zur Spiritualisierung apokalyptischer Terminologie im neuen Testament," *NovT* 25 (1983), 220–37
SIBER, P. *Mit Christus Leben. Eine Studie zur paulinischen Auferstehungshoffnung*, ATANT 61, Zürich, Theologischer Verlag, 1971
SIDER, Ronald. *Christ and Violence*, Scottdale, Herald Press, 1979
SIMON, Marcel. *Verus Israel. Etude sur les Relations entre Chrétiens et Juifs dans l'Empire Romain (135–425)*, Paris, Editions E. De Boccard, 1964
SMALLWOOD, E.M. *The Jews Under Roman Rule*, SJLA 20, Leiden, Brill, 1976
SMITH, Morton. *Jesus, the Magician*, London, Gollancz, 1978
Clement of Alexandria and a Secret Gospel of Mark, Cambridge, Mass., Harvard University Press, 1973
STEINMETZ, F.J. *Protologische Heilszuversicht. Die Strukturen des soteriologischen und christologischen Denkens im Kolosser- und Epheserbrief*, FTS 2, Frankfurt, Knecht, 1969
STEWART, J.S. "On a Neglected Emphasis in New Testament Theology," *SJT* 4 (1951), 292–301
STUHLMACHER, Peter. "Achtzehn Thesen zur Paulinischen Kreuzestheologie," *Rechtfertigung*, FS. E. Käsemann, Tübingen, Mohr, 1976
Suidae lexicon graece et latine, 2 vols., ed. G. Bernhardy and T. Gaisford, Halis, Sumptibus Schwetschikiorum, 1853
TACHAU, P. *"Einst" und "Jetzt" im Neuen Testament. Beobachtung zu einem urchristlichen Predigtschema in der neutestamentlichen Briefliteratur und zu seiner Vorgeschichte*, FRLANT 105, Göttingen, Vandenhoeck & Ruprecht, 1972

TANNEHILL, Robert C. *Dying and Rising with Christ. A Study in Pauline Theology*, BZNW 32, Berlin, Töpelmann, 1967

TINH, Tran Tam. "Sarapis and Isis," *Jewish and Christian Self-Definition* vol. 3, ed. B. F. Meyer and E. P. Sanders, London, SCM, 1982, 101–17

TONNEAU, Raphaël. "Ephèse au Temps de Saint Paul," *RB* 38 (1929), 5–34; 321–63.

USAMI, Kōshi. *Somatic Comprehension of Unity: The Church in Ephesus.* Analecta biblica 101, Rome, Biblical Institute Press, 1983

WEISS, H. F. "Gnostische Motive und antignostische Polemik im Kolosser-und Epheserbrief," *Gnosis und Neues Testament*, ed. K. W. Tröger, Gütersloh, Gerd Mohn, 1973, 311–24

WERNICKE, K. "Artemis," *PW* 2, Stuttgart, J. B. Metzlerscher Verlag, 1896, 1336–1440

WESSELY, Karl. "Ephesia Grammata aus Papyrusrollen, Inschriften, Gemmen, etc," *Zwölfter jahresbericht über das k. k. Franz-Josef-Gymnasium in Wien.* Wien, Franz-Joseph-Gymnasium, 1886, 1–38

WHITELEY, D. E. H. "Expository Problems: Eph. 6:12: Evil Powers," *ET* 68 (1957), 100–103

WILD, Robert A. "The Warrior and the Prisoner: Some Reflections on Ephesians 6:10–20," *CBQ* 46 (1984), 284–98

WILES, G. P. *Paul's Intercessory Prayers: The Significance of the Inter-cessory Prayer Passages in the Letters of St. Paul*, SNTSMS 24, Cambridge University Press, 1974

WILSON, R. A. " 'We' and 'You' in the Epistle to the Ephesians," *SE* II (= *TU* 87), Berlin, Akademie, 1964, 676–80

WILSON, R. McL. *The Gnostic Problem*, London, Mowbray, 1958
Gnosis and the New Testament, Philadelphia, Fortress, 1968
"Gnosis and the Mysteries," *Studies in Gnosticism and Hellenistic Religions*, FS. G. Quispel, ed. R. van den Broek and M. J. Vermaseren, EPRO 91, Leiden, Brill, 1981, 451–57
"Nag Hammadi and the New Testament," *NTS* 28 (1982), 289–302

WINK, Walter. *Naming the Powers. The Language of Power in the New Testament*, Philadelphia, Fortress, 1984
Review of W. Carr, *Union Seminary Quarterly Review* 39 (1984), 146–50

WORTMANN, Dierk. "Neue Magische Texte," *Bonner Jahrbücher* 168 (1968), 56–111

WÜNSCH, Richard. *Antikes Zaubergerät aus Pergamon*, Jahrbuch des Kaiserlich Deutschen Archäologischen Instituts, Ergänzungsheft VI, Berlin, Georg Reimer, 1905

YAMAUCHI, E. M. "Jewish Gnosticism? The Prologue of John, Mandaean Parallels, and the Trimorphic Protennoia," *Studies in Gnosticism and Hellenistic Religions*, FS. G. Quispel, ed. R. van den Broek and M. J. Vermaseren, EPRO 91, Leiden, Brill, 1981, 467–97
"Magic in the Biblical World," *TB* 34 (1983), 169–200
Pre-Christian Gnosticism, 2nd edn, Grand Rapids, Baker, 1983
"Pre-Christian Gnosticism, the New Testament and Nag Hammadi in Recent Debate," *Themelios* 10 (1984), 22–27

YATES, R. "A Re-examination of Eph. 1:23," *ET* 83 (1971–72), 146–51

AUTHOR INDEX

Abbott, T. K. 173, 190, 191, 193, 195, 198, 202, 210
Achtemeier, P. J. 208
Adai, J. 208
Allan, J. A. 136, 207
Allen, T. G. 196, 208
Allegro, J. M. 184
Arnold, C. E. 189
Arnold, I. R. 204, 205
Audollent, A. 178, 190
Aune, D. 19, 179, 180, 185, 189

Bammer, A. 26, 183
Bandstra, A. J. 198
Barrett, C. K. 193
Barth, M. 1, 81, 144, 160, 171, 173, 183, 187, 190, 192, 193, 194, 197, 198, 199, 200, 201, 202, 203, 204, 206, 207, 208, 211, 212
Baur, F. C. 7
Beare, F. W. 194, 195, 197, 198, 201, 210
Behm, J. 89, 199
Beker, J. C. 129–32, 141, 206, 207, 208, 212
Benoit, P. 34, 47, 186, 188, 197
Berkhof, H. 45, 48, 188
Bertram, G. 194, 200, 212
Best, E. 174, 196, 197
Betz, H. D. B. 3, 17, 20, 31, 57, 176, 177, 179, 180, 181, 185, 187, 190, 206
Bietenhard, H. 184, 189
Black, D. 208, 212
Bonner, C. 23, 181
Bornkamm, G. 176, 206
Bousset, W. 8, 125, 205

Bowersock, G. W. 186, 187
Braun, H. 203
Broughton, T. R. S. 174
Brown, R. E. 206, 211
Bruce, F. F. 11, 160, 176, 188, 190, 199, 200, 202, 204, 205, 209, 211, 212, 213
Bultmann, R. 7, 79

Caird, G. B. 45, 188, 203
Canet, L. 66, 192, 193
Caragounis, C. 135, 193, 206, 207, 211
Carr, W. 47–8, 162, 183, 188, 191, 192, 203, 204, 212
Carrington, P. 106, 202, 207
Cerfaux, L. 139, 208
Chadwick, H. 209, 211, 212
Champion, L. G. 201
Chapot, V. 176
Charlesworth, J. H. 31, 47, 184, 185, 188
Clark, K. W. 194, 201
Colpe, C. 8, 11, 80, 174, 176, 196
Conybeare, F. C. 55, 190, 192, 193
Conzelmann, H. 104, 150, 173, 200, 208, 209, 210
Cranfield, C. E. B. 188, 201
Culianu, I. 8, 174
Cullmann, O. 44–5, 46, 188
Cumont, F. 66, 179, 183, 184, 192, 193

Dahl, N. 92, 93, 173, 193, 199, 200, 201, 207
Daniélou, J. 184
Davies, W. D. 196, 202
Deichgräber, R. 100–2, 194, 201
Deissmann, A. 178, 181, 210
de la Potterie, I. 197
Delling, G. 189, 191, 192, 198, 201

229

INDEX OF PASSAGES CITED

Page numbers in bold print indicate an extensive discussion of the passage cited.